SELLEGRITY

Ethics, Skills and Selling Strategies

"Double" Your Sales

A Personal Achievement Program for the Christian Sales Professional

Robert L. Riker

ISBN-13: 978-0995848009

Published by First Page Solutions, Kelowna BC Canada.

Certain sections were first published in 1991 by McGraw-Hill Ryerson, Scarborough, Ontario under the title DOUBLING, A Guide for the Professional Salesperson – More Than 100 Strategies for Doubling Your Sales.

Riker, Robert L.

Yes, You Can · Your Doubling Strategy ·

TABLE OF CONTENTS

SECTION 2: DUTY

Preface

UNDER SIEGE...

There are seasons when the world is calm and there are seasons when it is not.

Today, it is not.

There is financial, political and spiritual turmoil on almost every front as world leaders try to get their collective houses in order. But as we approach what the Bible terms, "the end of days", most Christians believe that there will only be a brief calm before the true storm and that the "turmoil" is actually the labor pains preceding the birth of the new world order as spoken of in the Bible.

In this season, major governments seem to be ruled by opinions and secret agendas, by clever people on a mission to destroy the Word, or more accurately, to pervert it and give it an alternate meaning or understanding. The Christian is squarely in the crosshairs.

But truth is found in the Word of God, and it is the cornerstone of integrity, hope, peace and joy. Here's how it works...

"No Peace without Hope.
No Hope without Liberty.
No Liberty without Integrity.
No Integrity without Virtue.
No Virtue without Enlightenment.
No Enlightenment without Truth.
No Truth without God."

- *Glenn Beck*

Take away God, and truth is replaced with opinion and deceit.
Take away Enlightenment and we become accepting and confused.
Take away Virtue and we become perverted and self-absorbed.
Take away Integrity and we become schemers and liars.
Take away Liberty and we become enslaved or domineering.
Take away Hope and we become disparaged, depressed and cruel.
Take away Peace and we become frightened and enraged.

In a world where truth has been replaced often by a cleaver counterfeit or opposite, the Christian must battle daily to regain common sense and truth as God would endorse.

Have you noticed that many politicians, officials and even customers don't seem to "make sense" anymore? It's because their foundations have shifted; their ethics have changed and their version of common sense seems alien. Common sense is based upon a collective understanding of what is right and wrong, and if truth is replaced with a counterfeit, common sense (or lack thereof) reflects it.

The enemy seeks to torture, destroy and kill. Truth, dignity, common sense, honor and integrity all fall to his schemes. Satan is clever; he often works in very subtle ways, gnawing away at foundations and beliefs, switching fake for real, planting doubt where steadfast belief once stood. Our first clue: common sense seems to be missing.

Satan's a master counterfeiter. I used to develop "anti-counterfeiting" technologies for manufactured goods, currencies and documents. I know that a good counterfeit is virtually identical to the original. Unless you have the original for comparison, you can be easily persuaded that the counterfeit is the "real thing". Unless you know the Word – in context – Satan's counterfeits will take you in.

I am a Christian entrepreneur. I have tried to build Kingdom-based businesses and the more focus that went towards my principled efforts, the more Satan would take an interest. I have won and lost, over and over. Just when I think I'm safe, I discover I'm not.

Satan doesn't care about the Christian man or woman who isn't fighting for truth and Biblical principle – but he cares very much about those who do. He takes aim and begins to hurl those "fiery darts" we've all read about in Ephesians 6 – it's what the Armor of God is for: (emphasis mine)

> 10Finally, be strong in the Lord and in his mighty power.
>
> 11Put on the full armor of God so that you can take your stand against the devil's schemes.
>
> 12For our struggle is not against flesh and blood, but against the rulers, against the authorities, against the powers of this dark world and against the spiritual forces of evil in the heavenly realms.

> [13]Therefore put on the full armor of God, so that when the day of evil comes, you may be able to **stand your ground**, and after you have done everything, to stand.
>
> [14]Stand firm then, with **the belt of truth** buckled around your waist, with **the breastplate of righteousness** in place, [15]and with your feet fitted with the readiness that comes from **the gospel of peace.**
>
> [16]In addition to all this, take up **the shield of faith**, with which you can extinguish all the flaming arrows of the evil one.
>
> [17]Take **the helmet of salvation** and **the sword of the Spirit**, which is **the word of God**.
>
> [18]And **pray in the Spirit** on all occasions with all kinds of prayers and requests. With this in mind, **be alert** and **always keep on praying for all the saints**.
>
> \- NIV

Do you remember the story of William Wallace – Braveheart? He and his Scottish countrymen fought and defeated the British armies until the British deployed a new weapon – the longbow – that overwhelmed the Scots and for which they had no adequate defense.

Satan is like that. He tests you with a few fiery darts and if you defend successfully, and you are interrupting his plans, then he will bring out his longbows and fire a volley. If you are unprepared or ill-equipped for defense, the volley will overwhelm you, wound you and maybe even destroy you. Like William Wallace, you may be drawn and quartered in a spiritual sense.

I bring this illustration up because it comes from real life. It is what happens when you step out to stand for truth against an enemy that stands for deceit, destruction, dominance and death. It is what is loose in the world today.

Sellegrity is based on Biblical principles that, when used, will tend to turn the head of God in your direction. However, they will also likely gain Satan's attention, but for entirely different reasons.

As a believer, you always have a choice concerning your actions, just as God intended.

Sellegrity

You can float downstream with the majority of folks, and not even be aware of the current that is carrying you away from victory and truth. If everyone is going in the same direction, floating along that old meandering river, no one causes disruption, no one stands out. But roll off your raft and stand on the shallow river bed and see the commotion that ensues as others crash into you and the water swirls around your legs and fellow rafters call out for you to get back on your raft.

If you simply stop doing what the world is doing – it causes notice. If you go upstream, it causes disruption and chaos. This is what happens when you sell using Godly principles. You stand out. You become noticed. You are labeled as different. In God's eyes – a warrior. In Satan's eyes – an enemy to be destroyed.

Once you roll off that raft and stand on the river bed, everything and everyone will "encourage" you get back on your raft. I encourage you to let the raft go – let it float away with the others – and prayerfully take a step upstream. Then take another... and another. And thus begins your journey.

"I have written this so that you can grasp some of the issues involved in "standing" in the worldly system that expects and rewards you to be clever, complex, deceitful, politically-correct and poisonous. It is in response to a rapidly-deteriorating political landscape that will most likely herald the arrival of the antichrist. May God be with you all."

-Bob Riker

With thanks to all the participants in my training courses over the years – you have taught me far more than I have taught you! And thanks to my dear friends Cindy Anthony and Norm Sawyer for their help with the scriptural integration – so knowledgeable, so giving.

INTRODUCTION

The focus of *Sellegrity* is to inspire and equip salespeople who hold righteousness above self-serving success principles to prosper within a business system which values superstars, super deals, fast tracking and personal financial wealth. This means selling into a world that operates with a very different expectations and ethical standards than those that you may have as a Spirit-led Christian.

Sellegrity is devoted to those who serve God in their hearts but must also serve the world structure of commerce. It is about doing what is right, what is moral, what is truly ethical - all the time - and prospering both materially and spiritually.

In a world full of positive self-achievement that tends to lead to positive self-enrichment, *Sellegrity* offers another dimension: a purpose-driven achievement for God that leads to a life of positive self-sacrifice – also expressed as doing Kingdom Business. But surprisingly, the example that God sets for achievement is one that involves superior rewards – a "doubling" of worldly benefit – for those who act in an unselfish, diligent and proactive manner.

The first section of *Sellegrity* is devoted to the issues that impact the Christian salesperson's motives, actions and beliefs – your character and your purpose – and the dimensions of "Kingdom Business".

It explores the issues of how to act and react, what to accept and what not to accept and how you think about yourself and others. It deals with perspective because we always view and interpret our experiences, thoughts, attitudes and actions from our personal perch in life.

The **Duty** section of *Sellegrity* explores the skills and strategies that can be used by the servant-hearted, principle-based salesperson to build a viable profession that honors God, the client, fellow workers and management. It's about doing Kingdom Business.

The Duty section is based upon my original DOUBLING manuscript and its timeless techniques and principles. The section deals with the skills and strategies that lead to a doubling in sales effectiveness – or more, for this is what Duty calls for within the Christian – an obligation to provide a righteousness-based work ethic as if you are working directly for God – because you are.

The training sessions that accompanied the release of DOUBLING in 1991 proved without a doubt that if the content is understood, nurtured and applied, sales will increase, sometimes as much as ten-fold. "Duty" is how you fulfill your obligation to increase according to the **Parable of the Talents**, which is the scripture reference for the duty of doubling your sales.

These are the words of Christ as expressed in Matthew 25:14-30 (NAS) – commonly known as the Parable of the Talents. A talent is a measure of money.

> ***14*** *"For it is just like a man about to go on a journey, who called his own slaves and entrusted his possessions to them.*
>
> ***15*** *"To one he gave **five** talents, to another, **two**, and to another, **one**, each according to his own ability; and he went on his journey.*
>
> ***16*** *"Immediately the one who had received the five talents went and traded with them, and gained five more talents (he "doubled" because he had the ability and the confidence).*
>
> ***17*** *"In the same manner the one who had received the two talents gained two more (he also "doubled").*
>
> ***18*** *"But he who received the one talent went away, and dug a hole in the ground and hid his master's money (he worked from a "fear" base, did not have the ability, nor the confidence).*
>
> ***19*** *"Now after a long time the master of those slaves came and settled accounts with them.*
>
> ***20*** *"The one who had received the five talents came up and brought five more talents, saying, `Master, you entrusted five*

talents to me. See, I have gained five more talents. His master said to him, `Well-done, good and faithful slave. You were faithful with a few things, I will put you in charge of many things; enter into the joy of your master.'

22 *"Also the one who had received the two talents came up and said, `Master, you entrusted two talents to me. See, I have gained two more talents. His master said to him, `Well-done, good and faithful slave. You were faithful with a few things, I will put you in charge of many things; enter into the joy of your master.'*

24 *"And the one also who had received the one talent came up and said, `Master, I knew you to be a hard man, reaping where you did not sow and gathering where you scattered no seed. And I was afraid, and went away and hid your talent in the ground. See, you have what is yours.'*

26 *"But his master answered and said to him, `You wicked, lazy slave, you knew that I reap where I did not sow and gather where I scattered no seed. Then you ought to have put my money in the bank, and on my arrival I would have received my money back with interest. Therefore take away the talent from him, and give it to the one who has the ten talents.'*

29 *"For to everyone who has, more shall be given, and he will have an abundance; but from the one who does not have, even what he does have shall be taken away.*

30 *"Throw out the worthless slave into the outer darkness; in that place there will be weeping and gnashing of teeth. "*

This is a very powerful statement from Jesus concerning what we are to do with that which is entrusted to us, be it the Great Commission and the spreading of the Gospel message – its primary intent – or how we handle other issues, such as our money, possessions, responsibilities, obligations and profession.

God offers to the believer the opportunity to prosper. Notice that in the parable, no direction or instruction is given to the servants but there was an **expectation of duty** to be performed. He expects you to act out of faith, out of duty, and not out of personal fear, for the one slave that performed under fear in the parable was stripped by the Master of everything. God expects you to grow and to become more responsible, not less. He expects you to risk.

On the other hand, the devil wants to steal your authority – he wants you to hide the talent and to play it safe or to be so foolish as to lose through folly. God does not. Your "safety" does not come from hiding or just doing the status quo – it comes from the knowledge that you are doing what God has purposed for you in life, and if that is sales, then the expectation He has for you is to DOUBLE that which has been entrusted unto you by your employer. There is no shame or embarrassment in obtaining wealth and abundance as a result of service; it is God's common, earthly reward for those who are faithful and dutiful. God warns us about the love of money, not money itself.

Faith is your platform, not fear.

The slave who hid the talent in the ground told his master that he was afraid. This was not the fear of the Lord spoken of in Proverbs 1:7, even though in the parable, "master" represents God. The master called the slave "wicked" and "lazy". The slave was using fear as an excuse to avoid responsibility and to justify his laziness. If this was the fear of the Lord that signals the beginning of understanding and wisdom, then the slave would have been sought help or assistance to know what to do with the talent entrusted to him so that he could please his master or at the least, avoid punishment. If he had done so, even complete failure or loss of the talent due to inexperience would have likely brought compassion and mercy because he, at the least, sought to increase the value.

Instead, the slave did not pursue understanding, wisdom or knowledge, and instead despised the implied duty and instruction he had been given by the master. As Proverbs 1:7 states, "The fear of the Lord is the beginning of knowledge; fools despise wisdom and instruction". When we bury the gifts, neglect our God-expected duty and cover up our responsibilities is when we set ourselves up for a trip to the "outer darkness".

Let's have a look at the Parable of the Talents again, but this time, it's been re-written to become the "Parable of the Good Sellers":

For it is just like a business owner about to go on a long, well-deserved vacation, who called his salespeople together around him and entrusted his key customers to them.

To one he gave ***five*** *customers, to another,* ***two****, and to another,* ***one****, each according to his own sales ability; and he went on his extended vacation.*

Immediately the one who had received the five customers went and consulted with them, helped them to improve their own businesses and asked them for additional business and for referrals from which she gained five more customers and increased her business (she "doubled").

In the same manner the one who had received the two customers went and consulted with his customers, helped them to improve their businesses and asked for more business and for referrals and as a result he gained two more customers and increased his business (he also "doubled").

But he who received the one customer went away and visited his customer and did what was necessary to sustain business for he was afraid of losing the customer to a competitor or upsetting the customer (he worked from a "fear" base).

Now after a month the owner came back from his vacation and reviewed the key customer accounts with the salespeople.

The one who had received the five customers spoke up and brought five new customers, saying, `Sir, you entrusted five customers to me. See, I have gained five more customers from referrals and I have increased business with your existing customers. His manager said to her, `Well-done, good and faithful salesperson. You were faithful with a few things, I will put you in charge of many things; I am overjoyed with your performance and shall cut you a fat bonus check forthwith and free gas for the next month!"

Also the one who had received the two customers came up and said, `Sir, you entrusted two customers to me. See, I also have gained two more customers. His manager said to him, `Well-done, good and faithful salesperson. You were faithful with a few things, I will put you in charge of many things; I am well-pleased with your efforts and shall also cut you a bonus check forthwith and also pay for your gas for a month!"

And the one also who had received the one customer came up and said, "Sir, I knew you to be a hard man, expecting to

> *profit even where you have not invested. I was afraid that I might lose your customer to a competitor or perhaps upset them and so I serviced the customer as required and asked for no extra so that I would not cause concern. See, I have protected your customer and you still you have what is yours."*
>
> *But his manager answered and said to him, "You lazy man! You knew that I expect to profit all the time and in everything that I do and even expect to gain even where I have not invested. Then you ought to have at least shown the customer some new products and on my return I would have seen a small increase in sales from the customer. So take away the customer from him, and give it to the one who has the ten customers;"*
>
> *"For to everyone who creates profit for me, more leads shall be given, and he will have an abundance; but from the one who does not increase, does not create me profit, even what he does have shall be removed."*
>
> *"Send the worthless salesperson into the ranks of the unemployed; in that place there will be weeping and gnashing of teeth and no money for gas or for rent or even for thy cellular service or thy venti macchiato."*

Sellegrity helps you to develop your skills, strategies and attitudes so that you can do the very best job possible, in the sight of the Lord and in the presence of your employer and your family and your customers. *Sellegrity* does not use manipulative schemes or strategies nor does it diminish others in order for you to prosper; but it does involve hard work, smart thinking and dedication to growth and to duty. There are no shortcuts to growth: "no pain, no gain" is a common slogan for all honest achievers. Rewards will follow the application of genuine service, not vice-versa.

Sellegrity is an experience, designed to be a work-in-progress for the reader. It is a resource that can be accessed time and time again. It represents a process of growth. It contains strategies that, when enabled through skill, can result in an astounding increase in capability. It is an attitude of belief and personal commitment surrounded by developed capability. It is not hype; it is hard work, creative thinking, "meek" behavior and attention to duty.

God backs up the Parable of the Talents with a similar parable, the Parable of the King's Ten Servants in Luke 19:11-27, where the King rewards those who earned a return on their investment with authority over *cities*.

Sellegrity requires the reader to risk – time, talent, skill, emotion, trust, and enthusiasm in order to achieve the true rewards of genuine service.

Throughout the book, especially in the skill and strategy section, there will be many references to doubling your sales. It may seem that it is a simply a sales target, a goal and not a result of service, however, it is what "duty" calls for, according to the Parable of the Talents.

If you were to seek a doubling of your sales simply for your own benefit, your harvest will be enough to feed you and your family. If you seek a doubling of your sales to please your "master" because it is the dutiful thing to do, then your rewards will far exceed your efforts. The seeds you plant as a servant, without direct expectation of a personal and immediate return, tend to grow to become great fields that can feed many for a long, long time.

"Success" teaching focuses on self-achievement. "*Sellegrity*" focuses on selfless service with a Kingdom purpose. Both lead to recognition and even riches, but one "appropriates" it and through the other it is "bestowed."

Sellegrity relies upon having a servant's heart – one that is not concerned primarily about the self, but for the benefit of others. But let me make one thing very clear, the servant-based salesperson is anything but a "wimp". In the example of Moses, "the meekest man on earth," the servant heart is confident, skilled, professional, compassionate, honoring, respectful, willing, committed, trustworthy and without guile (craftiness). It seeks the best for all, but not at the expense of integrity.

Those who give from the heart, receive to the heart – in God's timing, not ours, and in God's currencies and measure, not ours. So although "duty" calls for a doubling of productivity, God may bless you with far more beyond the natural expected results and in many ways that can only be described as "priceless".

Double Your Sales

The challenge made in this book sounds a bit absurd; to "double" your sales. Quite frankly, it is a bit absurd to most. Not everyone can do it. But it's not because they can't; it's because they won't or simply don't know how. If you have the desire, what you will find within these pages can change your selling career forever. Yes, you can double your sales. You can triple your sales.

You can sell ten times as much as you are today. In sales, there is no limit to your productivity. There is only one absolute: *zero sales.* Everything above zero becomes a factor of previous performance. At some point in the past, you were only selling half what you are today. At some point in the future, you will be selling twice as much as you are today. This book helps you condense the periods of time between the natural doublings of your personal sales production.

Let's say that your natural doublings occur over a six-year period. The skill and strategy portion of this book shows you how to condense this time frame to six-month period, and in some cases, especially for those who undertake the Doubling Course, to a six-week period. It illustrates simple methods that are quite obvious and it shows you processes and strategies you probably would never run across during the normal course of doing business. Doubling does this while keeping in focus the integrity required of the Christian salesperson as he or she does business. You are always providing an example; a Christian witness to others.

This is not a read-it-once book: it was written as a foundational reference guide, as an inspirational and thought-provoking manuscript. It was written to be too inclusive for you to digest at one sitting. It was written to challenge you. Yes, you can double. You can do it again and again and again. Jesus provides a very vivid example of how we are to handle the responsibility of others' money: we are to use our talents and skills to provide an increase. In the Parable of the Talents, the *minimum* standard set, as a duty, is to strive to double. Rewards abound when you double.

As one illustration of the capability of the Doubling principles, I was contracted to design and facilitate a training program for a major computer service provider in Canada. I used the expectational selling format explained in this book – the group that was trained sold hardware service to business computer users.

The training took a total of just 15 hours spread over one month, but the results were astounding (and typical). Without adding any additional salespeople, service sales were up by 400%; more than half of the service sales force were selling at a rate three times their previous best or higher; the company's performance rating by the various watchdog agencies rose to put them at the top of best-performing companies. This all happened within three months of completing the training program!

If you don't think doubling your sales is possible, think again. This program didn't teach skills, only the strategies of expectational selling. With the addition of skill development, there is no limit to the increase. My personal increase was excellent – about $10,000 for 15 hours of facilitation, but my client's increase was astounding: an extra $3,000,000 per month in revenues! I brought everything I knew to the program; laid it "on the table" for the client. The client in turn committed their decision-making personnel to the project and carried the results of the program to the marketplace – and reaped their reward.

Sellegrity's Duty section combines five disciplines into one practical selling approach to help you achieve a doubling of your sales:

- Sales architecture (skill and strategy)
- Personality style types
- Preferential communication language
- Attitude development and control

- Goal setting and personal event management

These are molded into a unified, powerful approach that focuses on the most efficient method of selling known: *expectational selling.*

Sellegrity is a blueprint for increased sales: *your* increased sales. Each chapter contains strategies and techniques that can effectively double your personal sales. If they are learned and applied, the effect can be nothing short of astounding. Taken collectively or even independently, the suggestions in this book will assure you of a doubling in sales productivity if you plan and act as instructed; taken serially, one Doubling Point compounding the effect of the previous point, you can increase your sales by an astonishing thousand percent or more. Unthinkable? If you feel this is impossible, start opening up your mind to the realm of "What if?"

As a thirty-year-old “young” salesperson, I was selling recreational and business aircraft when a "what if?" thinking person introduced me to the strategic thinking that literally changed my selling career forever. He said, "Bob, you're good with customers, really good. What if you were to consider selling a 747 instead of a Cessna Skyhawk? What are the differences involved and ask yourself if you can realistically do it? If you can, then what if you try it? And more importantly, what if you succeed or fail? Ask yourself these questions and act accordingly."

I thought for a short time and then began to identify the components of the sale in relationship to the product and the end user. They were virtually the same. The skills were a bit up-scale but I felt I could handle that. Within one week, I had a serious potential client, had made purchasing and financing inroads with Boeing and had put many of the sales components together for a Cargo Version 747 sale. The client was only two doors down from my office and was in the business of shipping livestock worldwide. From a $25,000 to a $25,000,000 comfort zone; a thousand-fold jump! It was all in the thinking process and the actions that followed.

The sale didn't close due to a last-minute contract glitch, but it taught me a valuable lesson, as most “failures” do. It is possible to change your income level radically by changing your perception of selling and by changing your actions involved in selling. If you want a bigger view, find a higher perch. Today, the sale would have closed, for now I understand how to overcome the unmet expectation that effectively killed the deal back in 1975.

The important criteria for personal achievement has always been that you take personal responsibility for your actions, your thinking and your attitudes. Where you are right now is irrelevant: it's what happens from this moment forward that is really important.

For the Christian salesperson, it means merging your profession in with your purpose, for God has a personal plan for each of us.

> "*But as God has distributed to each one, as the Lord has called each one, so let him walk*"
> (1 Cor 7:17)

If your profession fits inside your purpose, then you can hit the home run. For most of us, however, our profession and our purpose in God seldom coincide, with the exception that God expects us to provide for our families and self, and to provide a witness for to the character and purpose of Christ, and this is where the profession and purpose always intersect. You are a living, breathing, walking, talking billboard for your life's philosophy.

Those who succeed in "merging" are those who can accept the responsibility of the witness, who can ascribe to the duty, and who will seek to become "meek", as Moses was meek, as opposed to becoming boastful and self-important, as most of the world expects you to become.

Passion comes from the desires of the heart. It should come as no surprise to the Christian, that God expects us to act passionately within our occupations, to work with our hearts first, then our minds. Having a passion for ethical selling is not an option if you are a salesperson by trade.

Anyone can coast with the crowd, to do what is expected by the masses, but it takes courage and boldness to break away and be different or to take a stand for righteousness. Intelligence is a nice asset but good character, perseverance, prayer and diligence bring more rewards.

> *"The plans of the diligent lead to profit; as surely as haste leads to poverty"*
> - Proverbs 21:5 NIV
>
> *"For the Lord gives wisdom, from His mouth comes knowledge and understanding"*
> - Proverbs 2:6 NAS

A warning, however: Once you decide that you will work to double your sales, you begin to stand apart from the average salesperson. This can bring pleasant or unpleasant results, depending on how much you disturb the status quo. Some managers and fellow salespeople will welcome your efforts; some will be intimidated; most will never notice.

My challenge to you is to find your own path to personal selling excellence. Yes, God has a great deal to do with the path, but it is your course to run – your decisions, your actions, your integrity at stake. I sincerely hope that you can double your sales but I fervently wish that you won't stop there, that you'll begin compounding until you experience a doubling each year, each quarter, perhaps even each month. Remember, approximately 80% of all sales are made by only 20% of the salespeople.

Your first challenge is to move into what I call Second Dimension Selling, where skills and strategies are the important tools of the professional salesperson. I encourage you to keep a diary to record your selling successes (and failures). In the future, it will become a part of your "selling well of knowledge."

Don't sell yourself short: take a realistic, optimistic view of your selling future and recognize that we all go through seasons where we have greater or lesser growth. Sometimes we even retreat. But these are just seasons, and they will change if you desire and seek growth that is worthy and inspired by God and not greed.

> *"He who pursues righteousness and love finds life, prosperity and honor."*
> *- Proverbs 21:21 NIV*

You have a mandate to fill, according to the Parable of the Talents – you must double at the minimum, and if you can do more, then the blessings will be even greater.

The important thing to remember is that you must strive for personal integrity in all you do because, in the final analysis, this is how you will be remembered by those whose lives you've touched.

Selling is the lowest paid and the highest paid profession. It can be the most relaxed or the most intense of positions. You choose.

YOUR "DOUBLING" STRATEGY

Doubling can mean doubling your income, doubling your sales volume, doubling your client base, doubling your profits, doubling your margins, doubling your per-sale amount or it can mean that you double your client satisfaction and retention. Doubling can be taken as a personal or corporate challenge, it can be directly related to sales or it can simply act as a philosophy of service, duty and accomplishment.

At the end of each chapter there is a "Doubling" summary. These suggestions recommend ways to develop the attitudes, strategies, tactics and skills necessary for doubling based on the material presented in the chapter. For the early chapters, the "Doubling" strategies are replaced by "Passion and Purpose" ideas.

The Increase

Sales increases can come immediately or they can come much later, depending upon your sales cycle. If your increases do not show up right away, examine the mechanics of the sales cycle to build a better appreciation of when the increases will come. Don't become discouraged if your customers' buying habits don't match your doubling expectations right away.

In attempting to double, you will need to make a lot of changes in your personal expectations, your management's expectations, and your customers' expectations. Some seeds that are planted may not come to harvest for ten years, twenty years or maybe never in your lifetime. A seed planted in faith will eventually sprout and provide return – but only God knows the timetable. A seed planted in greed will also eventually sprout and provide return – but you probably don't want to partake in the harvest because it will poison your spirit. The chaff imitates the wheat, but it has no nutrients.

> *"So are the ways of everyone that is greedy of gain which taketh away the life of the owners thereof"*
> *– Proverbs 1:19 KJV*

No Tricks

This book will not give you a simple, get-rich-quick formula for increasing your sales. Superior rewards tend to come from superior thinking and superior effort combined with an honest heart before God. There are strategies and skills that you can employ now that can have an immediate effect upon your sales, but most of your solid growth will come from dedicated study, practice and daily application of the principles and suggestions found within these pages. This book is a template for selling success; it is not a quick fix for missing skills or mediocre, sputtering efforts. Go it alone and you can have success; go it with God as your partner and your success will provide a rock-solid platform that will ensure that you can deliver, even under the most trying circumstances. As a Christian, you have a choice.

> *"Commit your works to the Lord and your plans will be established"*
>
> *– Proverbs 16:3 NAS*

VICTORY CAN BE YOURS

In Section Two, the "duty" portion of this book, where the actual skills and strategies are explored in detail, you can embark on a venture that can lead to success or frustration, depending upon how you act on the information. You can do one of three things upon reading the information, ideas and strategies:

1. You can decide to do nothing, in which case you've just wasted money on this book that you'll probably need when you retire, if you retire.
2. You can say, "Well, there are a lot of good things here, some really interesting ideas. I'm going to really make a go of it. Yes, I'm going to change my life starting right now! First thing in the morning, I'm putting this book into action!"

   You are <u>not</u> likely to succeed.

3. You can take one thing at a time and pay strict attention to that one thing for an entire week. You have to leave all other things alone, focusing and concentrating on that one thing for a week. Learn it inside out. Make it a part of your personality. In my DOUBLING courses, we practice each major skill continuously for three weeks!

If you follow it the advice in selection 3, you will be further ahead than if you try to enact all the ideas at once.

SECTION 1

CHARACTER, PURPOSE AND PASSION

The impact of character is truly your legacy. As I finish this, I am on the other side of 70 – so I have some significant life landscapes to survey.

With age comes a certain degree of wisdom, and a shocking realization that you really know very little about anything, or so it seems. Mortality issues begin to appear and thus, legacy issues as well. Life zooms by and in the blink of an eye, I find myself considering what else I can fit into it before God requires an entrance-interview with me.

The sad part is that you cannot go back and do it over, to erase the bad parts and grab more good parts. All we have is the moment – the day. If we can't make a difference in the moment then it will never be done by the time your life is summarized.

Character is built with one tiny stone at a time: one little pebble heaped upon another. God's instruction and Spirit are the mortar and if it's not there then the pebbles cannot gain any collective strength. They take no discernable shape and offer no structural support.

It's been said that good character takes a lifetime to build and a second to destroy. Any "upstanding citizen" who's been caught in deceit or fraud knows what this is all about: honor followed by disgrace; irrecoverable.

Character is built, not inherited or bestowed. We are not born good, we are born sinners, and sin is the cancer of character: sin is never benign.

"Good" character must be appropriated for it is not normal to be upstanding and faultless. Rather it is our base nature to be deceitful and sneaky and to lie and to steal. When you become born again, the Spirit of God infuses your soul and heart – and things change. You don't become "clean" but you do develop a hunger for righteousness – or doing the "right" thing. You see with new eyes, feel with a fresh heart and "character" becomes ever more important. When you "backslide", these are usually the first things to go – the hunger for righteousness becomes worldly lust, honesty transitions to deceitfulness and a humble spirit is overtaken by pride.

One of the Beatitudes say that those who hunger and thirst for righteousness shall be satisfied. Conversely, if you hunger and thirst after unrighteousness, then you will be unsatisfied and the cravings for unrighteousness will continue and intensify – like a cancer. Hence those who crave riches for riches sake, are never fulfilled. But those who were awarded riches as a blessing because they sought righteousness are satisfied. In many cases, these people give their wealth away – only to be blessed again and again.

Your character is a reflection of your choices in life: all of them.

It is the sum total of your choices, all the little decisions and the big ones too. Sometimes the little, seemingly unimportant and insignificant choices grow to become the giant-killers of life. Maybe it's an innocent e-mail to a long-lost flame that eventually spirals out of control to kill a stable marriage, or a little white lie that undermines the trust of a close friend.

However, seemingly minor choices can work the other way too. When I was 19, alone and living a thousand miles from my home, I decided to spend five dollars on a Cessna Discovery Flight at the local airport. In a short thirty minutes, a discouraged and lost young lad left his despair behind and was filled with a new vision and hope. Two years later I was flying executives in and out of New York City.

Section 1: Character, Purpose and Passion

Small decisions can trigger massive results.

This section is about the inner you. It is about the who you are under your skin, in the quiet times and when no one else is there but you and God. It's about your motives, your dreams, and your submission to God. It's about your soul and your passions.

Am I qualified to write about this? I don't know. It's not about me – it's about you. In some areas I am over-qualified; in others I may be as puzzled by life just as you are. Take what you can from it.

Personal performance is how you achieve your goals, your dreams, and your obligations. The difficult task is to distinguish which things are of God and which things are of you, because it's really easy to confuse the two. I have found that most things in life have a personal "flesh" foundation and God only steps in when you need a significant correction or epiphany.

Personal passion is about how you focus your energies, your talents and your emotions. Passion is about learning how to abandon yourself to a cause, to an outcome, to a process and to building your character.

At the end of every chapter, there are a number of summary points that challenge you in the area of Christian character and purpose. These are "pondering points", not recipes for success. They are ideas for you to consider concerning your direction, your character and your focus. Some could mean that a life-changing decision is required, others might draw a simple, "Hmmm."

This first section, four chapters, is to help you focus. It's meant to be a private conversation, something that triggers a dialogue between your heart and your head so that a unified, congruent personal plan emerges. The Bible warns us about being double-minded, about having one foot splashing in the mud puddles of the world and one foot resting in the green grass of God's garden. By aligning your head and heart in a singular focus, your life stabilizes, your character becomes dependable, your achievements become noticeable and you can leave the mud puddles to someone else.

ETHICS AND INTEGRITY

Ethics and Integrity Explained · Ethics are Driven by Spirits · The Cornerstones of Character and Duty · The Parable of the Talents · Faith Platform · The Parable of the Good Sellers

The Enron debacle in 2002 revealed the tip of an ethical iceberg that continues to impact the business and political world today. It, unfortunately, was just the harbinger of much bigger corporate greed and mismanagement issues to emerge, issues without end it seems, spreading deeply into politics as well. Personal greed, scheming and executive cunning have made a mockery of free enterprise, exchanging integrity for power and principles for private gain.

"*Sellegrity*" is about doing business in a world that seems to have a very difficult time in understanding what true ethics are.

ETHICS EXPLAINED

For most, "ethics" are simply the actions that reflect current acceptable business or social practices seemingly unfiltered though the application of righteous principle. For the Christian, it is the continuous application of righteous principle that is required and not "acceptable social practices".

Your ethics reflect your current belief systems: **what you do in secret <u>is</u> really who you are**.

The definition of ethics in the dictionary is fairly straightforward:

- the discipline dealing with what is good and bad and with moral duty and obligation

- a set of moral principles or values

- the principles and expectations of *conduct* governing an individual or a group
- a guiding philosophy

All of the above definitions apply to the Christian salesperson, as they apply equally to everyone else. However, for the Christian, "ethics" should be based primarily upon the righteousness principles, values, examples and philosophies found in the Bible. For the rest of the world, ethics are based on competing philosophies; some are religious-based, many are culture-based or politically-based.

In Genesis, we are told of the Tree of Good and Evil. We are not to participate in this arena. This is where the "do good deeds" religiosity springs forth and it is the Devil's playground, tricking many into believing that heavenly worthiness is found in "doing good works". It is not. When a person is born again, born of the Spirit, they now belong to the Tree of Righteousness and your heavenly worthiness is found in your personal relationship with Christ and nowhere else.

The Christian salesperson is under considerable peer pressure to substitute popular "success" teachings for Biblical principles or to mix them to form some form of hybrid philosophy that diminishes the intensity, purpose and clarity of the Bible. Most popular success teachings endorse self-centered behavior; the Bible does not, it endorses God-centered behavior.

The servant's heart should give no play to vanity or personal power schemes and self-help writings should be treated as practical tools and not as heart-borne core values or beliefs.

In practice, ethics has become a reflection of the acceptable practices of society, either in a micro-society, such as within a board of directors or in a specialized business segment, or in a macro society, such as in "North America" or "Canada" or in "third world countries." This dangerous practice eventually leads to an unrestrained quest for personal gain and power that compromises so many innocents along the way. Social traditions are not meant to be the foundation of ethics. They form a part of the base, but not *the* base.

Ethics

Principles	Traditions	Attitudes
Absolutes	Accepted Social Practices	Goals
Self-Evident Truths	Local & National Laws	Self-Image
"Unshakeable – Unbreakable"	Peer Pressure	Position
Right or Wrong	Group Dynamics	Power Issues

When the Principles are left out of the equation, then the foundation is made up of shifting expectations and attitudes that reflect the current trends of society. This is what is known as "situational ethics." Every time this occurs, a societal collapse eventually follows. This is where most of the world finds itself today. If the Principles are restored, then both the Traditions and the Attitudes reflect a balanced and productive society. When the Principles are removed (or replaced with false principles) then the Traditions and Attitudes are free to follow the path of least resistance towards greed and power and self-indulgence.

Principles based on Biblical Righteousness are meant to identify, restrain and condemn unacceptable behavior, whereas personal, opinion-based attitudes only magnify "socially acceptable" behavior and the cultural traditions legitimize (or condemn) personal or group behavior. The breakdown in society occurs when the Righteous Principles are removed, restructured, restated or diluted. Today, our society has "legally" removed, restructured, restated or diluted the Righteous Principles from the law, from the school and from the home.

Most of today's modern democratic societies, including those of both Canada and America, used Biblical principles as the primary foundation for their societies. In a few hundred years, the founding principles have been attacked, quarantined or eroded so as to limit or remove their consequence and guidance mandates. Personal power, progressivism and achievement philosophies have replaced them. It's absolutely no surprise to have an "Enron" event – it was the natural consequence of removing righteousness from the backrooms and boardrooms of business. If you take the levees away from the river, it floods the city and the countryside and the land becomes uninhabitable and disease becomes dominant. It is the picture of today's society.

From Jude 1, we can gain a glimpse of a society that has abandoned righteousness in favor of personal pleasures, as God described it:

> 7 *In a similar way, Sodom and Gomorrah and the surrounding towns gave themselves up to sexual immorality and perversion. They serve as an example of those who suffer the punishment of eternal fire.*
>
> 8 *In the very same way, these dreamers pollute their own bodies, reject authority and slander celestial beings.*
>
> 9 *But even the archangel Michael, when he was disputing with the devil about the body of Moses, did not dare to bring a slanderous accusation against him, but said, "The Lord rebuke you!"*
>
> 10 *Yet these men speak abusively against whatever they do not understand; and what things they do understand by instinct, like unreasoning animals—these are the very things that destroy them.*

11 *Woe to them! They have taken the way of Cain; they have
rushed for profit into Balaam's error; they have been
destroyed in Korah's rebellion.*

12 *These men are blemishes at your love feasts, eating with
you without the slightest qualm—shepherds who feed only
themselves. They are clouds without rain, blown along by the
wind; autumn trees, without fruit and uprooted—twice dead.*

13 *They are wild waves of the sea, foaming up their shame;
wandering stars, for whom blackest darkness has been
reserved forever.*

14 *Enoch, the seventh from Adam, prophesied about these
men: "See, the Lord is coming with thousands upon
thousands of his holy ones* 15*to judge everyone, and to convict
all the ungodly of all the ungodly acts they have done in the
ungodly way, and of all the harsh words ungodly sinners
have spoken against him."*

16 *These men are grumblers and faultfinders; they follow
their own evil desires; they boast about themselves and flatter
others for their own advantage.*

17 *But, dear friends, remember what the apostles of our
Lord Jesus Christ foretold.* 18*They said to you, "In the last
times there will be scoffers who will follow their own ungodly
desires."*

19 *These are the men who divide you, who follow mere
natural instincts and do not have the Spirit.*

20 *But you, dear friends, build yourselves up in your most
holy faith and pray in the Holy Spirit.* 21*Keep yourselves in
God's love as you wait for the mercy of our Lord Jesus Christ
to bring you to eternal life.*

22 *Be merciful to those who doubt;* 23*snatch others from the
fire and save them; to others show mercy, mixed with fear—
hating even the clothing stained by corrupted flesh. "(NIV)*

According to the above, God doesn't leave much to the imagination concerning His position on immoral and unethical behavior.

ETHICAL FILTERS

Look at ethics as your filters for decisions, actions and ideas. The outer filter should be the Principles filter – the one that deals with ultimate right and wrong. If you hold to Principles, your decisions are easy and your actions are deliberate; your plumb line for living is strong and straight. If you ignore the Principles, then your decisions and actions will only have personal attitudes and social traditions as your filters. Your plumb line is gone, replace by situational thoughts, others' expectations for you, fickle feelings and dangerous desires. These are forever shifting and changing as situations change and societies soften and sicken. If you rely on societal norms then anything is possible – and probable.

Principles, however, can also have an unrighteous base, such as those held by terrorists like ISIS, in which case principles can empower extremism, destruction and martyrdom. Because principles can be strong enough to cause a man to give his life for a cause, a principle can become more important than life itself. For the Christian, we are told this; that our lives are the price that will be extracted for our allegiance to Christ. But likewise is the ISIS soldier taught, but for "Allah". Both are willing to die for a cause. One dies to preserve life and goodness, one dies for self-glorification.

Ethics Are Driven by Spirits

Since this book is about ethical selling for the Christian business person, it is concerned about the spiritual world as well as the natural world. In the example shown, "Righteous" Principles, Attitudes and Traditions are empowered by guardian spirits and are the domain of God.

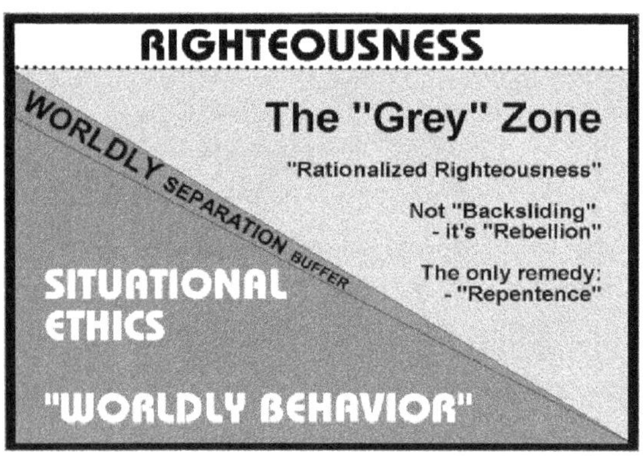

"Unrighteous" Principles, Attitudes and Traditions are the habitation of *strongman* spirits and are the domain of demons. That means that there will always be a battle raging within the Spirit-filled Christian when dealing with worldly matters – such as doing business.

If the guardian spirits of righteousness-based Principles are removed, replaced or ignored, then you unleash the strongman spirits that inhabit the unrighteous Principles, Attitudes and Traditions of society. It is then that you begin the slide into the "Grey Zone" of Rationalized Righteousness, where your behavior may be better and purer than that of dominant culture, but it is not at the level of purity expected or illustrated through the Bible. Its commandments and instructions are clear, precise and leave little or no room for personal interpretation but a lot of room for personal application.

An inch at a time, many of us creep farther away from what God expects of us and we move closer and closer to the acceptable social behavior of the world. It's like the illustration of the frog and the pot of boiling water. If you drop a frog into a shallow pan of boiling water, he will immediately hop out – somewhat singed, but nonetheless, alive. If you put the frog into the pot when the water is simply lukewarm, he will remain. Turn up the heat on the pot and the frog will acclimatize all the way to a boiling death without any attempt to escape his fate.

Similarly, when the Christian strays from righteousness and rationalizes his or her behavior one small moral breech at a time the day eventually arrives when true spiritual death is just one more breech away. The "buffer" – the supposedly distinction between worldly behavior and Christian behavior – becomes thinner and thinner until it merges with worldly behavior and there is no outward or spiritual distinction between the rebellious Christian and society in general. The deeper and steeper the incline, the harder it is to repent and recover until it becomes virtually impossible without a miraculous intervention.

THE CHARACTER OF THE SERVANT HEART

You're a Witness · Your Character on Trial · Twenty Character Traits · Clean Thinking · Honorable Actions · Being Trustworthy · The Principle of the Second Thought · Passion and Purpose

YOU'RE A WITNESS

Once you become a Christian, you offer yourself as a witness for others. Everything you do, say or even think becomes the subject of examination by others. Because you confess Christ to be your Lord and Savior, you immediately stand out. You cannot be anonymous. You have an identity in God, and He will hold you accountable for your actions as they affect others and yourself.

You are different from the non-Christian, for as soon as you accept Christ into your heart as your Lord and Savior, you now become "in the world, but no longer a part of it". You are expected to be an example, a work-in-progress, expressing the character of Christ to others through your "walk". When the world goes crazy and Christians are persecuted and killed for their faith as the Bible prophetically declares, and you are fingered and charged, you do not want the charges dismissed for lack of evidence! Guilty is good.

Being a witness for your beliefs is a delicate issue for salespeople, for most sell in a spiritually-hostile territory, sometimes expected to push for sales in an unethical manner by an equally-unethical sales manager, and asked to entertain or join the client in a non-Christian setting, such as in a bar or even in a strip club. You have to be able to determine when and how is the best way to exhibit your foundations, for there are times when your beliefs will offend others and there are times when your beliefs will attract others.

Your Character on Trial

Let's have a look at what makes up good Christian character. The Bible is devoted to provide examples of both good and bad character, because that is the bottom line for the Christian: to develop Christ-like character and to spread the Gospel (the Great Commission). Christ was the servant of humanity and of God, so as an example of the servant's character, there is no better. As a Christian, it is now your nature to lead by serving, to show example by personal deed, to be humble without bringing upon yourself humiliation.

What you think about most of the time is who you'll become.

Or, as the Bible puts it, *"what a man thinks in his heart, so is he"* (Proverbs 23:7). There is a very clear distinction between the thoughts of the mind and the thoughts of the heart, for it is the purposes, foundations, loves and directions that dwell in the heart that are the key to your character. God knows that the mind can be manipulated, He knows that man uses the mind to deceive and bamboozle. And because of our "earthly" nature, He is concerned with the pureness and integrity of your heart – personally.

Character does not spring from what you are, it springs from who you are, and God is in the business of putting a mirror in front of your face each day so that you can have a deep gaze at the reflection.

Twenty Traits of Character

Consider these twenty defining areas of "character", especially important when seen in the context of *Sellegrity*. Rate yourself on a scale of one to five, add up your scores and you will come up with an "Integrity" percentage.

1. **Congruency**, meaning that what you project to others is really who you are; your "head" and your "heart" act in unison. It also means that what you say about another when they are absent is exactly what you would say about them if they were present. Congruency also means consistency; you are reliable because you are predictable, and this is important for both your clients and your management. Congruency leads to

   [/]

trustworthiness, an essential ingredient for long-term success in selling, management – or life in general.

2. **Honesty**, meaning that deceitfulness is not present in any form. Transparency is the cornerstone of honesty, while conspiracy is its enemy. Omission has an equal or greater effect that lying has. Being fully honest is a tough task in a world that seems to run on white lies and bold deception. However, can you picture Christ being caught in a lie? We all know the embarrassment that it brings, the extra effort it entails to remember the lie that's been told, and the damage it can do. Trust is immediately sacrificed when a lie is uncovered. /5

3. **Integrity**, meaning that you stand by your word and deed regardless of the consequences. Integrity is earned, not declared or bought. It comes through a process of testing and is declared by others about you and not by you for yourself. I am always distrustful of a person or firm that boasts or promotes integrity as their motto. It usually means the opposite. Integrity is the result of character trial; a reputation that should be highly-prized, a banner worn humbly, for as hard as it is to achieve, it is far easier to lose. Once lost, it is almost impossible to regain. Integrity greatly depends upon a virtuous and wholesome nature. /5

4. **Accountability**, meaning that you accept the responsibility for your actions and promises. In today's business world, accountability is a term used to describe the actions necessary to bring a deceitful person to justice, rather than its positive meaning and purpose, and that is to act in a manner that declares transparency and correctness. A servant-hearted salesperson is one who at all times offers accountability for his or her actions and decisions, without hesitation. Accountability means truth in all things, including expense accounts that are not padded and client reports that are accurate and complete. /5

5. **Trustworthiness**, meaning that you do not violate or expose the intimacies that others have entrusted to you /5

for safekeeping. Being trustworthy is the cornerstone of the salesperson-client relationship. It means that an economic relationship can be established that will withstand the test and trials of time and competition. Clients will easily switch suppliers if there is no trust bond established, but are always reluctant if trust has been firmly established. Trustworthiness is a complex issue, made up of ingredients such as honesty, integrity, congruency, accountability, responsibility, timeliness, diligence, respect, honor and most of the other character traits.

6. **Timeliness**, meaning that you are respectful and will work with all available effort to meet or exceed the expectations of others concerning the performance of an agreed-to task, meeting or deadline. Timeliness shows respect for another, and it indicates that you truly care about the other person. For some personality styles, timeliness is a problem and must be consciously monitored to ensure it is not violated. /5

7. **Diligence,** meaning that you are careful in the allotment of your resources so that you finish those things that have been promised by you to others, first; that you do not start things and then leave them unfinished, and that you do not over-promise and under-deliver. Diligence looks after the little things as well as the big picture; it ensures that things are correct and on time. Diligence is a cornerstone of trust and integrity. /5

8. **Sincerity,** meaning that you express personal issues and concerns with your heart and not your head; that you don't talk down to another or patronize. Sincerity is the foundation of true service, along with its counterpart, **empathy**. Both work together to form a platform of a willingness to understand the position of another. Without this platform, talk becomes product-centered and not customer-centered, goals become selfish and actions become weak and half-hearted. /5

9. **Respect**, meaning that you allow for other views and opinions, harbor no feelings of bigotry, racism or malice /5

towards others, and refrain from judgment in your heart of another person's soul. Respect is evident when you refrain from conspiracy against another's character or position, even when you know that you can do the task better, faster, more effectively.

10. **Resourcefulness,** meaning that the lack of an apparent solution does not mean the termination of effort. Clients adore a resourceful salesperson, one who constantly thinks of ways to overcome problems or finds solutions using extraordinary, "extra mile" effort. Resourcefulness means that as a salesperson, you get to know the people in your business who can make a difference to your client; the production managers, the accounting supervisor, the truck driver. When extraordinary expectations are on the table, you must be able to draw upon extraordinary resources and relationships. /5

11. **Discernment,** meaning that you carefully weigh the issues before engaging your mouth; hesitation and balanced thought help prevent the tongue from tripping you up. As in broadcasting, the seven-second taped delay is a valuable tool for trapping the unwholesome word before it has impact. Discernment is most critical when you have a ranting client who needs to vent. Engaging in a shouting match only adds fuel to the fire; discernment would look at the larger impact and you would carefully look for ways to diffuse the situation rather than to immediately react. Discernment looks for the reasons behind expressed issues or behavior and seeks to deal with the root causes. /5

12. **Compassion,** meaning that you respond to help others in need without extraordinary thought or consideration; you just do it. It also means that you seek no glory or recognition in doing the deed; anonymity is a virtue and a true test of the pureness of the motivation. Compassion is at the core of the servant's heart. /5

13. **Expressing a Servant's Heart**, for it is the example of Christ in action. To lead by serving is the most powerful and respected example; to sell by serving is the ultimate gift to your client and to your employer, for it leads to long-term client relations and retention, increased profitability and selling insight that cannot be achieved through pressure sales. /5

14. **A Passion for Excellence**, for doing things right the first time is always beneficial. Present your talents as unto the Lord, for He is the final judge of your good works. Every employer and client respects a job well done, on time and as promised. This should be your skills and strategies goal professionally; that you learn how to achieve excellence as judged by your employer, your customers and your industry, and, of course, God. /5

15. **Humility,** meaning that you don't allow pride or a sense of undeservedness to become your shield or defense, and that a simple yet sincere, "Thank you" or, "I appreciate that" will bless the giver. Humbleness is a great strength for the servant seller, for it disarms the aggressive and endears the passive. It is harder to be humble than to be proud, but true humility expresses itself in thanksgiving for opportunities, for trials and for blessings. /5

16. **Demeanor,** meaning that you have the ability to express yourself in a manner that speaks positively or negatively to others; choose to be positive, expressed through prosperity, laughter, joy, smiles, lightheartedness, encouragement, blessing, honor, compassion, excitement, enthusiasm, interest and most of all, love. /5

17. **Loyalty**, meaning if you make a commitment to another, for a purpose, that you remain true and honorable to the commitment, and to the person. Loyalty always demands sacrifice, accountability and responsibility. Loyalty stems from *covenantal* liaisons, and not so much from agreements, as covenants are made between hearts and /5

between minds. Loyalty is not meant for causes or ideals, it is meant for people. Misplaced loyalty is the playground of the devil, and many relationships can be destroyed because loyalty is misunderstood or manipulated. See "Maintaining Covenant" below.

18. **Patience,** meaning that God does not always work on your timetable, but that your character is worked out in trial and in persistence. Waiting is sometimes the hardest work of all, and the ability to discern when patience is appropriate is a virtue. /5

19. **Giving,** meaning that your purpose in God will always have a component of giving, sometimes way beyond what would be expected. Giving means not holding back; providing what is needed from what you have or can get. It is the professional salesperson's hallmark for client satisfaction, but accomplished with wisdom, always. /5

20. **Maintaining Covenant,** meaning that most arrangements between parties are contractual, agreement-based, and that covenant-based agreements are reserved only for relationship issues, and only after a substantial period of character examination (ten years or so) and then when made, for a lifetime: irrevocable. Covenant is never to be considered lightly. Marriage is covenantal.. /5

/100

Your Character Score

Adding up the scores, you will come up with a number out of a total of 100. Call it a percentage if you will – a rating of character. No one hits 100. This is your number; something to be worked upon, to be raised. Since each of us is a work-in-progress, every increase is a cause for celebration. When I first took this "test" – honestly – I was shocked to find myself at a dismal 53.

KEEPING THE COMMANDMENTS

Many salespeople are faced with temptation every day. If you are "on the road" then a sense of invisibility can lull you into thinking that you can get away with actions and thoughts that you would not consider at all if your spouse (or your mother) was nearby.

The Ten Commandments lay out the foundations for moral behavior. These are the absolutes that God expects of all mankind, not just born-again Christians, yet it seems that our society has little regard for them any longer. Some commandments are broken regularly, even applauded by Hollywood and the media. Divorce now affects more than one-half of all marriages. Murder results in a slap on the wrist. Theft is commonplace and in some societies, expected. Lawlessness has replaced order in many parts of the world and the cheaters are rewarded.

It is easy to fall into the societal lure of joining in; going to the strip clubs, engaging in drunkenness and lewd behavior, having a one-night stand in a far-off city, watching porn on the internet, flirting with a fellow employee or traveler, and many other issues of incorrect behavior that diminish your character, usually in private.

Keeping the commandments is strictly a personal issue. In Old Testament times, it led to rigidity, religiosity, and societies driven to strict rules and laws, and numerous sub-sets of laws. This interpretation of the commandments into daily rituals and governing laws that no one could keep gave rise to those who constantly judged others. It is why, when Jesus came, God blessed us with *grace.*

It's time that we all took a look at the foundations that God meant for mankind and took them to heart. You'll find the Ten Commandments in Exodus chapter 20: 3-17. (KJV). As you read them, perhaps for the first time, drink in the unmistakable qualities of clarity and steadfastness. These are commandments – absolutes, not suggestions – given to Moses by God:

1. *Thou shalt have no other gods before me.*

2. *Thou shalt not make unto thee any graven image, or any likeness of any thing that is in heaven above, or that is in the earth beneath, or that is in the water under the earth: thou shalt not bow down thyself to them, nor serve them: for I the* **LORD** *thy God am a jealous God, visiting the iniquity of the fathers upon the children unto the third and fourth generation of them that hate me; and showing mercy unto thousands of them that love me, and keep my commandments.*

3. *Thou shalt not take the name of the* **LORD** *thy God in vain; for the* **LORD** *will not hold him guiltless that takes his name in vain.*

4. *Remember the Sabbath day, to keep it holy. Six days shalt thou labor, and do all thy work, but the seventh day is the Sabbath of the* **LORD** *thy God: in it thou shalt not do any work, thou, nor thy son, nor thy daughter, thy manservant, nor thy maidservant, nor thy cattle, nor thy stranger that is within thy gates: For in six days the* **LORD** *made heaven and earth, the sea, and all that in them is, and rested the seventh day: wherefore the* **LORD** *blessed the Sabbath day, and hallowed it.*

5. *Honor thy father and thy mother: that thy days may be long upon the land which the* **LORD** *thy God gives thee.*

6. *Thou shalt not kill.*

7. *Thou shalt not commit adultery.*

8. *Thou shalt not steal.*

9. *Thou shalt not bear false witness against thy neighbor.*

10. *Thou shalt not covet thy neighbor's house, thou shalt not covet thy neighbor's wife, nor his manservant, nor his maidservant, nor his ox, nor his ass, nor any thing that is thy neighbor's.*

These should not need any explanation to the Christian or the Jew. These are simple, rules for maintaining integrity and peace in a society.

Yet in today's society, every single one of these commandments is compromised by the laws of the land, placing man above God and bringing judgment upon those nations that permit the subversion. This, of course, makes it even more difficult to uphold the character expected by God when everything and almost everyone around you – maybe even your spouse and children – see no harm in the secular.

However, grace is not based on the law, it is based in God's character to forgive and to absorb those things that you cannot. Grace is boundless, cannot be measured and is unexplainable in human terms. Yes, the ten commandments are valuable – they form a foundation of ethical living. But we are all flawed, no one is perfect, and we fall far short of the mark suggested by the ten commandments. That is the miracle of Christ: that wherever iniquity shows itself in our personal lives, that the Spirit of God is more than able to cover us with grace and forgiveness.

Reflection

1. Decide to honor God. Do not compromise, but follow His commandments by faith. This means praying, tithing, and helping those in need. Giving is the antidote for greed. It means that your work is accomplished in a manner that will please the Lord as if He is your only audience, your closest confidant, your mentor and sole judge concerning your destiny – because He is.

2. Have a look at your character. Review each of the character issues brought up in this chapter and rate yourself as to your 'character success" or your "character lacking". There are always "character lacking" issues, and you need to list these and work on one at a time until they are conquered. Don't take them all on at once or even picture yourself as having all of your character faults at once – it can be depressing – but always picture yourself as a work-in-progress. One at a time, and take the time to slowly correct each area.

3. Look at the qualities of excellence in your life and decide where you are going to make immediate improvements. These are usually quick-decision issues, like the way you dress. One morning you're dressed like a slob and that afternoon, you can be completely tidied up, and everyday thereafter you can simply choose to be well-dressed and "a cut above". There's no learning

curve (for most) – just a decision, and maybe a new wardrobe. Isolate the excellence issues and make the quality decisions that need to be made – and stick by them. You literally can become "the new you" very quickly.

4. Good guys DO finish first. A recent study by Jim Collins in his landmark book, Good to Great[1], shows that the very best performing companies in the USA over an extended period of time (15 years or longer) were run primarily by conservative, brave, honest people who trust and praise their staff and who accept responsibility when things don't work out. These are people who believe in good character FIRST, and performance second. Good character and striving for personal excellence is respected, does pay rewards and is the ultimate measure of a person.

5. A Japanese industrialist once penned the words as a creed for his business life and his company:

   "The creation of value is the only and everlasting source of profit"

   To double your sales and more, concentrate on the meaning of "value". If you truly discover its meaning past the dollars and cents relationship, then you will have discovered the key to everlasting benefit. Write it down – "Value" – and everything that you think is associated with the term. Clue: there's a lot of "character" in "value". If your character has no value, then your access to resources will eventually be denied.

6. There is a great deal of emphasis today on personal independence and assertiveness. Unfortunately, this also tends to result in personal aggressiveness, defensiveness and self-centeredness; issues that are counter-productive to the building of a good character. We are all "personally independent" by design. Unique. It's God's plan. But it is what we do with our independent nature that sets us apart. Look at what you have

control over – make a list – you'll probably be surprised at how much you actually DO control. Personal independence means personal accountability. Want to double your sales? Then be prepared to double your accountability. As an exercise, isolate the things in business for which you are accountable – and why. Then look at those things you could be accountable for that will make a difference in the sales arena, such as promotion, advertising, customer service, trade shows, client feedback surveys, new product development input, etc.

7. There has been an entire industry created out of helping people to reshape and refocus their lives. Twelve – step programs abound, endless retreats and purpose-driven programs draw participants towards a gradual new confidence. However, as good as these programs are, there have also been cases of instantaneous change – people being overhauled in an instant because of God's intervention through His Holy Spirit, or – and it's a big "or" – they just simply, radically, decided to behave differently – and stuck to their decision.

It sounds too easy, but it happens every day. It's not complex – it just takes inner boldness and resolve. It happened to me once – when I decided to become a pilot and leave the "dopey" mentality I had been living in behind. It was an instantaneous and remarkable change. The mind and the heart have an incredibly powerful effect upon the body – as does God – and if you can accept a sudden change event as being possible, then you likely can achieve it.

Don't worry about what others may say, just hold firmly to the new you in your head and heart and move on with your "new self." This does not work when you are trying to develop new skills, however, because they tend to be acquired gradually, layer upon layer. Strategies and tactics – the "how" you use your current skills – can be instantaneously formulated and put into action. As in my case, I decided to become a pilot, could see it happening, but had no skills. They took years to acquire. But I was there in my head and my heart long before that final check ride for my professional certification.

In a spiritual sense, God's Spirit can also change you, but in much greater sense than just a "job" change. He changes your heart... and then that changes your head. In 1980, He took a middle-aged alcoholic skirt-chaser and in an instant drove the cravings from him. In an instant. His Spirit and my personal conviction have kept those cravings at bay for 37 years and counting.

The character of the servant heart must be protected and fed the Word if it is going to survive and grow. It takes awareness, prayer, submission, effort, diligence and forcefulness. As in Ephesians 6, you MUST stand.

PURPOSE AND PLANNING

God Has a Purpose for You · The Difference Between Purpose and Goals · The Five Principles of Purpose · Goals · Difficult Habits · With a Dream in Your Heart Expectations · Goals · Timing · Long Goals · Short Goals · Immediate Objectives · Priority Action · Resources · Accountability · Commitment · Revise, Reset and Recharge · Magnificent Obsession · Only You? · Self-Motivation · The Beethoven Grip · Passion Points

GOD HAS A PURPOSE FOR YOU

Each of us was known to God before we were even conceived. A purpose was created by God for every individual on the earth and you fit into His master plan. Unfortunately, you will never get to know your plan unless you can dialogue with God through meditation on the Word of God or through prayer and fasting. God just doesn't seem to hand out a set of instructions with a step-by-step guide for a perfect Christian life. He sends us on a journey of discovery to learn about ourselves, others, and Him.

The journey lasts forever and the only true goal is submission to Jesus as your Lord and Savior. His only requirement – *"who do you say that I am?"* and *"do you love me?"* It is the only fixed road marker along the way, all others are dangling carrots as God pulls us ahead to greater and greater capability in Him.

You, of course, have a choice. You can submit to His purpose for you, or you can go your own way, which is what the majority of us do. Our own path consists of the goals and achievements that are important to this world: position, profession, possessions, beauty, power, influence, money. These are not to be dismissed totally as being the opposite of what God wants for you, for we do have to live in the world even though once you are born again, you are not of the world any longer, having been separated from it by the Spirit.

God's path is very different. His purpose is divine, his goal is to see you walk in the fullness of His blessings, to achieve a harvest of souls for the Kingdom. Every person's path and purpose is unique and God truly cares about you as an individual. He won't tell you what to do, for you get to choose your own course, to run in your own race, but the purpose of your race must be grounded in serving God.

The Difference Between Purpose and Goals
Purpose is defined by the Oxford Dictionary as, "the object for which anything is done or made, or for which it exists". In reference to God, it is why he made you – the objective He has in mind for you. But we are not robots; we have a free will and mind and can choose to do good or evil, to bless or to curse, to submit or rebel, to be responsible or carefree, to work hard or loaf, to embrace God or to embrace humanism.

Just because God makes us in His image with a specific purpose in mind, does not mean we will ever find it, because we first have to submit, then seek. In today's world, that means swimming upstream, against the flow of worldly expectations and rewards.

Goals tend to be man-conceived targets that pull us ahead in tangible areas; a new car, better job, money in a savings account, a house. There is nothing wrong with having goals; I devote an entire chapter to achieving them because they are important as a tool for you to use for personal growth. But they must never be confused with, or replace, purpose.

Goals are simple and easy to understand. Purpose is not. Goals can be surrounded by achievement language, such as completion date, milestones and task priorities. Purpose is surrounded by motive, by effect, by principle, by service.

Purpose is more important than achieving goals; it always supersedes goals as the final reason for life. Worthwhile goals may or may not be directly related to your purpose and many times they are required to provide decent living conditions for you and your family. But when "secular" goals, those accomplishments or possessions you desire for your own gratification, replace your desire to serve God or to serve your family, then trouble looms. Your path will veer from God's path for you and a period of trouble will loom ahead.

Goals are well-explained in this book. You should have goals, in a priority order, but they should always be tested against your God-based purpose. Recognize them for what they are and be wary of those goals and desires that draw you into the humanistic thinking that you are at the center of the universe and that you can achieve anything that your mind can conceive and believe, as Napoleon Hill so boldly states in his "bible" for secular success, Think and Grow Rich.

David Kalamen, in his book, Life Purpose, explores five "principals of purpose" for you to consider. I highly recommend this book if you are struggling with trying to find out what God has in mind for your life. It's available from Kelowna Christian Center in British Columbia, Canada (Telephone (250) 762-9559 or go to www.kcc.net)

- God's purpose and plans are achievable.
- Every purpose has its fullness of time.
- Every purpose in God has an enemy.
- All things work together for good.
- Rejecting the call may mean being replaced.

His Purpose and Plans are Achievable.

God does not make mistakes. If He has called you to a purpose, then He will make available the resources and stamina for you to achieve the purpose and to work His plans. He does not tease. Not everyone completes their purpose, but those who strive to do the will and the work of the Lord will find true joy in life and reward in Heaven.

Every Purpose has its Fullness of Time

We do not know the Lord's timetable for us. It is the one thing that tends to be hidden from view, but we know that there will always be an appropriate time for the Lord to work through you. Your job: be available, be listening, be vigilant, be ready to act. Disappointment sets in when we set a timetable to God's purpose in us. Who knows, in the extreme God's purpose for your life may only be revealed upon your death!

In the Bible, young Joseph was shown his purpose early in life. It went to his head; he paraded his favor in front of his brothers, who in turn, plotted to do away with him. As the narrative goes, Joseph was sold to a trader's caravan, then to Pharaoh's household where he became a slave. His purpose, to save Egypt, his family and the Hebrew nation from starvation and extinction, did not emerge for many, many years of service as a slave and imprisonment. It was only when Joseph submitted himself totally to God that his purpose was allowed to be fulfilled. God has a "right time" for you, He has a "right place" waiting and He will assemble the "right people" to allow your purpose to be fulfilled, but only if you are submitted and willing.

Every Purpose in God has an Enemy.

God's work is always opposed by Satan. Whenever you step into your purpose, you will stir up opposition. The bigger and bolder the step, the more irritated and crafty the opposition becomes. The enemy will throw doubt, fear, illness, temptations, lies, deceptions, entrapments and blockades in your path to try and pull you off course. But your strength and conviction in God will always see you through. The more you overcome, the more God entrusts with you. He starts you with one talent, increases it to two then to five. Wisdom and character are gained in overcoming. But you've got to understand, as a Christian, you have an enemy

God's Purpose and Plan for You

Many of us make the mistake of seeking our plan and purpose by declaring it and asking God to bless it. Wrong. We must seek God's plan for us and then submit to it.

Firstly, you will never know God's plan and purpose for your life unless His Spirit dwells within your heart – the "born again" experience of salvation. (John 3:3)

Next, you must begin a season of prayer and intercession to seek the intimacy of the Father. He will not reveal His plans for you until a relationship is established. God wants you to seek His face before you seek. His hand. He wants you to seek relationship before you pursue purpose.

biting constantly at your heals. With an understanding of and commitment to God's purpose for your life, he will be right in your face.

All Things Work Together for Good

...to those that love the Lord and are called according to His purpose (Romans 8:28). We often forget the second half of the verse. Once you understand God's purpose – His "call upon your life" – and your heart is committed to Him through love, then everything that happens to you will be for the purpose of completing the "call". Whether it be good or bad, prosperity or poverty, success or failure – it won't matter, because you have accepted that the purposes within your life of God supersede all other issues.

This does not mean that you let everything go: responsibility, accountability, providing for your family (which is your highest earthly priority if you are married – higher than striking off on your own to do the will and work of the Lord), personal appearance, hygiene, finances, etc. God expects you to be on top of things, to set an example of diligence, dutifulness and responsibility. He expects you to do your very best at all times but understands when personal failures occur.

Rejecting the Call *May* Mean Being Replaced

God is patient, but He's also a good manager. If you balk at getting involved, that's your choice: it won't hinder God from achieving His master plan. God always has replacements available or He has an alternative plan. It's not that He doesn't care about you and your purpose, it's just that He's not going to baby sit you. He's involved in a war on earth, there's a prophetic agenda to be fulfilled, and if you won't help, He'll offer the opportunity to another.

That doesn't mean that God abandons you. He always has other "jobs" available and won't starve you of vision, passion or purpose.

But if you are willing, if you do pick up God's marching orders and you are successful in the mission, it just might mean that you will be in line to pick up someone else's dropped assignment. That's how God grows saints. Be willing, able and available and God will use you. Hide in a corner, reject His offers and you'll be benched for the time being. But for some, God turns His back deliberately and completely – leaving them to defend their foolish ways to all. (Romans 1). You don't ever want to be there.

GOALS

Goals are an excellent and accepted method of encouraging personal achievement. They are the tools of those who accomplish great things for God and for themselves. The difficulty is when they become our reason for living. If they replace purpose, then you are in trouble. Many super-successful people are very unhappy, yet they seemingly lack nothing in their world. "More is Never Enough" becomes the creed, and desire turns rapidly into greed. Their hearts grow cold, the poor become invisible, and life is simply there to support expansion.

Goals must be treated carefully. They tend to act as dangling carrots, pulling us ahead. Without them, it is easy to become reactive and stray off-course. With them, combined with purpose and faith, great things can be achieved.

The remainder of this chapter deals with setting and achieving goals. Throughout, the word "success" is used to describe the completion of a worthwhile goal and to describe those who have achieved: "successful" people. This sometimes makes Christians uneasy, and some look upon success as a negative. If understood, it is not.

God always encourages us to achieve, to step into the difficult roles, to do the things that others would shy away from. Success means that you have accepted a challenge and you have completed the task. If it is a worthy challenge, if it is a worthy goal, if it encourages others to become greater in God, if it equips you as a giver and supporter, if it does not cloud your heart and mind with self-importance, then use the term with honor and understanding.

However, if "success" means stepping over others to get to your prize, if it means planning and plotting to take away another's position or possession, if it means acting on a covetous desire, if it means increasing your self-importance and ego, then "success" is a dangerous term for you to use. Again, you get to choose the emphasis and the definition.

I choose to use the word "success" in the Biblical sense: to mean that you are submitted to God and to fulfill His purpose for your life is your ultimate agenda. Your goals are purpose-related, purpose-driven, linked to the responsibility of providing for your family and to develop abundance so that you may freely give when the opportunity is presented. "Success" means that you are doing thing right, in the sight of God, without regret or selfish desire.

DIFFICULT HABITS

The common denominator of successful people seems to be their ability to do the things that unsuccessful people don't like to do or are unwilling to do. It's not that successful people like doing unpleasant or difficult things; most don't. It's just that they have made personal commitments to become successful and they realize that there are just some things they have to do that can't be passed on to others.

They make it a habit to do the *unpleasant* tasks, such as personal accounting, forecasting, planning, decision making, hiring and firing, financial negotiations, banking and dealing with bank managers, taking risks, investing their personal money and investing their personal time. Few people like to do these things, but by doing them you take another step closer to achieving your goals.

Many people choose to enjoy the safer, more predictable side of life, foregoing the tough tasks for the easier activities. Much like the grasshopper who played the summer away while the ants worked to gather food and supplies for the long winter ahead, the non-striving person plays and sleeps and does the "easy" things while his or her passion-driven counterpart works hard towards tomorrow. When the winter of life sets in, the unsuccessful go pleading and begging while the successful relax and enjoyed the fruits of their efforts and diligence.

By forming habitual routines to take care of the "not-so-much-fun" tasks, you can take a great step towards personal accountability. One of those "not-so-much-fun" steps is goal planning. Of all the things that contribute to a successful person, the timely setting of personal goals play the biggest part.

With a Dream in Your Heart

It usually starts with but a wisp of a thought. A suggestion. An idea, a concept, a purpose. Then the idea begins to transform itself into a picture featuring you and the future. Color begins to flood the scene and sounds and action bring it to life. It is your dream for tomorrow, a hope and a vision of things better, life more fulfilled, less struggle, perhaps even honors and acclamations, recognition for a job well-done. For the Christian, it usually means being able to spend time in missions work, helping the poor, feeding the hungry, evangelizing – the things we want to do to explore and fulfill our purpose in God.

Nothing great was ever accomplished without someone having a vision deep in his or her heart that saw the final result long before anyone ever knew that an idea was beginning to bud.

Dreams and visions are what make us great and what keep us achieving. They take us through the tough times when everyone said that it couldn't be done, that it was finished: a failure. Dreams give us that last ounce of energy to pick up the pieces after yet another setback and to start building again.

Without a dream, there is no growth. Without a dream, there is no goal for which to strive. Without a goal to meet, there is no achievement. Without achievement, there is no real purpose to life, for God made man to achieve.

Dreams set the whole mechanism of performance in place: for the Olympic athlete, for the star salesperson, for the award-winning stage performance, for you. Dreams draw us through the storms of life. When you see a person who is stalled or bogged down, not moving, growing or achieving, it is because the dream has faded, like a forgotten old photo in a seldom-visited album.

Where is your dream? Is it out in the open for all to see? Is it worked on like an art masterpiece, carefully, consciously and with a purposeful hand? Or is it put away in some moving carton marked "old business papers," left to be discovered on some rainy day when you finally set about cleaning the attic? Or will it lie undiscovered until found in sorrow by your next of kin? Dreams are the path through the haze, the inner breath of an individual materialized for the world to see. They cause us to build, invent, design, teach, perform, outperform, strive, strain and stretch until the dream comes true. Without the dream, there is no better tomorrow, only another today. But dreaming without substance and purpose is as bad as not dreaming at all.

Dreams must be turned into something concrete, something that can be measured, divided into attainable parts, achieved and acclaimed. Most of all, dreams must be honorable; they must be purposeful and positive, and beneficial to all. For if one soul, one single person, is injured intentionally by your quest, then your dream is destructive, damaging and negative.

Ethics that change for each situation do not belong in the belief system of the Christian. You can't change the rules to suit each problem or opportunity. Draw your ethical boundaries with great care. Make your opportunities, desires and actions conform to your ethics, not the reverse.

When my children first learned how to do jigsaw puzzles, they were only three or four years old. The best they could manage was a 10- or 20-piece puzzle with simple, colorful designs. My wife is the master of jigsaw puzzles, and prefers 1,500-piece, difficult ones. Dreams are like jigsaw puzzles: either we pick easy ones that offer little challenge or complicated ones that we may never be able to complete without help from others or by having a wealth of experience and patience.

If you pick a dream that is far beyond your personal capabilities, your likelihood of quick accomplishment is low and your disappointments will be many. It is important to build your dreams within the logical extensions of your talents and interests, stretching yourself but not becoming ridiculous. For instance, it is likely for a welder to dream of becoming the head of the local union or owning a fabrication shop or even a factory or foundry. It is unrealistic for the welder to dream of becoming the dean of humanities at Harvard, a supreme court justice or head of a bank.

It is likely that your dream might involve something to do with sales management, executive management, owning your own distribution or sales firm, becoming a sales trainer or public speaker, or something similar. Your dreams tend to flow from your current interests and experiences and your desire to explore and fulfill your purpose in God. Sometimes, however, your current interests and experiences don't reflect the real dreams of your heart or the true purposes of God. In this case, you had better have a long and serious talk with yourself, with God and your closest family members or friends to see what it is that will pull you forwards. It might mean a shift in occupation.

Your dreams, your goals and your actions must align to form a straight path. That path leads to fulfillment and personal satisfaction as your goals are achieved and the dream blossoms into reality. If they do not align, then disappointment creeps in and steals away your happiness, joy and motivation.

Go down to the basement, find that old business box and retrieve the dreams of yesterday. Or, start building your new dream right now. Make it a serious venture, one to which you can dedicate a substantial amount of time, effort and resources. Choose your dream script carefully, fill it with detail, color, sound and characters, then start directing!

EXPECTATIONS

Expectations can easily be confused with goals. Goals are the destination; expectations are your feelings and personal reactions to how the goals are achieved (or not achieved). Expectations represent how you respond, feel and react to achievement.

Your personal satisfaction will be related directly to the expectations you develop concerning the events and activities that lead to accomplishing your dreams.

Many of us have had our dreams suspended or shelved, or have temporarily lost sight of the paths that leads us onwards. Because of this, many harbor deep, personal sorrow and perhaps anger and bitterness towards those things or people who somehow got in the way.

These negative feelings express themselves physically and emotionally, usually to those who are closest to us, yet without revealing why they erupt. For most of us, our teens and twenties left us with idealistic expectations but without providing the substance or skills for their realization.

Until we can level with ourselves and start afresh, the bitterness and sorrow over the un-fulfillment of these expectations will remain to dissolve and thwart any future plans. "Once bitten, twice shy" has a foundation in fact. The past can be a millstone hung around your neck or a milestone marking the growth and experience of a maturing individual. Millstone or milestone: you choose.

Extended Potential

Build your expectations to fit your extended potential, that is to say, the natural extension of your current skills or interests. Don't defeat yourself by setting unrealistic expectations. Most of all, ensure that your personal expectations concerning the future are indeed attainable. After all, the odds of becoming president of the United States is less than one in 40 million. The odds of owning and operating your own firm is better, probably around one in a hundred.

Goals

Dreams become realities when they are turned into concrete goals or objectives. Goals are the guideposts for success. It is a widely known fact that fewer than 3% of all people write down and actively pursue personal goals. These people, coincidentally, out-earn all 97% who don't record and pursue active goals. The power of goals and the mechanism for their achievement cannot be understated. For this reason, define your personal goals in the seven life categories that affect your life the most:

1. Spiritual;
2. Family;
3. Health;
4. Financial;
5. Business;
6. Community;
7. Personal.

These are arranged in a specific priority order that will help you to keep your life in balance. Each of these life categories can be subdivided into particular areas of growth. Take the business category, for instance, and look at adding separate subcategories of skills, position, industry, responsibilities, authority, recognition, etc. The financial category might be broken down into salary, commission, bonuses, net income, savings, home purchase account, vacation plan, etc. Each subcategory carries with it its own goal set. Each goal set carries with it an activity set.

1. Spiritual

What are your deepest beliefs about your soul and your being? Why are you here? What is your purpose in life? What is God asking of me? These are some of the questions that you must answer at some point in your life. The sooner you make these decisions, the more accurate and complete your goal structure will become. These are the most important goals to a human being, for without a personal spiritual commitment, understanding or decision, all of the goals in your other life categories will become hollow victories. Your spiritual purpose should pervade all that you do and all decisions that you make. They are your top priority goals because they affect everything in your life.

2. Family

Next are the family goals. The attention that you pay to your family as it grows is all-important to your overall success as a person. Too many times, high-driving, workaholic business people neglect and starve their families of time and emotion. Goals should include family-strengthening projects, vacations, special trips, celebrations, family rituals and daily interpersonal communication. Put the family goals above the business goals, for it is more important and satisfying to have good relationships than a sack of money and a title on the door. Don't accept the easy paths that society affords for child care. Take the time, make the sacrifices and do it right. Don't let strangers raise your family.

3. Health

This is pretty self-explanatory: set goals for how you would like to feel, look, act, exercise and eat. Health is very important, because without it, all things are compromised. At the age of 53, I had two heart attacks. My life, at the time, was surrounded by high-pressure corporate politics and delicate finances; the result was that I lost my capability to govern my business and eventually lost the business to those who wanted the fruits of my hard work. I restarted a new business, in poor health, and after two years of rapid growth went to have a triple coronary artery bypass to "fix" my health problems that were due to under-exercise and poor diet.

While I was on the operating table, conspirators set in place a masterful plan to rob me of my efforts again. They were successful. If my health was in good shape, I would not have lost either business. However, God is good, and He removed me from a business that was full of conspirators and greed, to a position of helping and teaching others – my purpose in life.

4. Financial

Financial goals are important for stability and for being able to take advantage of opportunity, but they are a poor substitute for a life purpose. They are part of the mix, an important part, but just a part. Set goals in the areas of income, investments, property and assets, possessions, taxes, tithes and free-will donations, etc. Finances tend to be the fuel that enables you to reach your goals, so treat them with respect.

The Bible has over 2,000 references to finance, so it is an important issue with God. He wants you to have abundance, but only when you are capable of handling it wisely. I am a firm believer in the tithe –

giving 1/10th back to God of your "harvest", for I believe that all resources are given by God; besides which, He commands it for our own good.

Your commitment to tithe triggers God's promises of protection from the devourer and promises of abundance. In fact, God taunts you to test him in this area. When you tithe, God fights your battles for you.

There are excellent teachings and courses on financial stewardship that can "re-train" you to think and act in a manner that will build financial abundance and stability, for most of us never have had any form of constructive financial planning instruction.

Set goals for gaining personal financial education first so that you understand how to manage assets, cash flow and debt constructively.

Above all, make the commitment to tithe as an unbreakable, unshakeable part of your being. Nothing gets paid before God gets paid. It anchors your financial destiny.

5. Business

This includes your job, your education, your working habits, your business possessions, ownerships, partnerships and anything else that is connected with your occupation. The business category tends to be the area that people set goals in first, but it must stay positioned behind spiritual and family in order to receive the proper perspective and balance. It is a difficult area to balance with God's life purpose for you as an individual; sometimes it is simply a way to put bread on the table. Other times, it is your purpose expressed through your skills and talents. God can and does work in either situation. *Ecc 11:6*

Many who are living a God-purposed life to its full extent have work that is totally unrelated: the dishwasher who supports a missionary in Indonesia, the lawyer who spends his vacation teaching at summer bible camps, the waitress who saves her tips so that she can work in the orphanages of Mexico for a couple weeks each year (that's my daughter!). Business should be considered as the means to an end, the "end" being founded in God's purpose for your life.

6. Community
How do you provide for the growth and function of your community? It should be in a person's heart to give of his or her abundance in order that others less fortunate may survive. Search for areas where you can provide time, money or experience to help your community prosper.

7. Personal
Last on the priority list are your personal desires for possessions and position. This is the area of the ego, and you must be careful not to let it get out of hand. Most people shy away from egotistical and boastful personalities. A recent survey indicated that the top executives in the country are, for the most part, conservative and exhibit a posture of giving rather than getting. Define goals in terms of leisure time projects, personal dress and appearance, personal (non-business) education, hobbies, reading, and other pursuits that affect only you.

Small Steps
Seven goal categories are overwhelming to most. I suggest that you take one area per month and dwell on understanding it, exploring it and finally identifying the goals that would be worthy to achieve. Pray about them; lay them before God; ask for insight and wisdom; seek His input and blessing. When you feel satisfied in your heart that the goals are "in tune" with your life purpose, then you can craft the final goal statements and set an achievement timetable.

The key to goal achievement is to break big goals into little ones, so that achievement and accomplishment have a chance to gain a toehold. Help yourself achieve by giving yourself steps that are large enough to show progress yet small enough to accommodate your stride. Make your goals achievable, measurable and rewarding. If getting there is half the fun, make arriving there the other half. Reward yourself for achieving and meeting your goals, setting in place a Pavlov-like stimulus-response reward system for achievement.

Rewards can be used on a daily or even a task-by-task basis. I personally use a task-by-task "mini-reward" system because, being a great procrastinator, I truly require short-term (hourly) goals and rewards to make it through the day successfully. I usually dangle an edible "real food" treat as a reward.

Declaration

The most important aspect of setting goals is to define them correctly. Most people define goals as "being wealthy" or "happiness and good health," but these are only the results of reaching goals. Goals must be tightly defined, with a measurable objective, a time for completion and a complete set of activity and achievement-related expectations. Then make a goal declaration and sign it.

> *My long-range financial goal is to have the sum of $20,000 in my personal savings account by January 1, 20--.*
>
> *I expect to reach this goal through personal hard work (50 hours per week), good financial management, taking personal initiative and using original and inspirational thought.*
>
> *I expect to have others to help me achieve this goal and to this end I will provide rewards to those people who help. I expect that the growth will begin slowly with a rapid acceleration towards the end of the allotted time. I will reward myself with a vacation for myself and my wife that costs no more than $5,000, to be used from this fund. The balance of these funds shall be used for the down payment on a home.*
>
> *I fully expect to achieve this goal using the talents and skills I currently possess and fully understand that there may be setbacks and disappointments along the way, but I shall not lose sight of the purposeful goal hereby set.*
>
> *I hereby pledge that I shall in no way intentionally diminish any person in the pursuit of this goal, but shall demonstrate a willingness to share, build and help those along the way.*
>
> *Signed,*
>
> **Sandra Sales**
>
> *(Current Date)*

The purpose of the goal declaration is to clarify and isolate your key objective and what you are willing to provide for its completion. By surrounding your goal with ethical and moral considerations, it ensures that the accomplishment of the goal is to the benefit of all involved. It makes the "action" decisions connected with the goal easier and clearer.

For each of the seven life areas, construct goals in concrete terms. For your lifetime and long-range goals, the highest priority is to make them consistent with your life purpose and if possible, reflecting your overall talents and interests. You must also construct a stream of more immediate objectives: plateau goals, annual plans, quarterly plans and monthly objectives.

These take time and a lot of effort to construct, so I recommend that you spend no less than a full month considering and constructing each goal area (Spiritual, Family, Health, etc.).

TIMING

Goals can be divided into incremental stages. I recommend the following three levels of goal development:

Long Goals:

- Lifetime goals
- Long-range goals
- Plateau goals

Short Goals:

- Annual plans
- Quarterly plans

Immediate Objectives:

- Monthly objectives
- Weekly objectives

Daily objectives

Long Goals

The long goals tend to be described as concepts, principles and destinations for achievement. They offer an infrastructure for your future; they help define your purpose, character and path in life. They feature three time frames: lifetime, long-range, and plateau goals.

Lifetime Goals

Lifetime goals help to define your character and your purpose. They are you: the person, the principle and the future you want to become, you need to become. Their completion will be the legacy you leave behind. Carefully define goals for each of the seven life categories: spiritual, family, health, financial, business, community and personal. These goals are conceptual targets that are real to you and are worthy to accomplish in the eyes of God. Keep adding details to them, refreshing and renewing your life purpose every year.

These goals represent the light at the end of the tunnel. Put a concentrated and continuous effort into defining, building and believing in them and the light will shine brightly to guide you through darkened times. Although you likely won't realize any daily progress towards these goals, slowly and incrementally you will move towards their completion through the use of your more immediate goals.

Lifetime goals are more general than long-term, plateau and annual goals, and tend to deal with lifestyle concepts or categorical statements rather than with tangible achievement. Some may be a tangible target, such as obtaining a certain amount of savings; others may be more of a life statement, describing how you will live and act. They surround and affect all your goals and objectives. For instance, your "health" lifetime goal might be stated:

> *My lifetime goal for the purpose of personal health is to exercise for at least 20 minutes three times each week, to vigorously walk ten miles each week, and to have a balanced diet that features "real" food, and is low in*

grains and sugar and rich in fiber and vegetables and that is not "processed". I will not eat "faux food".

In all things concerning personal health and especially eating, I will be moderate and temperate.

I will have a complete physical once per year.

I will restrict my skin's exposure to the sun to a minimum and avoid smog and other air pollutants. I will use common sense for my continued good health. I will avoid complex food chemicals and preservatives wherever possible, and respect the unclean foods as described in the Bible (Acts 10: 9-6) as being naturally dangerous for human consumption.

Think seriously about who you are, who you intend to be, what effect your goals might have on other family members. Your first goal step is to organize your lifetime goal statements.

Long-Range Goals

The long-range goals are similar to lifetime goals but tend to be more concrete and precise. They start organizing your lifetime goal statements into tangible targets. Set these goals for a time frame that is proportionate to your age, but never further away than ten years. You see, the passing of time is relative to how long you've been alive.

Remember when you were three or four years old. Half a day seemed like a week when you had to wait for something special, such as going swimming or taking a trip to the zoo; a week seemed like forever and summer stretched endlessly on. When you were a teen, a year was a long time, hard to see past. In your twenties, maybe the longest you could project yourself into the future was two or three years. Then, when you're 40, 50 or 60, time just seems to fly past.

Time *is* relative. At five years old, another year is equivalent to 20% of your life. When you're 20, it's 5% of your life. At 50, it's a mere 2%.

This pattern led me to create the *relative time span system* for goal planning, and it works for everything EXCEPT the Lifetime Goals, which have no time point for completion.

Long-range goals should be set at 20% of your current age; plateau goals should be set at 10% of your current age. So, set your long-range goals at four years if you are 20, six years if you are 30, eight years if you are 40, and ten years if you are 50 or older.

Make your long-range goals tangible, with a definite completion date and reward system in the definition.

> *My long-range business goal is to attain the position of National Sales Manager for a major computer retailer by June 1, ----.*
>
> *For this, I am willing to devote up to* ***40*** *hours per week in honest and concerted effort. I will attend training programs to enhance my personal abilities to perform the job as required and to prepare myself for advancement and promotion.*
>
> *Upon achieving this position, I will reward myself and my family with a trip to Hawaii for two weeks."*

Obviously, as soon as a goal is within reach, it is time to organize a new long-range goal that can take over as the current one is completed. It is important that all your goals be aimed at fulfilling your lifetime goals.

Plateau Goals
Plateau goals define intermediate levels you plan to reach on the way to completing your long-range goal. If you're a salesperson now, maybe your plateau goal is to become a field sales manager. Plateau goals are set at 10% of your current age (two years if you're 20; four years if you're 40, etc.).

Each of the seven purpose categories should carry a series of plateau goals on which you firmly set the groundwork for your assault on the next level. These are very important to success. They represent your most aggressive grip on the future. Choose them carefully and define them accurately.

My plateau goal for health is to attain a body weight of 165 pounds, a waist measurement of 32 inches and be able to jog three miles in 20 minutes or less.

I will devote as much as one hour each day if required to achieve this goal.

I expect to achieve this goal by August 1, ----.

I will reward myself by purchasing a new suit, shirt, tie, shoes and silk socks.

Short Goals

Short goals are set on two time frames: an annual plan and a quarterly plan. These goals represent targets that are far enough away to make you reach out but close enough so that you can still see them: out of reach but not out of sight.

Annual Plan

Design your annual plan to accomplish a portion of your plateau goals. An annual plan is exciting and meaningful to have. It provides for celebration, for hard work and for adjustment.

Design your plan to incorporate changes and occurrences that happen to you as you are growing. Perhaps your position changes, or you get married, or you purchase a house. These events might change the strategies required to achieve your plateau and long-range goals. For instance, a new baby in the house might limit your availability for extra-hours work, thereby causing a change in the method you use to reach your goal.

Annual plans take into consideration the changes and movements that you make on the way up (or down) the ladder. They allow you to adjust your strategies so you reach your plateau and long-range goals.

Quarterly Plan

Quarters are typical time frames for business planning. It is a natural cycle in which you should adopt aggressive projects and activities so you will complete your annual plan on schedule. Break your annual plan into four quarterly sections: January-March, April-June, July-September, and October-December. Call them quarters one, two, three and four.

The quarterly plan is based exclusively on your annual plan, and involves strategies, specific objectives, scheduled dates and a very close monitoring of the achievement path. At the successful completion of each quarter, carry the unfinished objectives or activities into the next quarter. Dangle a nice reward (such as dinner on the town) for yourself and your family for the successful completion of each quarterly plan.

Immediate Objectives

Immediate objectives are short-term, tightly monitored targets that quickly lead to tangible results. They express your quarterly plans in terms of prioritized activities and events. The immediate objectives are indexed into monthly, weekly and daily objectives.

Monthly Objectives

Your quarterly plan can be divided into three monthly objective plans. This is where dynamic activities and strategies are planned with day-to-day effectiveness and monitoring. Because these objectives stem originally from the plateau and long-range goals, you can be assured that the monthly objectives will lead you, step-by-step, towards the completion of your higher goals. Use a monthly pocket planner and a wall scheduling chart to track your goal activities on a daily basis.

Weekly Objectives

Weekly objectives are used as a monitoring process to ensure that you don't put off things or miss them altogether. Transferring your objectives and tasks from the monthly plan onto a weekly schedule will ensure that the high-priority items get done first and foremost. Those items that don't get completed this week either get rescheduled at a higher priority for next week or get dropped altogether.

Daily Objectives (Hourly)

Daily and hourly achievement objectives are especially helpful for procrastinators who tend to get sidetracked and lose the opportunity to complete the small tasks that lead to getting the bigger ones done. Most salespeople benefit by controlling their personal time and activities on an hourly basis. Most successful people have to do this, even after they are successful. It is one of the "difficult habits" successful people learn and practice.

Use daily calendar apps to keep financial records and to schedule your appointments and tasks. Then follow the daily outline as if your life depended upon it. All tasks should be prioritized. Each task should be scheduled and crossed off as it is completed. I can't emphasize more the importance of daily, hourly planning to the overall success of your major plateau, long-range and lifetime goals.

Personal Productivity Management

Goals represent the destination, and actions (tasks) represent the type of transportation we use to get to the destination. Because there are many different types and modes of transportation, you must be careful to select the right type at the right time to maximize the distance you travel for the time involved. Similarly, you must select the right type of action, used with the correct amount of effort and energy, at the appropriate time. It is called priority action, combining the physical act of doing with the strategic planning and scheduling of priorities.

Mason Jar Management

I was taught a simple, visual, effective method for managing activities during the day. I do not remember where it came from and I do not claim the system as my own; my apologies and appreciation to the designer of this simple system.

Goals are accomplished through scheduling and completing tasks. Most “issues” that impact us during the day are also tasks. Time management is also concerned with tasks. If you can sort and manage the tasks, you can learn to become both efficient and effective.

The most important action you can take during the day is to sort all incoming requests or tasks into one of three classes:

1. Dump it

2. Delegate it

3. Do it

Dump it means exactly that. Throw it away, shred it, dispose of it – immediately – and never consider it again.

Delegate it means that you find someone else who is ready, willing and able to take over the task and be accountable for its completion. If you can't delegate it, then you must dump it or do it.

Do it means that the task will now be subject to a priority process, so that the important things get done first and the unimportant things can be scheduled for lower priority times.

Here's where the Personal Productivity Management (PPM) program gets interesting, because it is in the assigning of priorities and the scheduling of tasks.

Rocks *Urgent and Important* (both time sensitive and directly related to the completion of your goals).

Pebbles *Urgent* (time sensitive only: if you do not act right now, an opportunity may pass that can not be recaptured, such as getting a pair of tickets to the seventh game of the World Series or completing a daily skill development program);

Sand *Important* (not time sensitive but directly related to the completion of your goals or to the establishment of a "difficult habit," such as doing your accounting);

Water *Routine* or *Relaxing* tasks (neither time sensitive nor goal-achieving).

For every activity you plan each day, assign a PPM quality next to it (Rock – Pebble – Sand – Water). Consider your day as a resource of time, in this case, visualized as a Mason jar. Mason jars, popular for the canning of jams, jellies and pickles, come in various sizes. The longer your day is, the bigger the jar is. A 12-hour day would be a 12-ounce jar; an 8-hour day would be a smaller, 8-ounce jar. You get the picture. The size of the jar determines how many tasks can be accommodated.

Into your jar, you can put any combination of rocks, pebbles, sand or water until the jar is full. Go past full and your life begins to go out of control. This is where the personal productivity management program gets interesting, because most of us prefer doing the routine and relaxing tasks first – the "water".

If the water fills your jar first, guess what – there's no room for the goal-achieving tasks, or you have to find time to do them outside of your daily time allowance. That means burnout, if it continues for too long or if it becomes a habit.

To maximize your efficiency and effectiveness, the correct method of scheduling tasks for completion is to put the rocks in first, the pebbles next, then the sand and finally the water.

Because rocks represent the things that tend to be hard or unpleasant to do, they can easily become a point of procrastination. If you don't do them, they begin to pile up on the "to do" shelf, where someday they will come crashing down on you, usually causing injury, sometimes paralysis, always disruption. Put the rocks in your daily jar first. Do them first. Take them out one at a time and deal with them.

The pebbles aren't as intimidating. They tend to fall into the gaps in the jar formed between the rocks. Sand is similar, it can flow into the spaces between the pebbles and the water can soak into the entire jar, eliminating any wasted space. They all have a sequence of entry and of retrieval.

It is a simple, effective time management principle that is amazingly effective. In my home office, I have four wall-mounted file folder holders that are arranged one above the other, one the wall next to my desk, facing me as I sit at the computer terminal. They are made of an attractive black metal screen design, and each has a different color tab in the upper right-hand corner. Hot pink is for rocks (it draws my eye first) and it is the top holder, purple is for pebbles, yellow tab for sand and blue for water, the bottom holder. I always work from the topmost holder down, and that way all items are completed.

The system works with the priorities flags in Microsoft's Outlook daily scheduling program, the rocks are assigned the "high" flag, the pebbles become the "normal flag and the sand becomes the "low" priority flag. Water? Well, after I've completed the rocks-pebbles and sand requirements, everything else should be water – relax and enjoy.

To eliminate procrastination from your daily life, do the rock tasks first, the pebble tasks next and then the sand tasks and finally the water tasks. Generally, most unsuccessful people do the absolute reverse of this system because it is the routine items that offer safety and an unthreatening workday: no risks.

App's

There are literally hundreds of "app's" available for your phone, tablet and even your watch that can integrate your schedule and tasks, rate them in priority and alert you when they need attention. They can even alert others who are involved. Powerful CRM's – Customer Relations Management programs – can organize an entire sales force. But they all are only as good as the input. "Garbage in = garbage out" is still valid.

The key is to schedule actions according to their priority to assure the most important things get done first. In this way, the routine, who-cares-if-they-get-done-anyway items are sacrificed for the goal achieving activities that lead to success.

Prepare for tomorrow by scheduling activities and by assigning priorities the night before. This gives your subconscious mind the entire night to work out the solutions to some of the more subtle and challenging tasks that lie ahead.

Resources

Seldom does a successful person make it to the top without help from others. Sometimes this help is in the form of advice, sometimes it is a partnership, other times it is financial resources. Whatever you need, it is available if you'll look and honestly request assistance. The important aspect of getting help is that you reward people for the help they give. Don't take and run, but make a concerted effort to repay *twice* what you have received.

Where do you find your resource people? Start with people who know more about your future goals than you do. If it is for business, ask for help or seek advice from people who are already there, already occupying the next plateau. If it is financial, seek advice from people who have already obtained similar goals; chances are they will help you plan your financial portfolio to enable you to get there. Do not rely on bank managers or accountants for advice on investing; rather use them as sounding boards to temper advice obtained from financial planners.

Check to see if there is an organization for retired executives in your community that offers "wise" advice at a reasonable rate.

The internet offers a real Catch-22 dilemma: it's fast, it reaches around the globe, but the information sources are not supervised, meaning that you can find seemingly good information, but have no idea about its credibility unless you can be sure of its source. I use the internet all the time for research, but I am very cautious concerning its content.

Avoid the advice of people who have not been where you are trying to go. The natural tendency of people, unfortunately, is to try to keep you where you are now. "If I'm not growing, you shouldn't be allowed to grow either," echoes their thinking. Many dreams and desires have been dashed due to a neighbor's snide comment or a spouse's disbelief.

Go to those who share your belief systems and who have already made their dreams come true. This is where good advice resides. Seek God for His wisdom through prayer and fasting.

I personally find a lot of solid, reliable advice and wisdom through studying the Bible. To many, the Bible may be compared to a lottery ticket that's been tucked away in your desk drawer for months. You see it every time you open the drawer but for some reason you just couldn't throw it away. Then one day, an article appears in the local newspaper about unclaimed lottery tickets that could be worth millions.

Checking the numbers carefully, you realize that a million dollar ticket has been yours all this time. Almost every day that ticket caught your gaze, month after month, maybe even for years, but during all your struggles, you never took the time to see if that old ticket held the resources that you needed. The Bible is like that ticket: the numbers match, if you'll only take the time to check it out. Every conceivable circumstance of humanity is noted and a solution exists for every problem and opportunity. Its wisdom is beyond compare. As a Christian, you have a source for all the answers.

ACCOUNTABILITY

Every authority entails responsibility and accountability. The successful achiever realizes this relationship and deals with it in a routine manner. Every action you take must be justified, and the results of every personal action will eventually come to rest in your lap.

The more you shirk accountability, the less grip you have on the future and on personal success. Unsuccessful people are those who hold themselves unaccountable to others for their actions and behavior.

Make accountability part of your personal portfolio. Take responsibility for every single one of your actions without exception. Don't hide behind others or pass the accountability off. If you started it, it's yours. This is the way character is built, and, unfortunately, there is far too little character in today's world. The truly successful individual is one who can face up to all things, positive and negative, that come about as a result of his or her actions (or inactions).

COMMITMENT

The Christian sales-achievement personality, Zig Ziglar, tells the story of two southern boys who stop to fetch a drink of water from an old hand-operated cistern pump, the kind with the two-foot long handle and big spigot faucet.

Through a most illuminating word picture, Zig describes the quest for cold water that lays 200 feet below the surface. To get the water, you have to keep pumping because you can't see how far up the water has climbed inside the pipe below the pump. As soon as you stop, the water begins to fall back down, so you've got to keep it up until the water gushes forth. You might have to sweat and toil with seemingly negative results for a long time before any positive signs appear. Once the water gushes forth, however, all it takes is a slow, even motion on the pump handle to produce all the cold, clear water you could ever use.

It's a story of commitment and perseverance. It's a story of seemingly un-rewarded effort being put into a project that doesn't yield short-term results. How many have given up when the "water" was only half way up the pipe? How many have given up when the "water" was only a foot away from the top? An inch away? Under what conditions would you give up? How *strong* is your commitment? Can you *persevere?*

Would commitment dissolve as soon as you miss your first regular paycheck? Would it go after the first mortgage payment couldn't be made? How about the second? Third? Would it be after foreclosure? Would it be when they take your car? How about the first day you can't afford gas to get to that important meeting? Would it be when threatening calls from the collection agencies become your dominant incoming communication? Would it be when your phone is disconnected? Would it be when there is simply nothing left: no job, no food, no home, no car, no cash and nothing in sight but a dream? What is your give-in, give-up point – and is it actually worth the price you are paying?

These are the serious parameters of entrepreneurship - the steps found between a paycheck and a personal income. These are the steps that almost every successful person has had to face at least one time in his or her life. The only thing that brings you through is a "gorilla grip" on commitment. This is why priorities are important: so that commitment is placed in the right perspective. Cars can be replaced, houses can be refinanced, your friends and relatives will feed you (for a time). Someone will give you enough money for gas to make it to that meeting.

I tell you this because I've been there, more than once. I've had it all, and lost it all for the sake of my commitment to an idea. Sometimes, the commitment was misplaced; sometimes it was justified. Every single time it hurt, it penetrated, it cut, it tore and it made me agonize over the lives that were being affected, because it wasn't only me that went through it, but my family, friends and those who trusted me. There's a huge mountain of personal pain in the words, "we lost it all."

But the dreams can pull you through. Your spouse shores you up, your kids restore your laugh, and a friend lends you an extra fifty dollars (Thanks again, Trevor!). Then your struggles pay off, the dream turns into reality and another experience has been added to your portfolio. A hundred times you wanted to quit and a hundred times you denied yourself the pleasure or the pain. You might be in one of these seasons right now. If you are, you have captured my empathy. Take heart, persevere, and give it one more try, for the season will change.

Careful planning and fervent, heart-based prayer is most critical at times when commitment is tested. Rest assured, if you step away from the crowd, your commitment will be tested. This is why goals and goal-related priority activities are so important: they give you a measuring stick to see just how far up the pipe the water has climbed.

Revise, Reset and Recharge

Goals change, interests sway and time alters the perspective of the future and the past. This is why you must maintain a constant vigil on the appropriateness of your goals and actions. Without making major changes, keep your goals up-to-date and realistic. Keep them in line with your developing skills and experience and adjust them as conditions change. Reset your goals to reflect your current desires, but avoid the temptation to make radical changes on a whim.

It is a good idea to have a personal goal review process where you must wait 30 days before changing any of your plateau, long-range or lifetime goals. This will help protect your goal path from changes as a result of temporary emotional conditions and will help to stabilize your activities and decision making.

MAGNIFICENT OBSESSION

There is nothing more powerful than a person obsessed with a purpose. Mountains move, buildings sprout, jobs are formed and the creative process thrives.

To activate your purpose and your goals fully, become obsessed with their completion. Make the purpose an integrated extension of who you are. Talk about it. Explain it. Write about your goals. Find pictures that describe your goals and hang them where you can study, dream and plan. Most of all, manage the goals, the dreams and the purpose.

A Caution

Make sure that *you* control the goal, however, and that the goal doesn't control you. Too many times, the inexperienced allow their dreams and goals to possess them. They are just tools for achieving, not the purpose of achieving. This is when reality can sneak away and craziness can creep in.

There is little danger in having an obsession, a strong desire and commitment to see the completion of goals that lead to the realization of a positive, productive, worthwhile goal linked to your God-implanted purpose. It is dangerous to allow the obsession to slip to a possession, where the dream takes over your actions, thoughts and desires. It is a fine line; make sure you stay on the manageable side.

ONLY YOU?

There is a trend in "success" thinking that is attractive, and yet dangerous. It is that you are at the center of all things; that you are or can become a "little god" among men. A free will to choose means placing a lot of responsibility upon your shoulders for making right decisions and taking personal action, and this can lead you down the road to spiritual troubles if you are unaware of the traps that are set for the unwise and unknowing.

Striving to become successful does not mean that you have to also become the center of the universe, for centering the universe around yourself likely will result in the development of an uncaring individual with standards and ethics that change to suit his or her particular needs and situations. As a Christian, God is at the center of your universe – period.

This section is a personal warning for those who believe in a sovereign God: respect the occultic aspect of many success teachings and programs. These groups are looking for people who want to achieve and prosper. They prey on your weaknesses, dreams and emotions and most of all, exploit greed. They offer shortcuts to personal success, boost your self-esteem and stroke your ego until you feel like a million. But I don't think you'll like where the path eventually leads. Be careful: most programs offering mind control, personal power, positive thinking, unlimited riches, and even peace and tranquility usually have hidden agendas that are cult-based and dangerous. There really is no such thing as a free lunch.

You can do everything in this book without any involvement with dangerous liaisons involving questionable success formulas. You can become a happy, successful and contented individual without sacrificing your soul, friends, family or future. You don't *have* to walk on fire or be bitten by a poisonous viper to prove anything. Just remember, there is always a price to be paid for taking the shortcut.

Your responsibilities include choosing and defending your personal belief system. Mine is based on the Bible, with Jesus as my Lord and personal Savior as you already know. Yours may be different.

Yes, you must make the individual decisions, take the individual actions, accept the individual responsibilities and be accountable for your life in general and specific terms. Only you can be responsible for you.

SELF-MOTIVATION

Accept the responsibility for getting yourself going and keeping yourself going each day. Realize that motivation is an emotional force that varies from day to day, and if you depend upon external motivation (such as recordings, videos, motivational speakers, books, etc.) to keep your spirits high, you will be riding on a roller-coaster of emotional highs and lows. Yes, there are good resources. Yes, there are interesting and thought-provoking speakers and videos. There is wisdom available from these sources, but for a more secure, consistent inner motivation, concentrate on the purposes of God for your life. Every day, review your purpose-driven goals and the benefits of achieving these goals and then make a daily commitment to their completion.

If you can learn how to kick-start yourself each morning, then the day will move quickly, smoothly and productively. One incredibly powerful strategy: spend 30 minutes first thing in the morning reading the Bible. No interruptions.

Preparing a daily schedule helps to keep your motivational energy in line and keeps it from being wasted on unproductive areas. Motivation does not have to be in the form of an emotional "hit" that sends you out the door in a cloud of euphoria.

The safest type of motivation is the self-assurance that you are going to accomplish your daily tasks and accomplish them with enthusiasm that comes from deep within your heart. This is the type of motivation that can carry you through the depths of desperate times. Look at those lifetime and long-range goals. Concentrate on the next plateau. Minimize the consequences of defeat and concentrate on the rewards of success. Always move forwards and always give thanks, for you don't make it there alone. Always be considerate, kind and caring of others.

THE BEETHOVEN GRIP

"I will grip life by the throat!" was Beethoven's moving response when he found out that he was going deaf.

It didn't leave room for laziness, mediocrity or partial effort. Grip life by the throat. What a way to approach everything you do, with supreme and intense concentration and a focused view! You can live life to the fullest when life is not taken for granted; each day amounts to a separate lifetime.

What if you knew that you would be dead in 30 days? For some strange reason, you were given a glimpse of tomorrow and could see that in exactly 30 days you would die suddenly. How would you react? Would you be passive and sullen, knowing the end was near and there was nothing you could do to avoid it? Or, would you be like the composer who took life and gripped it by the throat? Which would be you?

Personally, I would like to live my last days to the fullest, renewing friendships, taking care of business, loving my family, making my peace with God and doing what I could to give rather than to take.

Facing the reality of death is a sobering and in some ways, calming, experience. In 1999, I experienced two heart attacks. The damage left me in constant pain and gasping for breath for the next two and a half years as I fought to regain my health and reverse the effects of heart disease. Finally, I was scheduled for a triple coronary bypass and I regained my health virtually overnight. During that period, when my life depended on a narrow10% passage remaining open in the "widow maker" coronary artery, certain death was only a platelet or two away. Priorities shift. Perspectives change. Realities reform.

We won't know when our last day comes – that's in God's omnipotent hand, for man is *appointed* once to die. Wouldn't it be better to be prepared? To achieve all we can achieve, to have all things accounted for at all times, to express our love and affection for one another while we still can? To grip life by the throat? It might be a good idea, just in case.

This chapter has dealt with achieving your purpose in God. It has dealt with perspectives. It has dealt with an important aspect of success: setting and attaining goals. Your strategy involves carefully planning goals in the seven life categories and in the eight levels involved in goal achievement. Your strategy involves making a habit out of personal goal management and developing other difficult habits that take care of business.

Of all the chapters, this is probably the most important because it provides a solid foundation for everything in the future. Build your house on the solid Rock.

Passion and Purpose

1. Identify the difficult habits and tasks that you must do to break away, to be independent, to stand apart from the crowd. Make a complete list, following the seven life categories described in the goals section.

2. Define your dreams. What are they, where do they lead, who and what do you want to become? Take a full month for each of the major goal categories and present them to God for comment and wisdom. Take your time to think each life category through, then describe how you would like to be remembered to others when you pass away. Your achievements, your demeanor, your purpose in life: these dreams are the basis for your lifetime goals. Write down your dreams, goals and purpose.

3. Construct your seven lifetime goals, one for each life category. Write them down and create a goal declaration for each one. Sign them and put them in a goal file where you can also record all your other goals and achievements. As old-school as it sounds, I suggest a large loose-leaf binder with seven dividers for the seven categories. Keep all your goals in this binder and record changes and progressions monthly.

4. Now start on the long-range goals that will help you achieve your lifetime goals. Use concrete terminology and following the example in the chapter. Clearly fix in your mind the goals and set them for no longer than 20% of your current age. Describe them clearly and concisely. Describe what you are willing to give in exchange for the achievement. Describe what rewards await you upon attaining your goals. Be specific: don't describe your future in generalities.

5. Now look at selecting the plateau goals (10% of your current age; half-way to your long-range goals). Make this a stepping stone to your more important long-range target. Again, use concise, concrete, tangible terms to describe each goal.

6. After the plateau goals are completed, work out an annual set of goals that reach towards the plateau goals. Describe these goals with definite dates for completion (I suggest keeping on an annual January 1 renewal schedule). These goals should be realistic: just out of reach but definitely possible to achieve with a little extra effort. If your goal is to have $50,000 in the bank by year's end but you've got nothing right now and you're unemployed, chances are that your goal is unrealistic.

7. Once the annual plan has been organized, start breaking it down into quarterly plans, with completion dates and approximate scheduling. The quarterly plans help you adjust for seasonal distractions and allow you to apply emphasis when needed to ensure that you achieve lagging annual goals on time. Further break the quarterly plans into active monthly objectives. Make these objectives accurate, and attempt to accomplish as many as possible during the first two weeks of each month. Plan your monthly activities on wall charts and by using a daily scheduler. It's advantageous to get a good visual perspective of your month at hand.

8. Construct goal-achieving activity plans on a daily basis and assign priorities to each activity of the day. Highlight all goal-related activities. Schedule activities for tomorrow the evening before.

9. Discover and describe your personal level of commitment to your goals and to your activities. What is your breaking point for each goal you describe?

10. Devise your personal "kick start" program for ensuring that your motivational level starts off strong in the morning and remains constant throughout the day. Avoid relying on outside or external motivational products. Instead, look towards your goals and goal activities to provide a more natural enthusiasm. Exercise is a great way to naturally raise your motivation and achievement levels. Thirty

minutes with the Bible first thing in the morning promotes continuing contact with God, the author and finisher of your faith.

BREAKING STRIDE

CHANGE

Most of us have watched world-class athletes competing in the mile run. For most of the race, the runners follow one another around the oval track in a tightly knit pack. Finally, there is but one lap left to run. The track official's bell signals the start of the last lap. It is a final call to strategy, effort and will for each of the runners. As they come down the back stretch, several begin to make their break-away moves. Kicking in that extra power and straining against pain, the top milers break stride, slowly moving away from the pack to seek the lead and the victory. Increasing the pace, the leaders actively attempt to break through previous boundaries. They feel it is necessary to achieve the victory.

This example demonstrates in graphic terms what you also face if you seek victory in sales: you must make deliberate adjustments to your skills, your goals and your attitudes. But most of all, you must make adjustments to your actions.

To double your sales, you must break stride with those who surround you. You must kick away from the average salesperson and fix your eyes firmly on personal victory. Those who reach the top in their professions have learned to break stride and take the lead. They have learned to change habits, attitudes and actions. They have learned not only to accept change... but to manage it and master it. You, too, will have to master change if you want to accomplish what this book proposes: to double your sales. You can far exceed this doubling, however, if you have a firm desire and actively commit yourself to accomplishing your goals.

Don't be intimidated by the suggestions in this book. You really can accomplish every single one if you apply yourself to the task. The first thing that you must do is decide to change. That decision takes courage for many people.

The second thing that you must do is decide consciously to erase the boundaries with which you, as a salesperson, are currently familiar and comfortable. If you are making $4,000 per month, erase this limitation as a boundary. You can make much more. If you are used to working from nine to five, erase this as a boundary. If you are used to driving a four-year old car, erase this as a boundary. If you see yourself as a mediocre, "average" salesperson, erase this as a boundary.

Erase these boundaries. Consciously. You cannot rise above the invisible ceilings that you place upon yourself. Identify the boundaries that contain you or restrain you and erase them. Write them down and physically remove them from your life: the boundaries of income, performance, position, possessions, security, relationship, race or color, past failures, housing, neighborhood, education, speech or language, size or stature, appearance, clothing, bank accounts, debt, prison records, past marriages or affairs, bankruptcies or business failures, personal attacks and slanders and anything else that enslaves you.

Search for those things in your past that are useless baggage. Because they bother you, they evoke fear and restraint. You can choose to let go of old baggage, such as poor decisions, old romances, sickness and money problems. However, you cannot change the past; you can only change the future. By changing the way you react to and think of the past, you will change the way you act towards the future. I hereby give you permission to sweep the past away, to toss the baggage overboard, to lighten your load.

> *"Therefore, if any man is in Christ, he is a new creature; the old things have passed away; behold new things have come."* – II Corinthians 5:7 NAS

Replace fear with faith.

Replace your old boundaries with new foundations upon which you can grow. The former boundary of $4,000 per month income becomes a foundation of $4,000 per month, a minimum amount that you can count on. It is a plateau from which you can begin to build toward a higher income. The boundary of ten jobs in five years becomes the foundation of diversified experience. The boundary of having only a high school education becomes the foundation for adult education courses. Each negative boundary has a corresponding positive foundation if you will only look for the brighter side.

As each restriction is replaced with a positive foundation, you will experience growth and confidence not possible in the past. Now the former restrictions are working for you rather than against you.

However, be careful to hold on to those ideals, ethics and morals that express truth and goodness. Use them as mortar for your new foundation and once you have established your ethical platform, do not move from your position. In a world of situational ethics and moral decay, you can stand apart and above by contributing strong moral fiber to your business and personal life. If you won't stand for "character," then who will?

Don't Settle for Less Than You Can Be

Many people, especially in sales, settle for much less than they could be. We all possess the energies and talents to become great in whatever fields we choose, so why don't most of us make it to the top? For the majority of people, their levels of commitment don't match their levels of desire. For others, the dreams have faded away or have been put on the shelf for later attempts. Still other people have accepted failure as final defeat and have chosen not to pursue their dreams any longer. Some people are comfortable with guaranteed weekly paychecks and old-age security benefits.

Are you in one of these groups? Did an unplanned event interrupt your rise to the top? Were you fired from that key position? Did a merger snuff out your chances for promotion?

If you answered "yes," you are excusifying, my personal term for accepting the blows of life instead of fighting back and seeking God's vision for the next step. He always provides an answer, although many times we don't agree with it and seek our own path.

> *"Many are the plans in a man's heart but it is the Lord's purpose that prevails"* – Proverbs 19:21 NIV

The concepts, ideas and strategies found in these chapters are for people who can overcome personal fear and will risk taking a chance – in faith – so that something new might change their lives. Don't settle for less than you can be. Don't be satisfied with substitutes. Don't listen to the vast majority of people who tell you that you can't. You can.

Don't play into Satan's hands, but work with what God has purposed for you. It takes hard work, it takes courage, it takes faith in yourself and in God and it takes discipline. Most of all, it takes desire and commitment bound together by your personal covenant of conviction. Dust off that dream, go get your goals out of storage, have a chat with God about your purpose in life and start the growth process going again.

FEAR

Fear is a powerful motivator. It makes people leap from 20 story buildings to avoid fires, it pushes the heart to beat at three times its normal rate, it releases powerful chemicals into the bloodstream, it kills, it destroys, it incapacitates. By contrast, it also protects and alerts against real danger.

Fear is a complex emotion, both useful and destructive. "Spiritual" fear traps and holds back; it incapacitates, intimidates and destroys opportunity; it saps your strength and spiritual potency. To reach your God-purposed potential, you must break through the spiritual fear barrier and tackle many "practical" fears as well. You must step out of your familiar surroundings into foreign and sometimes hostile territory. You must enlist faith and with it, courage and conviction.

Practical fear is a natural reaction to an unplanned, unfamiliar or unexpected situation. It is usually a good thing, protecting us from harmful and dangerous situations. Stop, Look, Listen. It protected us from whizzing cars as a child.

Spiritual fear is very different: it is one way that the enemy works in the life of a Believer to rob him or her of the achievement potential and prosperity that God desires for his or her life. This is clearly illustrated in the life of Moses (Acts 7:20-37). Already implanted in Moses' heart was the desire to be the deliverer of the Hebrews from the oppression of the Egyptians. He thought that when he came to the defense of one of his brethren, and killed the Egyptian, that the Hebrews would understand who he was.

However, they did not understand and instead played right into Satan's hand with their cutting words, "Are you going to kill me like you killed that Egyptian yesterday?" It was part of Satan's strategy to stop God's purpose in Moses from being accomplished. In an instant, Moses' heartfelt identity as "deliverer" was savagely stripped away and "murderer" implanted in its place.

One act sent Moses "off course" for almost 40 years, because he listened to Satan rather than to God. God always wins in the end, however, and with his mandate restored, Moses led the Hebrews to the edge of the promised land. We have to be careful that Satan does not divert our heartfelt identities, planted by God, so that we, too, wander in the desert for the majority of our lives, robbed of our glory in God, sapped of our strength, unsuccessful.

Fear is also a reaction to a familiar, unpleasant situation like going to the dentist. You have comfort zones in all areas of your behavior, many of them confined and contained by experience. Comfort zones are feelings that let you know that you've been here before and that you are equipped to handle the situation within a certain range of behavior. For many comfort zone behaviors, you can plan and practice your way through and create new, expanded comfort zones. This is one way that you can establish "break-through" behavior that effectively deals with "comfort zone" fear.

In a simple sense, this is what sales training role-play sessions are designed to do. They help you establish an embryonic comfort zone concerning a new skill or technique.

Let's have a brief look at the two types of fears, spiritual and practical, to see the difference.

	Spiritual Fear	**Practical Fear**
Foundation	Satan's plan to destroy your walk with God	God's natural protection for mankind
Reaction	Incapacitation, doubt, lack of authority – based on emotion.	Logical cause-and-effect, based on physical laws.
Solution	Prayer, faith response, spiritual warfare, steadfast resolve	Analysis of situation; physical "stretching"
Result	If *not* overcome; death of vision, death of the spirit	If *not* overcome; a limitation that must be planned around
Result	If overcome; victory and spiritual confidence	If overcome; an expanded comfort zone = new capability

And then there is the fear of the Lord. This is both a spiritual and a practical fear, for as the Bible says, "The fear of the Lord is the beginning of knowledge (wisdom)." How intriguing. It is the one area in which a spiritual fear is a positive for you. You could substitute "respect" but it just doesn't do God justice: no, we should be very much aware that God can destroy and punish as easily as He can create and bless. He is the Almighty, beyond our comprehension. This fear comes from knowing God and understanding the spiritual laws that govern our lives.

An example would be the law of sowing and reaping, and it is inevitable that you will harvest primarily from that which you have planted. Planting for a harvest on rocky, infertile ground yields no harvest at all, for the seeds cannot establish roots. Disappointment, discouragement, wasted time, money and effort is the end result.

You should have fears about investing your life and talents into areas that cannot produce a return because the spiritual "soil" was not present. You can also sow good effort but with perverted intentions, like a farmer planting opium seeds rather than seeds of wheat. Both grow, but one carries the seeds of greed whilst the other carries the seeds of grain.

The fear of the Lord matures as we get to know Him. This fear helps us make right choices along the way, sometimes to avoid discipline from God, and sometimes to please God. It is just the beginning of knowledge and wisdom.

As we mature in our walk with God, our motivation to please God broadens into a deep abiding love for Him and all of His creation. Fear is actually replaced with Love. Wisdom would teach that God wants you to act on His behalf, and not your own. Doubling His investment in you is a very good start.

Here is an effective formula for breaking through the practical "comfort zone" fear barrier:

- Verbalize and write down what it is that you want to accomplish and what things or situations produce anxiety or fear within you. Believe in faith that you can achieve it.
- Isolate the strongest fearful elements and examine them carefully to see why you are afraid or concerned. Write your emotional and your logical reasons down separately. If it is a spiritual fear then you must seek a spiritual solution. If it is a practical fear, then proceed with a logical approach that "expands" the comfort zone barriers.
- For each point, ask yourself, "What if I fail?" and "What if I succeed?" This strategy isolates the consequences.
- Plan strategies for each negative consequence. Try to turn the negative consequence into a positive experience. Look for the benefit available through each possible negative result. Write these benefits down. Eliminate every single negative by converting it into a positive.
- Select a plan of action to take you through the situation. Practice it and concentrate on the rewards of its successful completion. Do not dwell on the negative possibilities or upon the results of failure but concentrate on

the benefits or rewards of success. Accentuate the positive.

- Take the action you have planned. Record your all of your successes. List your achievements. Build upon your successes; learn from your failures and setbacks.

Faith is used to deal with spiritual fears. Here are a few attributes of faith:

- It is impossible to please God without faith– Hebrews 11:6.
- Faith is a gift of the Holy Spirit – I Corinthians 12:9
- Faith is not one of the fruits of the Holy Spirit – Galatians 4:22,23
- Faith is not the power of positive thinking – Proverbs 21:30
- Faith is not "mental ascent" – James 1:22-25
- Faith is not the ability to believe – James 2:19
- Faith is believing with the <u>heart</u> (not the head) and confessing with the mouth – Romans 10: 8-11
- Faith without action is "dead belief" – James 2:17
- Pray with thanksgiving, believing you received it; you'll have it – Philippians 4:6

If you are a spirit-led Believer in Christ, then this is your platform. If you use it, God will reveal your purpose and path. If you do not, Satan will reveal his purpose and plan.

At the end of the apostle Paul's life, he states that he has fought the good fight, he has finished the course and he has kept the faith. The "fight" is spiritual, emotional and physical; the "course" is your personal path – your purpose – and the "faith" is his unshakeable allegiance to God.

The DUTY section of this book worked wonders for secular salespeople to help them improve their skills and their productivity: it has been proven in courses from coast-to-coast. For the Spirit-led Believer, it can only be better.

Desires

Desires, like fears, come in two forms: spiritual and practical. Practical desire tends to be the flip side of practical fear. It is crucial that you have a well-defined and articulated practical desire or dream before you start trying to break through practical fear. Desire tends to lessen fear. For your desires to be powerful enough to break through the fear barrier, they should be defined into practical goals. Commitment and enthusiasm for your practical goals overpowers practical fear. Read carefully the chapter on structuring your goals. Exactly what do you want, when do you want it, and how much of it do you want? What are you going to give in return? Practical desires tend to be based in the head and the wallet, they tend to concern tangible items, and they tend to be satisfied if enough money is thrown their way.

Spiritual desires are very different than practical desires. They are desires born and carried deep in the heart, and they come from God. When a person is "born again", the Spirit of the living God invades his or her heart. Until that time, the heart is occupied with worldly desires and concerns.

When God is invited into the heart – the "born again" experience that Jesus describes in John 3: verses 3-16 – then the desires of the heart change because God's Spirit is now present in the heart. There will be battles within you between "good and evil" or "the flesh versus the spirit", but by being born-again, you will begin to understand the spiritual consequences of your choices and desires. You've *moved* from the Tree of Good and Evil to the Tree of Life and Righteousness.

If you are not born again, then much of this book's authority and impact will remain undiscovered. If you are born-again, then the full power and authority of God is available to you so that you may pursue your purpose in God through your skill and a salesperson, manager, entrepreneur or business owner. There is a very big difference.

If you are not born-again, then I urge you with all intensity to read the gospel of John and before reading, with a humbled and honest heart, ask God to make the words of the gospel plain to you and to speak to you and you alone.

Reading the Bible is like finding God's website and having a look around. Lots of interesting stuff but you just can't understand it. Then you discover that there's a "Member's Entrance" that entitles you to an inside look, complete with interpretations, revelation, insight and access to God's power and authority. You click to enter only to be faced with the password box. When you're born-again, you get the password. Check it out – John Chapter 3.

If, in doing this, you are moved to act, then Jesus tells you to believe in your heart first that you have welcomed Jesus as your Savior, your spiritual master, and then to confess with your mouth to someone. If you've no one to share this with, then send me an e-mail: roberetriker@sellegrity.com and I'll be pleased to respond, for this is the greatest of all responsibilities for the Christian.

Spiritual desires are based in the purposes of God. They are ethical, moral and good. They almost certainly present a higher calling upon your life; to move upward and forward; to grow and develop in the understanding of God and in the realization of your personal strengths and weaknesses. Spiritual desires lead to spiritual goals which lead you into spiritual battles – Satan's domain.

If you intend to grow, especially in the knowledge and wisdom of God then you will have to fight, like the apostle Paul. As Ephesians 6:12 declares, we struggle not against flesh and blood, but against the rulers, against the powers, against the world forces of darkness, against the spiritual forces of wickedness in the heavenly places.

This is what awaits you and me in the marketplace as a salesperson: deceit, lies, schemes, corruption, manipulation, unhealthy expectations, greed, lust, theft and countless other expressions of "evil". Galatians 5:19 expresses these evil issues in more descriptive words:

> *"Now the deeds of the flesh are evident, which are: immorality, impurity, sensuality, idolatry, sorcery, enmities, strife, jealousy, outbursts of anger, disputes, dissensions, factions, envying, drunkenness, carousing, and things like these, of which I forewarn you, just as I have forewarned you,*

> *that those who practice such things will not inherit the kingdom of God."*

If your desires, spiritual or practical, are based on any of these, then you will constantly struggle as a Christian salesperson. Your spirit life will die, your bones will dry up, you will be slain as a Saint, and the only thing that will bring you back is the breath of God (Ezekiel 37) blown back into you by a Spirit-filled Believer. I have been there.

Choose your spiritual desires based on the purpose that God has revealed to you for your life; if He hasn't revealed it to you it's because you haven't asked with a humbled heart. He will not hold back. Your safest position is to launch your spiritual desires based in the results it will return – the "harvest". If the result is manifest in one of the fruits of the Spirit, then you know you are on safe ground:

...love, joy, peace, patience, kindness, goodness, faithfulness, gentleness, self-control; against such things there is no law (Galatians 5:22-23).

SUCCESS LEAVES CLUES

Successful people tend to do things in similar ways. Your best chance for success is to find someone who is successful at doing what you would like to be successful at doing and simply play copycat. Emulate success by doing what successful people in your business do. Conversely, if you wish to remain in your current state, continue to do what you are already doing. To climb the ladder, you must reach upwards and change position. You go no higher by standing on the same rung and hoping the ladder will somehow grow or extend.

But sometimes, you have to climb all the way down to the bottom to reposition or extend the ladder so that you may gain a loftier perspective or goal. Sometimes, your goals may require an industry change, a job change or a complete professional change to be satisfied. These changes should all be made after careful consideration and risk evaluation.

Discover the things that “successful” Christians do differently than you do now. Decide to include these in your role model profile. If you can't find a real person to emulate, then “invent” one. Read stories, biographies and autobiographies of successful Christians to gain insight and to search for clues. Your mission is to extend and grow. You may need to find a *new* ladder altogether. You are mainly looking for *character* insights, not skills or strategies. Study the great men and women of the Bible who were faced with difficult personal choices and impossible obstacles. God is still in the business of moving mountains; He can and will help.

PLANNING TO SUCCEED

Most of us do not actively or thoroughly plan for personal success and so, by default, we actually plan to fail. We play "not to lose" rather than play to win or achieve. We fail by playing safe, by accepting the status quo, by not risking to win or achieve.

Failure is not the opposite of success; it is the result of not succeeding or accomplishing the things that you know that you are capable of achieving. However, today's setbacks can be considered as the building blocks of tomorrow's success if you sincerely look for the elements of success within each apparent failure.

Your most effective tool for success is a carefully devised and executed plan, surrounded by personal prayer and faith. Just as conductors keep music sheets in front of them at all times, pilots keep instrument landing approach maps at their sides and carpenters constantly refer to blueprints, so must you as a salesperson develop a plan and follow it to completion.

As an amateur carpenter, I have attempted many projects, from constructing dog houses and backyard decks to doing a complete home renovation. Sometimes I thought I knew "building" pretty well, so I would start into a project with just an idea or a rough drawing. It wouldn't take long until trouble arrived in the form of too-long, too-short or not-square. The remedy usually included tear-down, re-plan with detail and rebuild. It took three times the amount of effort to do it right the second time because I had to clean up the mistakes made during the first attempt.

How often we attempt to succeed without a carefully designed plan! God has a plan. The Bible tells us that He knows the beginning from the end and all the possible paths of every individual alive, dead or yet to be born! It is truly beyond man's comprehension, as it should be. But the bottom line remains: God has a plan; so should you. Now, if you can tap into what God has planned just for you, you can begin to realize the unlimited potential available from Him. It's called walking in His purpose, and it's powerful.

You must conceive and construct a personal plan that will map out your future years, your "course". Start with a long-range goal and break this into sub-goals. Put detail into the plan to give it substance and activate the plan through purposeful activities. Assign realistic deadlines for each activity to be completed. Some goals are spiritual, some practical, some physical, some financial.

As you progress through each chapter of this book, recognize that you must develop and build a personal achievement system that will help you accomplish the doubling tasks. They do not happen to you just because you read: you must apply considerable effort and you must apply it consistently, logically, intelligently; with faith and prayer and sometimes, fasting..

Dottie Walters, a consummate professional speaker whom I hired to present a seminar for a new women's sales organization in Calgary, wrote to me after her presentation and enclosed a copy of a new book she had just published. Inside, she wrote, *"To Bob, remember a dream come true is a goal plus a deadline!"* Let the simplicity of those words sink in. A goal plus a deadline results in a dream come true. Dottie implies that as well as dreaming, you have to take action.

TAKING ACTION

Many of us are full of ideas but short on taking constructive action to put these ideas into play. Many of us try something once and meet with apparent failure because we did not think and plan the action through. First-time failures abound in selling, as in most things worthwhile. The first time I raced a car on a professional track, I slid off into the grass and had to follow behind the pack for the rest of the race. It didn't make me feel very good. The first time I tried to sell my product, the customers said "no." The first time I asked a girl out to a high-school dance, she rebuffed. If you stop taking action, you lose all chances at succeeding. A popular lottery runs a TV ad campaign that ends with the quip, "You can't win if you don't buy a ticket." You must take personal action.

But taking personal action isn't all that's necessary. You must take quality action that is focused and purposeful, not clumsy, half-hearted or vague. You must adopt a mental position of clear, accurate and truthful thought. You must clearly identify what you want to do, how you want to do it, when and where you want to do it and why you want to do it. And then ask yourself, “Where’s God in this?”

Take focused action and lock all other things out. Prepare yourself, define your goal and set a deadline for its accomplishment. Focused attention and action can double your sales.

Enthusiasm and Passion

Enthusiasm comes from the Greek word meaning "God within." As a Christian, it speaks volumes to me as it should to you. Many times enthusiasm can take you where no amount of skill, planning or experience can. Enthusiasm is the companion of passion, the two great success builders. Whereas enthusiasm can be the presence of God within you, passion is your *commitment* to God’s purposes.

When was the last time you were truly passionate about your job? About your spouse? About anything? I think everyone, at one time or another, has had a deep, passionate relationship with an idea, a concept or a position. It was you and you were it! Your enthusiasm was over-whelming and sometimes even sickening to your less enthusiastic friends, but it took you into areas in which you never dreamed you could go.

Many of us experience passion without God being involved. Consider the depth that passion can take when you are totally committed to doing God's plan and purpose as it applies to you – personally, privately.

To be great, to reach the top, you must have passion for your "mission." Passion brings on enthusiasm. Action brings on enthusiasm. Enthusiasm sets things on fire! Enthusiasm alone will sell more goods than any other single personality attribute, but passion will keep you in the fight long after the others have quit and your enthusiasm has been exhausted. Quiet resolve sets in: you will win.

Ask God to fill you with an extra measure of His strength, wisdom, authority, compassion, understanding, eloquence, enthusiasm and passion – do it before every sales call, before every meeting, and before every presentation. Ask Him before you write every proposal. Ask Him for an anointing to be upon you so that others can see and feel something different about you.

Ask Him for an extra measure of boldness and intelligence; ask Him for an extra cup of courage, that you may drink from it when faced with the really tough situations. Ask Him to protect you from the discouragement that the devil will always throw at you. Ask Him.

THE COVENANT

You need a covenant: a binding, unbreakable, unshakable agreement between your current self and your future self. This covenant will be the basis for your commitment to your goals. It should be a written agreement that hangs in your study, your bathroom, your office or wherever you will be reminded daily of your commitment to your profession, to your family, to yourself and most of all, to God.

In your covenant, describe the person, the goals and the rewards that you seek. Describe the time frame and deadlines that you have given yourself to achieve these goals. Describe the character that you wish to become in Christ.

Endorse it with two signatures: the current you and the future you. Date it and display it. To help the commitment process, explain your contract to a confidant, someone who shares your thoughts and desires. Discuss it with your pastor or priest, with your wife. Put it in the open for all to see. It will become your testimony.

We Seldom Choose Selling

Every salesperson starts out the same: basically unskilled and unsure of what lies ahead. Few people choose selling as a profession. It's not generally found on the career counselor's list of good and worthy occupations. Most of us stumbled into sales through one door or another and most of us arrived without the purposeful intent of establishing a lifelong career.

However, many people stay in sales because of the challenges and freedoms it offers, not to mention the potential and the elation. Others stay because they don't know what else to do. The problem with most salespeople is that they continue to hold on to the idea that selling is just a stepping-stone to something better, such as sales management. Most salespeople regard selling as less of a "profession" than of a "position." This book is for those of you who wish to turn your position *into* a profession.

There are some common, accepted estimates that show the influence of effective selling skills: 20% of sales are made by 80% of the salespeople; conversely, 80% of sales are made by the remaining 20% of salespeople: the "pros."

Why do the salespeople in one segment sell four times more on average than the salespeople in the other segment? In a few cases, they work four times harder. In another few, they work four times faster. Some salespeople work harder and faster. But most of the 20% of salespeople that sell 80% just work more skillfully and strategically. They take time to plan and to think before they act.

Hidden in the top 20% of salespeople is a small percentage of ultra-professionals who represent the pinnacle of selling success. It is estimated that only about 5% of all salespeople fall into this category of the "super salesperson." I refer to them as Third Dimension Sellers. They are not found in every industry, but tend to be in industries that can take advantage of technology for leverage.

Because most salespeople consider themselves "positional" rather than "professional," they do not personally seek ways of improving their abilities to sell, even though just little changes in behavior could bring about extraordinary changes in income. However, those that *do* seek to improve their skills can take giant strides in sales productivity. Many attend training seminars and conferences and these help. But the real gains begin with new attitudes.

The attitude of personal achievement begins with the recognition that selling requires the truly professional application of planning, skill, wit, intelligence, timing, personal action, strategy, tactics, faith and courage. It also begins by accepting the attitudes and actions that make you a Professional Sales Corporation.

THE PROFESSIONAL SALES CORPORATION

Think of yourself as an all-in-one sales development company. Your corporation devises and completes product and service transfers under contract to an employer. You are responsible for strategy, design, sales, customer service, bookkeeping, personnel, advertising, promotion, marketing, management, maintenance, data processing and finance.

You are that one-person show. You do it all. You've accepted the responsibility, you've been given the authority and you will be held accountable for your actions. You are a Professional Sales Corporation.

Thinking of yourself as a Professional Sales Corporation is the first step in recognizing that selling is more than just a job. It's a career: the ultimate private, professional corporation. And just as every corporation runs using plans and rules, so should you. Just because you might "work" for someone else doesn't lessen your responsibility to yourself for growth and extension.

As soon as you adopt the posture of becoming more than what you have been in the past, you will begin to grow and achieve.

Look at some of the areas that you should be concerned with in becoming a Professional Sales Corporation:

- Organization, planning and scheduling;
- Unique knowledge of product, service or industry;
- Marketing, advertising, promotion and sales;
- Market positioning;
- Competition;
- Production, order processing and shipping;
- Customer support and service;
- Human resources, training and career path planning;
- Financial forecasting and profitability;
- Financial support and operating capital;
- Budgets and tracking;
- Auditing and financial statement to shareholders;
- Return on investment;
- Board of directors;
- Advisory board.

All of these subjects demand personal thought, application and action. You must apply them to yourself. For instance, as a salesperson you can identify many ways to improve. Use a successful corporation's actions as your guide. How often does it plan? How does it schedule and assign activities for the most effective flow? How does it organize departments for maximum efficiency?

Think of yourself as having personal departments, such as finance, production, sales, general management, etc. Look at each department to discover its weakness or strength.

Every category deserves your attention on a continuing basis. Create a corporate profile that defines you as a Professional Sales Corporation.

THREE DIMENSIONS OF SELLING

Salespeople fall into three broad but neatly segmented categories or "dimensions." These dimensions cross all selling situations and affect all salespeople. They are known as the First, Second, and Third Dimensions

It's perhaps easiest to think of the three dimensions as the attributes of a box – length times width times depth.

Length would be what most salespeople start with – personality. Some are "long" on personality with much expression; others are "short", with little defining characteristics. A "linear" salesperson, one selling on personality only, has little chance of making it to the higher productive states.

Width would reflect the skills that salespeople develop and the product and customer knowledge they absorb. It also reflects a certain degree of experience that allows the salesperson to mature and develop into a professional, maybe even some sales management experience is involved.

Depth would represent the experience, strategies, tactics, inspiration, entrepreneurship and growth that they develop within the individual.

Many salespeople never evolve past the First Dimension – they remain as flat as a sheet of copy paper. This is where the new, untrained salesperson begins his or her career and where most salespeople tend to remain. It is where most salespeople still reside: an estimated 80% of all people who are involved in selling are First Dimension Sellers. The "sales professionals" with focused skills are Second and Third Dimension Sellers; they represent about 16-19% of all salespeople. Only an estimated 1-4% enter into the super-salesperson category of Third Dimension Sellers.

First Dimension
When we first begin to sell, we use the skills directly associated with our personalities. For most of us, this means using years of personal communication learned within homes, schools, church and social environments. These are the "skills" we use as our selling tools.

First Dimension Sellers rely on personal, emotional and unstructured communication to deal with a job that requires insight, planning, strategy, focused interaction, quick thinking, conversational control and specific selling skills to be effective.

Imagine that you just learned how to drive the family car. Suddenly, you are asked to drive a 100-foot long semi-tractor trailer from Boston to Los Angeles, making a number of deliveries and pickups in Detroit, Chicago, Denver and San Francisco. You don't even know how to shift a standard, let alone maneuver a loaded semi with a pup! You'd feel anxious, reluctant and nervous because, although you know how to drive, you don't have the additional skills or experience required to handle the assignment.

Selling is similar: learning how to sell is not difficult; learning how to sell professionally is a different matter. First Dimension Sellers keep on driving the family sedan, year after year; Second and Third Dimension Sellers have learned how to handle the big rigs and how to drive in all road and weather conditions.

First Dimension Sellers tend to continue to use their personal, emotional and manipulative sales formats until they receive proper skill-based training and actually begin to use focused selling skills on the job. That is why 80% of all salespeople sell only 20% of all goods and services: they don't *use* the skills they've been shown. Out of every ten salespeople, *eight* are First Dimension Sellers! Hard to manage, susceptible to external motivation and low in sales productivity, the

First Dimension Seller is the stereotype with whom most people identify.

Second Dimension – Adding "Width"

Skills and strategies differentiate the Second Dimension Seller from the First Dimension Seller. By learning even the basic skills involved in selling, a person can double, triple, even quadruple sales productivity. Many people equate sales training with skill development. However, this is seldom the case. Many First Dimension Sellers have attended several sales training seminars and consider themselves "trained." In my many years of sales training, I've never yet come across a *seminar* that trains someone to sell in three days or less. The most a seminar can accomplish is to expose and explain skills or strategies. They cannot develop skills. Only constant, day-after-day practice and hard work for weeks or even months can build effective skills and replace old, unproductive habits.

The Three Dimensions of Selling

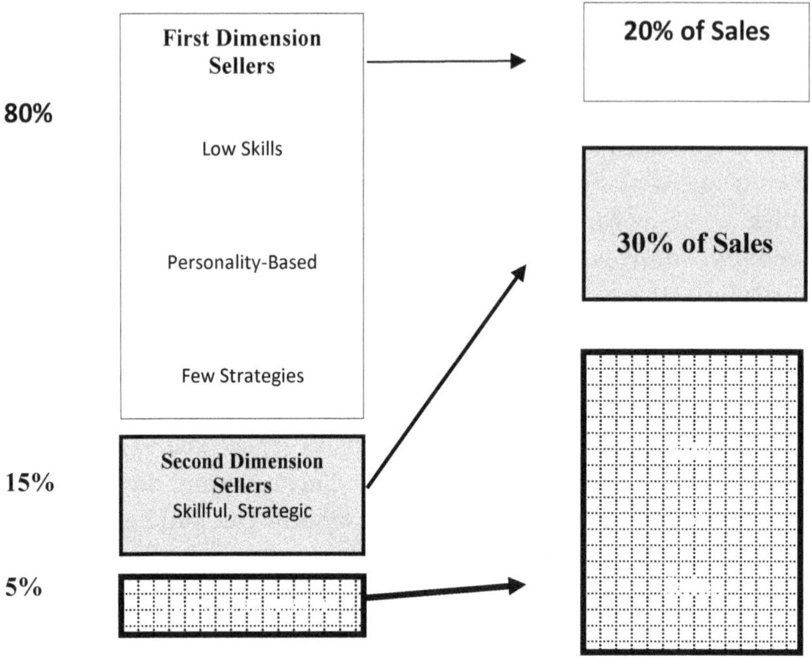

Second Dimension Sellers are the salespeople who have acquired and use professional selling skills daily. The maturation process from First to Second Dimension can be as little as several months or as long as a lifetime. More than likely, it will never occur at all. You have to make a concerted, positive effort to adopt and use professional selling skills and strategies.

The results are worth it, however. Second and Third Dimension Sellers sell more than all of the First Dimension Sellers combined, their incomes are many times higher and their promotional qualifications are much enhanced. These are the people who most likely become the sales management candidates. Easier to manage, consistent in production, responsive to management strategies and internally motivated, the Third Dimension Seller is a true sales professional. He or she concentrates on finding the value-added solution rather than simply on pushing product. Chapter 2 isolates the skills that will start you on your way to becoming a Third Dimension Seller.

Third Dimension
Just as the Second and Third Dimension Sellers sell as much or more than all of their First Dimension counterparts put together, so Third Dimension Sellers sell more than all of the Second and Third Dimension Sellers combined. What distinguishes a Third Dimension Seller? The initial clue is that they are recognized as experts within their respective industry: people with exceptional experience and product knowledge depth. This recognition gains them trust and acceptance.

But this recognition is only the result of what the Third Dimension Seller has accomplished. The characteristics that lead to this recognition indicate a rare person indeed.

Third Dimension Sellers are planners, plotters and strategists. They actively seek and establish industry-wide recognition as "the" person to talk with concerning their areas of influence (products or services). They may only actively "sell" for a few hours each month, yet their production at the end of the year is likely ten times that of the nearest Third Dimension Seller.

This is because they spend most of their time planning and influencing. It could be that they conduct value-added seminars for clients and potential clients. They might be writing articles for the industry trade periodicals. Maybe they are involved in social or political activities that take them closer to their target market buyers or influencers.

They may go three weeks, three months or even three years without a sale, but when the sales come in, they're real doozies! Inherent risk-takers and excellent risk-managers, Third Dimension Sellers look at the bigger picture and have a perspective that escapes their lower dimension companions.

They have reached the pinnacle of the selling professional. Incomes often reach into the six- and seven-figure territory. Don't look for them in the typical places, however, because they are atypical in behavior for salespeople. Tending to be polished professionals with a high degree of integrity, Third Dimension Sellers orchestrate complete sales from both perspectives: the sellers' and the buyers'.

They are expectational sellers, establishing and selling to expectations that were firmly placed through their groundwork efforts. What does it take to become a Third Dimension Seller? Read this book thoroughly: then act.

Your Doubling Strategy

In this chapter, you read about becoming a Professional Sales Corporation, acting like an autonomous corporation in which you play most of the key roles. Begin your Doubling Diary now by profiling yourself as a Professional Sales Corporation. List all those attributes identified earlier in the chapter and assess your capabilities in each area. Highlight both your strengths and weaknesses, but, more importantly, address the bigger picture. And answer....

- What do you, as a Professional Sales Corporation, see as your business future?
- Where do you want to go and who do you want to be?
- What ideals do you stand for?
- How does God surround your planning, decisions and actions?
- How can you use God's resources as your own?
- How can God use your resources as His own?
- What elements make up your personal integrity?
- What future ventures do you feel optimistic and positive about?
- What training and knowledge do you need and when are you going to get it?
- What attitudes can you alter to bring about positive change?

- What successes can you concentrate upon? (Learn from, but do not dwell upon, your failures.)
- What bad habits can you exchange for good ones?
- What physical things would you like to change about yourself?
- How would you like to change your image?
- What spiritual things would you like to change?
- What knowledge areas would you like to improve?
- In what areas does your lack of skill hold you back?
- What skills will propel you ahead?
- If you were to isolate three key things that you feel could help you sell twice as much, twice as fast, what would they be?

The answers to these questions comprise your Doubling Plan. Only you can do the work and only you can gain the benefits. But, that's what a Professional Sales Corporation is all about.

DOUBLING

Use these ideas in conjunction with the plans in the appendix for maximum effect. Each idea could affect your sales and your career by an unimaginable degree: your choice, your effort, and your return.

1. Master your fears by dissolving them. Each day, isolate the one thing that you fear or dread the most. Write it down. Then constructively develop ways to resolve the problems associated with the fear by replacing it with its positive counterparts: desire and purpose. Develop several actions that can actively, positively combat the fear. If it is fear of debt, replace it by concentrating on the rewards associated with positive performance and proper stewardship.

Pray for wisdom and strength to enact your plans. As a part of your fear-mastering strategy, it is important to get past your daily fears at the beginning of each day. Don't let them linger to pollute and paralyze your attitudes, emotions and actions.

Focus on the positive, productive side of things rather than the negative, fear side. Look at what can be done about each of your fears and concentrate on the resolution side of the issue rather than on the consequence side. Respect the consequence, but dwell on the resolution and your purpose.

2. Choose to sell. Don't perceive your position as temporary or even the result of happenstance. Make a positive decision: in or out. Having chosen, determine to become and act as a professional. Don't be fooled into thinking that you can get by with your persuasive personality: that's a typical First Dimension trap. You need tangible skills and strategies.

3. Decide that you will take on the responsibility associated with becoming a *personal* Professional Sales Corporation. You are the chairperson of the board and, as such, the ultimate responsibility for the success of your business rests with you. Isolate the departments you require to build your new corporation and start building an implementation plan.

Decide which skills you require first and which strategies you can start using now. Then set about the task of acquiring them. There are no short cuts: it takes hard work and repetition. You can't buy skills: you have to grow them. Keep adding new skills and strategies until you have a complete portfolio developed. This may take years, but you must start now. Your weekly plan involves the isolation and development of each department of your Professional Sales Corporation.

4. If you think you are a First Dimension Seller (most salespeople are), then decide now that within one year or less you will be a qualified Second Dimension Seller. Be committed to this goal. The more quickly you move away from personality selling towards skill/strategy selling,

the sooner you'll double your sales.

If you feel that you are a Second Dimension Seller, then begin to complete and round out your skill and strategy portfolio. Take one skill and strategy area each week and practice it until it makes you ill. Skills have to become second nature to become effective.

5. Analyze your particular selling situation so that you can choose the best combination of factors to create your Doubling Plan: volume, income, margins, units, dealers, distributors, territory, time, etc. Decide what your best doubling "mix" is and then start developing strategies to create that mix. Each day, keep track of your sales results; match these results against your Doubling Plan.

6. Decide right now not to be the victim of change but the master of it. Understand what is going on in your industry and your community. Get involved and be aware. Erase your self-imposed and peer-imposed boundaries and expectations. You can do better if you sincerely commit yourself to personal growth and are willing to subject yourself to risk and criticism Every week, consciously erase one confining boundary and replace it with a goal that is just out of reach but not out of sight.

7. Your level of commitment, or passion, must match your level of desire. Every achievement exacts a price from the benefactor. Decide what you are willing to give or do to achieve your new goals. Plan your future in stages so as not to bankrupt your resources before you can realize a return from your investment.

Devise and execute a good, workable plan on a month-by-month basis, keeping longer-term goals in mind. A good plan carried out with enthusiasm is far better than a perfect plan never enacted at all. Review your plan at the beginning of each week to ensure that your upcoming activities will contribute to the timely completion of your goals.

8. You must take action to make things happen. Action entails risk. Be prepared to risk criticism, ostracism and maybe even your job or some treasured assets. Almost every successful person goes through a

learning stage that involves a loss before he or she realizes a gain.

Taking action generally assures positive results; letting others take action almost always ends in negative personal results. Make a daily list of actions you are going to take that will result in positive resolutions. At the end of the day, review your actions and the outcomes. Learn, modify and try again if the results were not fully to your satisfaction.

9. Acting enthusiastically helps you to become enthusiastic. Never go into any meeting or interview unless you have first prepared yourself in prayer . Eliminate gloom and doom from your life. Just take control and banish it. Replace it with enthusiasm – “God within”.

Every day, every hour, act as if you love everything about life. Try to make the other person feel more important than yourself. Focus your enthusiasm in an infectious manner upon those around you. Get others excited by being excited for others.

10. Make a binding agreement with your future self as to who and what you want to become. Don't forget to take your family and your spiritual relationship in to account.

A balanced person functions more efficiently and effectively than one who is so strung out on work that there is no time for anyone or anything else. Rest and recharge your batteries at least one full day per week. *"And on the seventh day, He rested."*

SECTION 2: DUTY

SKILL AND STRATEGY DEVELOPMENT

The following chapters relate to the understanding and development of the skills that can take you from a First Dimension salesperson to a solid Second Dimension salesperson. If you were to measure your sales production in terms of greater sales volume and improved margins ("better" sales), the growth should amount to a sixteen times (16X) increase. Don't believe it? Here's the proof, based on the well-known Pareto (80/20) rule:

Sales force:	10 Salespeople
Total sales:	$100,000
80% by 20% =	$80,000
or, 80% by 2 salespeople =	$40,000 each
Remainder:	
20% by 80% =	$20,000
or, 20% by 8 salespeople =	$2,500 each

$40,000 is 16 times greater than $2,500 – that is the potential increase available to solid Second or Third Dimension salespeople.

This dimension is characterized by salespeople, "inside the box", who develop excellent communication skills, prospecting techniques, expectational probing and solution presentation skills, commitment and closing skills and customer retention skills. They employ strategy and tactics to best suit the selling environment and to take advantage of opportunities. They manage the sales process to achieve the win-win outcome. They work hard to achieve tough-to-get goals and corporate targets.

This section deals with these skills, strategies and knowledge. It is both a reference section and a template for personal growth. When we do the DOUBLING workshop program, it takes a minimum of six weeks to explore and anchor the skill sets.

Don't be surprised if this section seems intense: it is designed to be that way so that those who truly want to improve can extract the "meat".

My suggestion: skim it first to get the feel for the expectational selling process and how it differs from what you are currently doing. Then devise a plan of study to master each chapter. In the DOUBLING courses, this is accomplished by simply repetition that takes the participant past the common responses. In effect, the same "point" will be examined for 21 days so that every angle will have been explored and explained by the student, and by then they feel absolutely comfortable with their personal reaction concerning the point.

Since this book has literally hundreds of skills, techniques and strategies that are interwoven, the process is quite complex – but the end result is astounding.

The Duty Section is for those who truly demand more from themselves and are willing to put in the effort that can make a lifetime worth of difference to themselves, their family and to their community.

Essential Skills and Knowledge

The Essential Skills · Building on Sand · Building on Rock · Good Selling Skills · Developing Good Strategies · Full-Time Profession · Analytical Thinking · Taking Selective Action · Personal Training Agenda · Practice · Added Value · Product Knowledge · 20/80 · User Knowledge · Industry Knowledge · Be Results Oriented Keeping Up · Getting Ahead · Too Little, Too Much · Interpreting · Informing · Your Doubling Strategy

The Essential Skills

Imagine being asked to perform open-heart surgery or play a Bach concerto or fly a high-performance fighter jet. If you've been trained for these tasks, then they are familiar tasks. If you have not, then the thought of even a rudimentary attempt is ludicrous and absurd. Yet, in many ways, the comparison between top-notch selling and the above examples is justified. The skills may not be as obvious, but they are nonetheless as hard to learn and require a similar amount of practice to master them fully.

Selling requires a base of essential skills, just like piano playing does. I remember my mother when she decided to learn how to play the piano; she went up and down the scales for hours at a time. Similarly, when I learned how to fly a plane, I spent endless hours of repetitive practice to learn the basic skills of flying. Actually, anyone can *fly* a plane, but it takes skill to *control* it.

All worthwhile occupations involve fundamental skills that must be learned and practiced until they become second nature. Selling is no different. The primary difference between Second Dimension Sellers and First Dimension Sellers is that Second Dimension Sellers have developed a foundation of basic, professional selling skills. Later in this chapter these skills will be defined, but it is vitally important for you to understand that no permanent growth can take place without these skills.

BUILDING ON SAND

Every builder knows that a house built upon shifting soil is doomed to early destruction. I caution you not to build your business future on unsure or unproven ground. You must develop and use your common sense to discern between what is stable and what is emotional, especially in terms of business opportunities. Salespeople by their very nature tend to be highly emotional and susceptible to externally applied motivation. Trusting your career to emotional decisions and external motivational sources is akin to building a house on sand.

I was a young (30-ish) vice-president of a firm that promoted and presented large motivational rallies in major Canadian cities. We would use only the best speakers, household names to most salespeople. All day, our audience of several thousand would absorb the "you-can-do-it" rhetoric of the speakers. They purchased cassettes, books and videos until the shelves and boxes were empty. When the final speaker walked away from the podium, they shot out of the auditorium riding high on a cloud of positive slogans. Tomorrow the world was theirs!

But what really happened? I know, and perhaps you know as well, if you've ever been to a similar event. Tomorrow dawns and that feeling of being able to conquer the world has faded into a feeling of uneasy anticipation, maybe even into a feeling of anxiety. You try out some of the axioms and techniques and perhaps meet with faltering success. Then the custodian of your comfort zone issues a warning: you can't do it like they said you could. But it seemed so easy! They said anyone could do it. You have been deceived! You wander straight back to your old self, the custodian having done its job.

When external motivation is applied to an unskilled salesperson, the reverse effect (de-motivation) tends to be the eventual result. If you lack skills, it takes a remarkably short time for the motivation pendulum to swing to the opposite side and put you in the dumps. You remain as an unskilled, First Dimension Seller unless you make a determined, planned effort to escape. Relying on external motivation to revive your enthusiasm is like taking drugs: a life of silent despair accented by brief moments of hope-filled elation. They are no different.

External motivation is the sand upon which most salespeople build their career foundations.

The "house" built on sand awaits destruction from the first ripple of an objection. The foundation shifts with the elements and seasons. The dwelling is a mix of colors, having been painted time and time again by loosely applied motivation. A draft blows through unfinished and unsealed windows. The roof leaks whenever it rains, having hastily been built by untrained hands.

In the winter, the owner must spend all his earnings just to try and keep it warm enough to live in; in the summer, the sun stifles the inside. A sense of confusion, momentary panic and frustration builds as bills hang on the wall awaiting payment, but there is just never enough to pay them all. The phone hangs disconnected on the wall. Teenage music wails from a bedroom with an old blanket for a door and mixes with the somber tones of a TV newscaster to add to the general feeling of discomfort.

This is the house of the unskilled. It's been for sale for three years now, but no one has offered to buy it yet, not even a low-ball. Maybe next month. Yes, of course, there's always *next* month!

Building on Rock

Second and Third Dimension Sellers know that it is a combination of strategy, intelligence, perseverance, knowledge and enthusiasm acting upon a specific skill base with passion that makes them successful. The fighter pilot cannot execute complicated tactical maneuvers if he doesn't feel fully at ease with the basic operation of his aircraft. The surgeon will attempt new, more complicated and perhaps dangerous procedures only after she has completely mastered the basics. An Indy car driver won't push 220 if he doesn't feel competent at 215.

- Exceptional results come from exceptional ideas working through exceptional skills.
- Exceptional results come from ordinary ideas working through exceptional skills.

- Exceptional results come from exceptional ideas working through ordinary skills.
- Ordinary results come from ordinary ideas working through ordinary skills.

Prayer, or lack of prayer, modifies all of the above.

If you don't have a wealth of exceptional ideas and strategies to draw upon, then it might be wiser to develop a portfolio of exceptional skills. The foundation of any professional salesperson is composed mainly of skills: communications skills, interpersonal skills, presentation skills, interrogation skills, closing and commitment skills, discernment skills, product application skills and many others.

Without a fully developed set of basic skills, you can build only so far, only so fast.

Salespeople are drawn to motivational materials like tax inspectors to falsified returns. However, salespeople with a solid skill base look at motivational materials differently than do their unskilled counterparts. They glean the kernels of wisdom and the useful ideas. They listen for strategies they can incorporate. They search for that elusive competitive edge. They know instinctively that for every 100 punches that a boxer throws, only one will have any significant effect. Out of a hundred ideas, perhaps only one is useful and practical. But just one good idea can mean the difference between mediocre performance and a knockout victory.

One good idea, enacted skillfully, can easily double your sales.

The professional's “house” rests on a foundation of basic selling skills that are firmly and comfortably established. The foundation grows more solid and elaborate as new skills are added and infused with existing skills. The dwelling is built of strategy, perseverance, attitude and knowledge. It is decorated with the results of enthusiasm, courage and decisiveness. It is made warm and comfortable through the calming effects of wisdom, confidence and experience. Good organization is apparent throughout: neatness, cleanliness, a flow.

Smells of good things baking welcome the visitor and handshakes are genuine, firm but genteel. A hug or two is not uncommon. This "house" built on rock appreciates in value each year as new conveniences and additions are planned and added. Its landscaping reflects the private, professional nature of its owners. This is where you can stay for a lifetime, relaxing, growing, prospering and yet remaining at peace.

What kind of "home" are you building? What kind do you want? What do you have to do to change from sand to stone? When are you going to start? *Why not now?*

GOOD SELLING SKILLS

In my personal career as a sales trainer, I quickly discovered that sales training seminars don't train. They teach.

There is a vital difference: teaching shows you how to do something; training prepares you to do something. When I discuss skill development, I sound unconventional to most salespeople and managers because of the nature of accepted industry standards for sales training.

Selling skills take weeks, months and years to learn. It's not that they are that difficult; it's just that they have to be practiced sufficiently to make them second nature. When I was a commercial pilot, the job was boring. The only really exciting times were during takeoff and landing. I used to describe the job as many pilots do: 95% boredom punctuated by 5% terror. Most of the training for commercial pilots focuses on what to do when things go wrong. To fly a plane is simple. To fly a plane that is in trouble is an incredibly complex, demanding and dangerous task. Professional pilots are paid highly because they can handle problems effectively.

To sell is simple. To sell under adverse or highly competitive situations is an incredibly complex and demanding task.

Adverse conditions are what selling skills are all about, for brilliance in selling isn't developed under clear-sky conditions. The big bucks and recognition are earned during stormy, desperate and sweaty times, when perhaps hope is all that's left. This is when the salesperson must rely on second-nature skills developed through training, practice and experience. To face an angry committee or a vindictive, spiteful purchasing agent can shake a person to the very core. No one likes it, but it has to be handled. It's no time for an amateurish attempt at cute tricks learned in a seminar. It's time for proven sales techniques and strategies.

Here are the basic skills of selling. If you don't have them, you need them. They are your future, your rock foundation, your equity increase. You can double your sales by mastering each skill by itself and using them in strategic harmony:

- Rapport skills, recognizing and adjusting for the needs of other people;

- Observation skills, reading body language and the subtleties of non-verbal communication;

- Investigation skills, uncovering and implanting expectations, needs, desires, motives and parameters;

- Commitment skills, growing purchasing commitment and orchestrating a tension-controlled sale from beginning to end;

- Negative response skills, interpreting, responding and reversing negative opinions, actions or events;

- Presentation skills, making your solution sound attractive, exciting and complete to the prospective client;

- Expectation skills, exposing, implanting and fulfilling client expectations;

- Communications skills, facilitating the transfer of information from you to your client;

- Organization skills, operating your Professional Sales Corporation efficiently, effectively and profitably;

- Strategic skills, evaluating selling situations and planning tactics and actions that result in a bigger, faster sale;
- Technology skills, rising beyond the sales support boundaries that may eventually hold you back;
- Social media skills so that you can influence a much larger audience and help grow relationships;
- Training skills, providing added value to your customers and selling team;
- Product knowledge application skills, positively affecting your customers through your personal knowledge of your product and interpreting your product's features into advantages and benefits;
- Motivational skills, positively motivating individuals and groups during sales presentations;
- Attitude-adjusting skills, repositioning your personal attitude quickly when depressed or de-motivated.

These are the skills of a Second Dimension Seller. They are only headings, for under each one lies months of daily effort to develop each budding skill into a hardy perennial.

Developing Good Strategies

To become a Second or Third Dimension Seller you must learn to think in terms of *strategies*. A strategy is a selected course of action that will bring about a desired result. Most salespeople don't employ anything above standard selling strategies: *"I'll show him our top of the line and if it's too much money then I'll hit him with the super-saver deal!"*

It's not original thinking. It's all too common. The Second Dimension Seller is characterized by the use of original strategy: uncommon concepts for selling success employed on an individual basis.

If we do not use good strategic thinking it is because we don't train ourselves to think strategically. Defensive driving is a good example of strategic thinking, always visually and mentally mapping out an evasive maneuver should a vehicle under observation make the wrong (but not unexpected) move. Selling strategies are similar: what do you do if the prospective customer zigs or zags the wrong way? How do you steer your "ship of sales" through the rough waters? Are you prepared for the expected and the unexpected? Most salespeople are surprised, caught off guard and easily defeated by the unexpected.

But strategies only work if you have demonstrable skills to enact them. You might have worked out a great strategy to use should the customer give you a particular and specific objection, but what happens if you are tossed something that's outside of your experience and planning? Do you have the skill to handle an objection for which you don't have a prepared answer or documentation?

This is what I am talking about when I say that strategies must come from a foundation formed from skills. You must have been there before, experientially or experimentally.

Strategic thinking in sales requires that you develop the habit of thinking strategically. This is not as difficult as it may seem. Here are a few suggestions to help you develop strategic thinking:

- Before you go into any sales interview or before anyone walks onto your sales floor, picture in your mind what might happen. Create likely situations that might concern you and then work out imaginative solutions. Fill in the steps necessary to get from the expressed concern to the solution. What would be your most appropriate response?

- For every sales call, imagine appropriate customer concerns and then plan positive solutions.

- Consciously practice the skill of thinking ahead in everything you do during the day. If it is lunch, then think ahead about what you would like to eat and then seek it out on the menu. Don't simply react to the menu as most people do. If you are driving your car, think and plan your route in your head before you drive and as you drive. If you are buying clothes, think ahead of the color or the style that would please you and then search for it.

- Plan your day in advance. The best time is the night before because this sets the subconscious into motion during the night. Give your unknowns and your next-day problems to the subconscious and let it work on the problem. If you believe in the power of prayer, then turn the impossible problems over to God for His help. It's always worked for me.

- Always plan alternatives to your best course of action (or expected reaction). Have a contingency plan for everything you do during the day.

You are building new thinking skills so be prepared for some uncomfortable feelings. After a week it will begin to feel more natural and after a month of everyday use it will be second nature. An un-worked mind is like an un-mown lawn: eventually it goes to seed and becomes a haven for weeds and a target for finger-pointing neighbors. Never stop challenging your mind, for the day you stop growing is the day you start dying. I know people who, at the age of 80 or 90, are more alert, alive and challenging than many people in their 20's. You choose.

FULL-TIME PROFESSION

There are many ways to increase sales output. One is by bettering your skills so that you can improve your ability to sell and to close. Another is to increase the number or quality of people you talk to. Unfortunately, too many salespeople suffer from job switch syndrome, which works against both of these simple Doubling techniques.

What is job switch syndrome? It is thinking about your job only when you are required to be at work, turning "on" when you arrive at work and turning "off" when you leave for the day. In the off hours, no extra effort goes into planning or skill development. No extension effort is applied. Your entire sales effort is restricted to what happens during normal business hours. And in most cases, this effort is reactive. However, for most Second and Third Dimension Sellers, the job switch seldom is turned off. Instead of shutting completely down, it goes into a monitoring status, always remaining alert to possible selling or learning opportunities.

The job switch syndrome means that First Dimension Sellers only spend about half of their waking time actually engaged in their work, and most of that time will be centered on reactive situations and directly engaging the client in the sales event. Little time is spent on finding or culling potential clients or developing new skills and strategies.

Second Dimension Sellers spend about 80% of their time selling and 20% of their time searching for new clients, commonly called "prospecting." Their selling time primarily is spent with the 80% of their clients who already provide 80% of their income.

Third Dimension Sellers spend roughly 80% of their time searching, thinking, preparing, positioning, developing, creating and only about 20% (or less) of their time actually selling; their minds seldom leaving the priorities of creating new sales, contacts and markets.

The first task for all salespeople is leave the job switch on longer – your mind should be "engaged" 14 or 16 hours per day. Leave it on "monitor" during your social activities and your quiet times. Ponder and develop. Think past the common, everyday experiences of the selling job.

Determine that you are going to devote more mental activity to being better at what you do. Decide now that the job you have is your profession. You must wear it.

As a professional, you can glean considerable success from being able to think logically, creatively and clearly. You can't do this if you are on drugs or alcohol most of the day. You can't do this if you spend most of your free time socializing and being involved in non-productive activities or thought.

To rise above the mediocre, you must stand aside from the vast hordes of First Dimension Sellers. You must avoid the traps and trappings of those who do not want to see you get ahead. If you wish to become different, then begin to act and think differently.

Analytical Thinking

Analytical thinking looks at the cause-and-effect relationships of why and how people are attracted to your product or service. It deals with the types of prospects best suited to use your product or service, the ways to contact or meet these prospects, the ways to increase your contact numbers and how to get better contacts.

Analytical thinking explores the "numbers" of selling. How many contacts does it require to find a solid prospect? How many prospects does it take to produce a customer? How many calls does it take on the prospect to make a sale? How many posts on social media does it take to have one new customer walk through the door? What do the analytics tell you?

Analytical thinking is a simple but often overlooked step to doubling your sales. If you can analyze where your sales come from and increase the "input" side of the sales equation, then your "output" side will register higher.

> **The more or better prospects you can talk to, the more sales or bigger sales you will get.**

Also, if you enhance your skill base, then the number of prospects who become customers will rise.

> **The better your selling skills are, the more sales or bigger sales you will get.**

You have a choice: change the methods by which you locate prospective customers (enhance the input) or change your personal skill level so that the people with whom you talk are more likely to purchase (increase your closing ratio), or both.

Many sales programs picture the input side of sales as a huge funnel through which all suspects, prospects and other assorted bodies must pass. The dilemma faced by increasing the volume on the input side is that it increases your work load (screening, sorting and qualifying) while not necessarily increasing your sales output.

This seems as if I just said that it doesn't pay to increase the input side of the equation. You're right. It doesn't. If you don't think the input (or funnel) philosophy through thoroughly beforehand, you will wind up with too much to handle and the strategy will actually be counter-productive.

This is why analytical thinking must include selective action. You must sort out the good ideas from the not-so-good ones, increasing the input selectively. Here are some hints:

- Isolate the prime characteristics of your current good customers. These characteristics could include industry type, position, income, location, price sensitivity, quality requirements, product suitability for task, economic reasons (costing or profit), political alignments, environmental suitability, etc. Whatever factors caused your current prospects to become customers, will probably be the buying factors in future prospects. Isolate these factors and then seek prospects with similar characteristics.

- Prepare a prospect profile of the most likely type of person, company or industry to purchase your products or services. Write it down. Continue to add to the profile as you recognize factors that influence the buying process. After a while, you'll look for this type of prospect instinctively.

- Expand your profile to similar types of industries or people. If you are successful in selling to buyers in the automotive industry, should you not consider other transportation industries as well? In one move, you might increase your input potential tenfold. Select each parallel industry carefully and work with it cautiously so you do not undermine your current sales portfolio.

TAKING SELECTIVE ACTION

One step will immediately begin separating you from the rest: taking selective action. Selective action means that you search for the best method or activity to take in any given situation and then decide how and when to act.

Essential Skills And Knowledge

Most salespeople react emotionally to a given selling situation, thereby losing their control and possibly losing the sale. First Dimension Sellers react emotionally most of the time because their selling skills are based upon personality traits rather than upon focused communication skills. However, because they can logically recognize a selling situation, Second Dimension Sellers generally evaluate before formulating actions or planning redirection strategies.

Recognize - Formulate - Select Action - Act

Selective action involves strategic thinking. You must generate the alternatives and then determine a successful course of action.

Strategy fails when you have limited skills and options.

Pause to formulate a response completely *before* opening your mouth. All too often, an immediate response is emotionally based. If you pause, ponder and postulate, you will find an incredible ability to say or do the right thing.

Personal Training Agenda

All successful Third Dimension Sellers create their own personal training agendas. They do not rely upon others to tell them what they require in terms of personal growth. It is vital for you to understand that to grow you must learn and experience things that you do not know now!

To develop a personal training agenda, you must first know where you are and where you want to be. Obviously, there are degrees of learning and a learning curve is involved in whatever you do, so a good pinch of practicality must be a part of training.

For instance, if you consider yourself to be a budding Second Dimension Seller, then you are facing a considerable amount of skill development. It's like the example of the new driver and the transport truck. There is a learning gap that you must bridge through a combination of training, practice and experience. The more experience that you add (whether actually on the job or in practice sessions), the more comfortable you will feel with the new skill or knowledge.

You can't jump from here to there without effort and planning. You must decide where you are now and where you want to be in time increments. For example, if you require rapport skills, it might take you three weeks of intensive daily work to get you from here to there.

The learning process requires that you give new information time to absorb, time to adjust and time to mature within you. It also requires daily repetition if it is to become second nature.

In building a personal training plan, you should look at monthly, quarterly, annual and long-range time frames.

A monthly plan might include developing a specific skill, practicing on a daily basis throughout the month until the skill feels comfortable and useable.

A quarterly training agenda might see you reading selected books or listening to selling tapes or attending a local seminar or course.

An annual agenda might have you taking a university course or an advanced training program. It might also include taking a selection of training programs offered throughout the year.

A long-range training agenda might involve developing specific technical expertise or earning a degree or being hired by the firm that provides the specific training that you seek. Whatever your position, you can always grow. As my old friend, Memory Man Bill Clennan, says,

"You're either green and growing or you're ripe and rotting!"

Make training one of your "unshakeable unbreakable" personal goals and activities. Training provides knowledge. Knowledge provides insight. Insight encourages strategies. Strategies create sales. (And sales put money in your jeans!)

You and you alone are responsible for your personal education. No one else. Just you. You also are responsible for paying for your own education. You tend to learn better when it's your own dough on the line. Let it sink in a little deeper....

"You're either green and growing or you're ripe and rotting!"

Practice

Training results in knowledge; practice results in skills. The typical period required to absorb, internalize and acquire a skill is three weeks: three weeks of practicing every day in a conscious effort to "try." Depending upon the skill, it may require five minutes each day or five hours.

The important element is spaced repetition, trying the same new skill activity every day, day after day, until it becomes second nature. Only when it becomes second nature will it be comfortable, pliable and strategically useful.

Practice is what most salespeople will not do on their own. To double, you need to commit yourself to a practice period every day. Practice with your dog, your cat, your wife or husband, your friends or your voice or memo recorder. Be critical. Strive to achieve performance perfection. Always look for new and improved ways to accomplish the task that the skill addresses.

In one year, you can become fully proficient in every single professional selling skill if you will commit yourself to daily practice. Even just 10 to 20 minutes per day is enough.

If you practice conscientiously for one year, your financial and professional world will be so dramatically changed that the title of this book will seem like child's play. Doubling your sales is easy. But you can do much more, if you'll only take the time and make the effort.

Added Value

I remember one time going to a local lumberyard to buy a few building studs. I only needed six studs and, knowing the routine, I casually walked over to the lumber counter and paid for my studs before heading out to the yard to search out the best six. Lumber has always seemed overpriced to me, and there have been a few times when I have been furious with myself for allowing the lumberyard helpers to select and load "my" wood, only to wind up with twisted, split or warped lumber. That is why I now select and load my own. It seems to be the only way to protect the *value* of my purchase.

This trip was like most of the rest. I knew where the studs were located and pulled my truck right beside the pile, hopped out and began to sort for the straightest, tightest-grained studs I could find. Finding six wouldn't take long. Just then, the yard hand arrived to "assist." A big man with a quiet manner, he quickly noticed that I had a purposeful intent and did not force his priorities upon me.

In fact, he did something that made my trip quite memorable. Instead of scrutinizing me while I hand-picked, he said, *"Look, if you need some more lumber, there's a pile of discards right here that we'll be taking to the dump later today. Just help yourself; take as many as you like."* He smiled, took my delivery slip and signed it, and walked away with a nod of his head towards the considerable pile of studs in disarray not a dozen feet from my tailgate.

Standing there, speechless, and with an overwhelming sense of discovery, I began to load up. After a dozen or so, a sense of fair play began to creep in and I ceased loading, leaving behind a treasure for the next lucky lumber hound.

I have made many trips to the lumberyard before and since this incident, but I doubt if I will ever forget that single trip. Why?

It's called added value. Any time you receive more than what you expect, the experience becomes a positive, memorable one. The yardman didn't have to do what he did, but because he did, the accepted value of my original purchase became flooded with the extra, added value of the discarded "treasure" studs. I would never have taken them as my paid-for choice, but for free they looked marvelous. I subsequently never questioned the value of my original purchase because it had been considerably altered by the additional lumber. It cost the lumberyard little, yet it gained a secure and loyal customer, now lured into thinking that it just might happen again.

Salespeople who can create added value will alter positively their customers' appreciation of their purchases. People, whether they are acting on behalf of themselves or their corporations, react well to added-value programs. It has to do with expectations.

Exceed the expectation and positive results occur.

Fall short of the expectation and negative results occur.

It's the key to every WOW! – based business.

Added value is simply doing something to your product, service or personal involvement so that what is received or perceived to be received exceeds the expectations of the customer.

You must realize, however, that the basic value expectation must be in place before added value has any effect. Using the example of the lumberyard, I had already paid for my studs, and as I sorted through the new lumber, my expectations of the value received for goods purchased were firmly established. This is why with every free stud that went into my truck, the added value mounted.

Here are some added value areas that you could address individually or corporately:

- More product;
- Additional, related product;
- Additional, unrelated product;
- More or enhanced service;
- Coupons for additional product or service;
- Unusual service;
- Application assistance;
- Industry information;
- Financial discounts;

- Enhanced delivery scheduling;
- Enhanced installation;
- Training or enhanced training;
- Personalization of product.

There are many, many areas where you can make the difference between a normal, acceptable sale and a memorable, unforgettable sale. You must take the responsibility to do what it takes to create the added value in every sale.

PRODUCT KNOWLEDGE

As a salesperson, how many times have you been handed a product catalog and been expected to extract product knowledge from its pages? The information inside is really only a part of the product knowledge package. It more than likely expresses feature or function knowledge: weighs 23 pounds, has 119 channels, gets 50 miles to the gallon, is made of nickel-chrome alloy, etc. These are interesting and vital facts, but they alone are not enough to sell past First Dimension boundaries.

All Second Dimension Sellers have progressed past relying on product knowledge expressed as features and functions. They stress the results of the features and functions. They also have learned to surround the components of any product or service with application knowledge and industry knowledge. It's no good to have a widget unless you know how a widget is going to be used.

In my sales training programs, I have a device that was given to me when I was first involved in training. It's called a Torlo. I don't know where it came from and I don't know if it is still manufactured, but it gets attention in class. Oddly shaped it had two 8" white plastic "claws" encompassed by a large black plastic knurled ring that when turned, drew the "claws" together. It has perplexed thousands of salespeople from coast to coast. I describe it as a special device with a capacity of 1/4 inch through 1 inch, wear-resistant and waterproof. The best made. One-year unconditional warranty. Length: 8 inches; shank 1/4 inch. price: $9.95. Would you buy it? Probably not, because you don't know what it does. You don't know how it affects you. You don't know the value relationship. You might not be getting the best deal.

Product knowledge consists of knowing the features and functions of your products and how each of these features or functions affects your client. The effects can be functional, financial, emotional, safety, service-oriented, etc. This is the basic fundamental product knowledge that all salespeople should possess. If you don't have instant recall of product information (features, functions, user benefits and advantages) and how this information affects the client, you don't have sufficient product knowledge depth to develop overall professional selling prowess.

As well, if you do not interpret features and functions into benefits as a matter of habit, then you must develop the skill of benefit interpretation. This one skill will double your sales.

20/80

I once had a training task placed in my lap by an office furnishings company that had just experienced a major sales force overhaul. Only one of the original seven salespeople remained and six new salespeople had been hired. The task was simple enough to describe: bring the new salespeople up to speed on product within four weeks. The product was catalog and showroom based. The showroom exhibited executive suite arrangements, but the catalogs held all the component pricing and accessories. There were literally thousands of products.

There is no way to gain product knowledge depth when you have thousands of products to represent by trying to memorize it all. The solution: 20/80 – the Pareto effect.

> ***20% of your products probably represent 80% of your sales.***

Concentrate on learning the 20%. Review with your management which products are traditional sellers and which represent "fringe" products. This is exactly the technique I used when training the furniture sales-people. In one month of intensive on-the-job training, they acquired a sufficient product knowledge base to complete sales unassisted. Know your 20% inside out.

Know all the facets: customer use, product quality, product features and functions, user advantages and benefits, and economic parameters. Know the competition's strengths and weaknesses in relationship to your product. Know how your product is accepted by the end user or by the consumer, and learn about why and how these products are used from the customers' points of view. Become an *expert* concerning the key 20% of your product line. Then, add personal depth by learning how to integrate the remaining 80% of your product line with the top-selling 20%.

User Knowledge

The key component of product knowledge is *user knowledge.* If you do not know how or why your product or service will benefit or be used by your customer, then how can you possibly understand or empathize with your customer's position?

How will you understand or appreciate what constitutes added value to your customer if you cannot appreciate his or her personal position within the sale? That position includes the use of your product or service. You sell, they use. They use, you supply. However you paint the relationship, you can only be effective if you understand your product from the customer's perspective.

Once, when working with the newly appointed sales manager of an import automobile dealership, I suggested the concept of his salespeople becoming "personal transportation specialists" rather than new- or used-car salespeople. The results were quite astounding, simply because in adopting the position of a personal transportation specialist, the salesperson had to go beyond the "what color and how many doors do you prefer?" approach that was common to a "push" sale. They had to find out the why, where, when, how many and how often of the prospect's personal transportation portfolio. They had to get involved. Rather than pushing the red, four-door sedan, they sold a two-door coupe and a four-door wagon because it best suited the transportation needs of the customer.

Appealing to how and why people use your product is always a stronger technique than just presenting the product and hoping that it fits.

The dealership became the number one in the country (for that manufacturer) within one year, with individual salesperson productivity averaging about 30 vehicles per month. Contrast this with the national average of around ten cars per month and you can see why the dealership became number one.

The change was due to four key things:

- the development of a professional selling skills base;
- enhanced product and user knowledge;
- personal self-image enhancement;
- a dynamic, goal-driven manager.

"Steve" was young, aggressive and a team leader; he made the formula work by taking a personal interest in each salesperson and in each sale. He was not afraid to risk and he was not afraid to reward. Steve himself was selling over 40 cars per month!

You, too, can increase your sales by knowing the why's and the how's of your customers, your products and your services:

- Why do they use it?
- When do they use it?
- Where do they use it?
- Who uses it?
- How do they use it?
- How do they benefit from using it?
- How can they improve their jobs by using it?
- How can they benefit financially from using it?

INDUSTRY KNOWLEDGE

Industry knowledge is as important as user knowledge is. What is the prospect's industry like? Is the industry growing, receding or stagnating? Is the industry using or benefiting from your product or service now? What is the reputation of your product within the industry? Are there new industries that could benefit from using your product? What is the competition saying about your product? Is it true?

The more industry knowledge you gain, the better you will understand your prospects' and customers' needs, desires and frustrations. Industry knowledge is a sure way to understand what constitutes added value to your client.

You must communicate in terms relevant to and appreciated by the industry to which you sell.

For instance, I once was an operating partner (president) of a company producing a special security marking fluid that, when applied, would chemically identify an item to a particular registered user, be it a firm, a plant location, a floor or a department. The purpose was to deter internal theft by making company property identification impossible to remove. While the marking fluid cost users over $8,000 per gallon, it saved millions in potential losses.

The auto industry, petroleum refiners and heavy manufacturers were early users. As we gained expertise, we broadened our markets to include everything from public schools to electronics manufacturers.

Each customer saw a different use for exactly the same product. Steel mills and automobile factories drastically reduced theft of tools and equipment; laboratories protected computer components and irreplaceable instrumentation from misappropriation; and other customers saw it as a method of controlling warranty claim abuse. There were hundreds of ways the product could be used.

But each time we presented the product, a daub of oddly-colored paint, it bore the jargon and clothes of the industry for which it was intended. It felt "comfortable" to the person across the table from us when we made our formal presentation. To achieve this level of acceptance, we *first* had to learn something of the industry we approached.

If you deal with a product that is expected to cross industries, recognize that each industry has its own boundaries, its own protocols and its own language. One of the best ways to learn is to study trade magazines, attend industry trade shows or research them on the web. Listen to the industry, pretend you are a user yourself and gain an industry appreciation before going out to challenge new territory.

Be Results Oriented

If a product or service does not benefit you in some way, why buy it? If your product does not benefit your clients, why should they buy it?

Show a tangible result: something that can be shown on paper, held in a palm or presented to the financial officer as proof that a benefit was obtained. By making the intangible tangible, your sale will be easier.

All too often, salespeople rely on "presentation talent" (a fast mouth, quick hands and dancing feet) to instill a feeling that is supposed to say, "This is a good deal!!!" To many professional buyers, it means that the salesperson has not done his or her homework.

Becoming results-oriented means preparing for each and every sale and looking for the user payoffs surrounding your product or service. If you sell to a detail industry (such as laboratories, manufacturers and institutions), then you must seek verifiable, tangible evidence of results-oriented use. It is vital that you prepare the evidence before going into the "courtroom" of sales: your prospect's office.

If you deal in an industry that is more emotional, such as real estate, auto sales or retail sales, then your results are in the immediate personal application and appreciation of the product or service. Backed up by some simple support information (it looks stunning on you... this house will appreciate because of the excellent location... the acceleration will just glue you to the driver's seat), your result claims are cemented and appreciated.

Train yourself to think as customers think, see as customers see, feel as customers feel, and hear as customers hear. Train yourself to step out of your shoes and into theirs. Train yourself to be a shopper and a purchaser, while at the same time maintaining your poise as a salesperson.

Don't sell face to face; sell side by side.

Sell as if you were buying, and ask yourself, *"Would I buy from me?"* Why or why not?

KEEPING UP

Subscribe to stay alive. All industries have trade publications. Subscribe to and read them all. Read your product industry periodicals and your customers' periodicals. When you are in your prospects' reception area, see what trade periodicals are available. Write down the titles and subscription details and URL's. Ask if you can have copies to take with you. Request a copy of the client's annual report from the receptionist and, if they have issues of previous years' reports, try to get these as well. Obviously, research their websites.

Attend to comprehend. All industries have trade shows. Go, ask and listen. Gather literature, study it and then catalog it in a reference file. Ask your prospects and customers about upcoming trade shows. Ask them why they attend. By attending, you'll see who has the booths and who is trying to attract your prospect. You might want to put up your own booth.

Inspect to detect. All customers will show disenchantment, elation or normal satisfaction within a specified period of time after the purchase. By investigating the use of your product after it's been installed, you can gain valuable information, head off potential trouble or gain new sales through referrals. It's been shown that a current satisfied customer will purchase additional product much faster and with less effort than a new prospect.

GETTING AHEAD

Staying current with product, user and industry knowledge is demanding but necessary. Set aside a specific period during each week for product review and enhancement and for searching on-line for competitors and like-industries. Sometimes to get ahead you must sit on your behind.

TOO LITTLE, TOO MUCH

How much information is enough to trigger a positive buying decision? I guess if we knew, there wouldn't be a lot of work to sales. I know salespeople who are experts at the data dump. They give the prospect every possible bit of information pertaining to the past, present and future use of the product in question. They are a walking encyclopedia of little known facts. Yet, I know others who can whisk by on the personal assurance that it will do the job. How much is enough?

What are the negative consequences of both approaches? Let's have a look.

Too Little Information:

- It creates fertile ground for buyer's remorse if the sale is concluded too fast.
- Prospects can't make good value judgments.
- Prospects can't evaluate fairly against competition.
- Once the salesperson is gone, product insecurity develops.
- The product is intricately linked to the salesperson's presentation and personality. This puts the sales process in a very emotional context, which is hard to manage and control.
- Decisions become centered around emotional criteria and the presentation personality of the salesperson. Factual information may become distorted or omitted.

- If a decision must be made by a third party who is not at the presentation, the selling process is incomplete.
- Emotional presentations and pleas seldom work on all professional buyers.
- If the information is to be presented again by your prospect to internal influencers or decision makers, there is likely insufficient information to help make the presentation convincing.

Too Much Information:

- Some prospects can't digest all the material. They may react by not reading the information or proposal at all.
- Delays may occur due to an overabundance of un-essential information that now must be interpreted.
- Questions may arise due to information that was not in original purchasing agenda. This may trigger additional study or new purchasing parameters.
- More information might encourage additional competitive evaluation.
- The purchasing decision becomes attached to the evaluation of information.
- The information takes too long to prepare and is too hard to present.

There are also *positive* consequences of both approaches.

Too Little Information:

- The sale is faster and less complicated if the buying decision can be obtained early.
- Less preparation is required by the salesperson and less time is required by the purchaser to evaluate.
- Tightening the sales cycle means more sales per period.

Too Much Information:

- Presentation can be distributed quickly to decision makers.
- Factual buyers have time to digest and consider.
- Your information may physically "stack" better against competition because more tangible materials are presented.
- Many data points may lead to a negotiated, assumed-close sale, which is more appropriate for institutionalized businesses.

In the next chapter, we look at personality styles and how information affects prospects with different styles in different ways. For some, a deluge of data is important; for others, it is frustrating. Yet, some prospects won't be influenced at all, just as if your information didn't exist.

I once did a special training project for a health club that involved taking half their staff and training them to sell in a consultative manner. The remaining staff used the hard-close, no-holds-barred approach to pressured sales that the chain was currently using.

In terms of product knowledge, the hard-close group provided only the positive, only the attractive, only the irresistible. To get a decision, the prospective health-club attendee was taken to a specifically designed closing room, where he or she was made to sit on uncomfortable plastic furniture across a glass-and-chrome table from the "closer." The table and the closer were between the prospect and the door. With minimum information and with lots of embarrassing, arm-twisting sales pressure, the prospect either had to cough up a check or maneuver past the closer and out though the halls. It was an almost impossible and inescapable trap.

The result: 80 to 90% of prospects wrote out checks and signed a multi-year contract. However, payment on over 70% of the checks received was stopped by the customer. This was an expected consequence of the system: close ten to get three. Out of those prospects whose checks were cashed, fewer than 5% ever used the facility on even a part-time basis.

In comparison, the "consultative" sellers were trained to inform their potential members fully and to walk them through the facilities. Here, they could experience the ambiance and excitement that could be theirs if they joined. The salespeople were instructed to sit with their prospects by the pool and carefully explain the pros and cons of joining and using the club. The close was classic puppy dog:

"Stay for a while and try it out for yourself. When you're satisfied, I'll be glad to help you with the details."

It worked: over 80% bought and fewer than 2% of the checks received stop payments in the six months following the pilot project. Unfortunately, it worked too well! Most of the 80% who bought used the facility regularly, and within a short period of time it was standing room only.

This example highlights several factors in favor of realistic, responsible delivery of product knowledge:

- People need to know enough to make rational informed decisions; anything less risks buyer's remorse and its consequences.
- People need enough time to make their decisions and to interpret the product information in terms that they can understand. Rushing a decision before the information can be digested will result in undue pressure, buyer's remorse and cancelled sales.
- The more alien your product or service is to the everyday activities or experiences of a prospect, the more assimilation time is necessary for information to be digested and understood.
- Too much information causes overload and delay; too little information pressures the prospect into making an irrational and uninformed decision.
- Your sales approach and strategies should always be in harmony with your company's overall objectives

and purposes. You may have a better way, but will it be the *right* way for your employer?

INTERPRETING

Delivering product information can become comfortable and routine. However, it can also become a weapon without your being aware of it. This situation is especially prevalent with technically complicated products because salespeople often become immersed in the internal jargon of their industries. Some industries are so immersed in product-specific language that a whole pecking order can be established and maintained on fluency alone.

Be aware that the customer either knows *less* than you do or knows *more* than you do about your product or service.

If your customers know less than you do, you can intimidate and confuse them by using unfamiliar terms and language. It happens hundreds of times every day, in every industry: destruction by data, buzz word blasting, jargon jousting. Either you learn just the bare essentials to get by (so that you can't confuse anyone) or you learn so much that you can describe the complexities of your industry in simple, easy-to-understand, everyday language. Choose one path or the other, because the middle path, partial knowledge, is the most dangerous. There are three points to consider:

- In most cases, a simplified approach is safer than a complicated one.
- If you have a wealth of product knowledge, use it only when specifically called for by strategy or defense.
- Don't attack with language, don't patronize or intimidate and don't fill your ego with pompous self-worth based on a buzz word balance.

The translation of product qualities and applications into a format that is understandable to your prospect is a delicate, time-consuming and patience-stretching experience, but it is of utmost importance to the success of your sales relationship. Until you become aware of the little understood and seldom practiced skill of fluency control, it is possible that you won't even recognize that it could be costing you many sales.

INFORMING

Just how much "inside" information do you tell your prospect about your product or service? Every product has its positives and negatives, checkered history and hidden skeletons. This being the case, what information do you provide?

In terms of developing a long-term client relationship, I recommend that you provide both sides of the story, especially if the negatives can be presented as positives. It's far better to lay your cards on the table and state an open, defensible position than to have your competition come along and expose the soft underbelly of your product.

No one has a perfect product. Some are better in certain features or functions; some may give an enhanced financial enticement; others may have a better appearance. But none is perfect.

It is better to deliver a little bad news with a lot of good news than to have your product torpedoed when your customer is alone with your competition.

You alone determine how much information is enough for your clients. You determine whether your client relationship is strong enough to handle information praising your competitors' products while perhaps highlighting just a single, but important feature of your product. You determine whether your prospect will come to the same conclusion as you have regarding a multi-product survey or comparison. There are no easy answers. You *must* get to know your prospect or customer.

YOUR DOUBLING STRATEGY

Decide to develop the skills and product knowledge depth of a professional. This might take time, but if you're in the game then why not play like a pro? Top salespeople are not born; they develop. You, too, can develop into more than you are today. But only you can make that decision and only you can take the first few steps. Once you start, it's hard to stop.

DOUBLING POINTS

1. True added value can be provided by you only after you know why customers buy or use your service. Create an inventory of things or actions that could constitute added value to your clients. Go out of your way to include added value. Each week, develop a deeper understanding of how your product affects one of your customers. Learn it from the customer's side. Decide to start thinking like your customer thinks. Why should they use your products? How could they or their businesses improve by using additional product or by using the product in different ways? Create a customer viewpoint profile for one of your customers each week.

2. Added value erases the original value relationship and replaces it with a more positive, enhanced and memorable value. Examine how the added value you provide enhances this relationship and develop methods to introduce and explain the added value and its effect upon the overall purchase. Each week, learn one new way of expressing this added value to your customers in the form of an expectation.

Exceed your prospect's expectations and positive results occur; fall short and negative results occur.

Make it a conscious habit to set your prospect's purchasing expectations firmly and then to exceed them intentionally by including added value. Every week review your selling performance and isolate the areas in which your product falls short of meeting the customers' expectations. Develop a new method of presenting your product so that it meets or exceeds expectations (see Chapter 5).

3. Product knowledge consists of feature and function knowledge, user application knowledge and industry application knowledge. Start a personal growth plan so you will see advances in all three areas. Remember, it is up to you to take on this responsibility. Make it a habit.

Each week work on a new aspect of your product or service so that you fully appreciate your product from the position of your customer. User application knowledge is the most important to comprehend fully. If you don't understand your customers' businesses, ask to observe or even offer your services to a customer for a day so that you can better appreciate what his or her needs might be.

4. Subscribe to stay alive, attend to comprehend, inspect to detect. Build monthly and annual plans to attend trade shows, conferences and seminars pertaining to your customers' businesses. You be where they are. Use the internet to obtain background information. When visiting new prospects or before visiting new prospects, request a copy of their latest annual reports. Annual reports on major conglomerates and many local corporations can be found on-line and in your local library. Pick a time, perhaps once per month for a couple of hours, and explore.

Don't ignore the sales and personal development books either. Spend time reading and expanding your industry knowledge by reading trade magazines, attending trade shows and talking shop with your customers. Make a list of all current trade periodicals and subscribe to as many as you can. Read at least one trade magazine thoroughly each week.

5. Too much product information can confuse and delay the sale, waste your time and waste the prospect's time. On the other hand, it can help when a detailed proposal or complex product is being discussed by many influencers on an evaluation committee. Develop three basic information support packs: a normal portfolio for the typical prospect, a detail portfolio for the committee or "think-it-over" prospect and a highlighted piece for those not concerned with detail but highly concerned with bottom-line results.

6. Too little information can leave the prospect with only the "feeling" of your presentation and not enough rational data upon which to base a valid, informed decision. It can speed up the sale but can lead to early and severe buyer's remorse following the sale. Design a point-by-point summary of your presentation to leave behind with your prospect and to use as a selling presentation guide. Not only will a summary sheet

help the prospect to remember your presentation, you also won't leave out key issues, features, functions or user benefits.

7. A solid selling future is built on the rock foundation of basic selling skills. Make plans now to develop a complete inventory of skills. Don't be satisfied with what your employer gives you. It will generally lead only to average selling. You must take personal responsibility for skill development. Choose one skill weekly and practice it for at least 30 minutes each day. The optimum formula is to keep repeating the exercise for at least 21 days. See the appendix for information on self-help programs that are available.

8. One idea, enacted skillfully, can easily double your sales. Start a book of ideas and keep it with you wherever you go. Especially take it to places where you tend to think (restaurants, the bathroom, the den, etc.). Write down even the silliest ideas. It is important that you capture inspiration when it occurs. Schedule an "idea" time each day so that you can do some idea thinking. Then, just start dreaming of things that interest you and write your ideas down. Never throw an idea out! Often, ideas are years ahead of their time. Devote one clean page to each idea. Listen to successful people for inspiration and new ideas. Don't look to unsuccessful people or sources for successful ideas or strategies.

9. Start thinking logically and analytically. Improve the quantity or the quality of your prospects. Develop a customer profile that isolates the 20% of your customers who give you 80% of your business. Then use this profile to help you find more good customers. Each week, find at least one new prospect that fits the 20/80 profile. Study the analytics!

10. Switch yourself on longer. Make a commitment to your profession. Keep a log of how long you were "on" each day. Keep stretching. Decide that you are responsible for your future growth and education. Design a monthly, quarterly, annual and long-range personal training plan for yourself that will take you from where you are now to where you want to be at the end of each period. Learn a minimum of one new selling skill each month and learn it inside out. Take selective action rather than reactive action. Pause, ponder, postulate: then perform!

"WOW!"

For All Businesspeople · WOW! · Deming's Model · The Military Model · The Concentric Model · The Importance of Trustworthiness · "Outside the Box" Thinking · Taking Extraordinary Action · Personal Accountability · Corporate Commitment · Management Function · Team Considerations · Hiring Considerations · Failure Fixes · Daily Feedback Channels · Recharging the Front Line · Too Little, Too Much · Interpreting · Informing · Your Doubling Strategy · Doubling

For All Businesspeople

The chapter you are about to read is for business owners, sales managers, service providers and salespeople. In fact, it's for the entire corporation. It's about the philosophy and function of business, and why many businesses must work hard to change their operations – totally – if they are to compete successfully. It has a lot to do with the ability of a corporation to double its sales – or more.

It is placed in this location in the book because it demands consideration from management; if you are to get ahead and stay ahead, then this chapter is likely the most important in the entire book. It is philosophical in principle, but practical in application. It deals primarily with a thing that business leaders and teachers call, "The WOW!"

An overworked term, it still retains its impact to the customer and to the employee; something significantly positive has just taken place, be it a satisfied service situation, a sales bargain or a management negotiation, they all have their foundation in the simplicity of an expectation being exceeded.

This entire book is built upon the principle of establishing expectations so that you can, individually or corporately, meet or exceed them. It is the basis of "WOW!"

Since the microcomputer explosion that began in the mid-1980's business has had to deal with rapid change. Some succeeded, some did not. The buzz-words of management training dealt with managing "change" – those who could were heroes, whereas a decade earlier, they were outcasts, usually too radical in their thinking and actions to find approval from the "do not disturb me" management that preceded the computer revolution. New thought and dimension erased the traditional concepts of business, especially with the arrival of global internet commerce.

You, as a salesperson, may have had to deal with the changes. If you are new to sales, you are growing up in an environment of challenge as never before seen by business. You may be working for a recognized industry leader yet finding your competition coming from a sophisticated internet marketer whom you never meet, see or hear – but the impact is real.

Amazon.com started with a cash investment from Jeff Bezos' mom and dad… Apple Computer was developed in a garage… Many other success stories that now impact literally *everyone* started small. Tomorrow's competitor is getting ready to launch any day. Stay awake!

However, today is about dealing with the current realities of sales and service that impact the customer and now the challenge is far greater, is omnipresent, and nobody seems to be playing by the same rules: it's an open sales architecture. But sometimes to get ahead, it's wise to take look back, just to see if the ground has been covered successfully before.

A WOW! – based business is the ideal foundation for doubling your sales.

WOW!

The purpose of business is to sell products or services at an operational profit.

If your business cannot do that, it will not be in business for very long. As a salesperson, if you can't sell at a profit, you won't have a job very long. Anything will sell if it is priced low enough, but will there be enough profit to sustain operations and empower growth? Your "job" is to ensure that the company and the customer base survives, and that requires a careful appreciation of exactly how your products, services and operations interact with profit.

The most expensive customer to sell is the new one. I read one article, now long ago misplaced, that quoted Sam Walton of Wal-Mart saying that it cost him "thousands" of dollars to attract a new Wal-Mart customer, which is why he was concerned about making sure that the customer would always feel comfortable about returning merchandise, no matter the reason. It was always less costly to "retain" a current customer than to "gain" a new one.

"Wow!" is an expression from customers that is hoped for by all business operators. It represents a service or sale that has had a significant impact. It means that likely there will be word-of-mouth endorsement that can last for years, if not a lifetime. It means that new clients and customers could be influenced enough to try your product or service, all on their own. It means "success."

W. Edwards Deming

After the close of World War II, defeated Japan was embarrassed, destroyed, and humiliated. The U.S. military struggled with the rebuilding of Japan, but were failing as they tried to impose their military-model of business structure. By chance, Dr. Edwards Deming, a quality assurance statistician working with the U.S. government, was asked to address the Union of Japanese Scientists and Engineers in 1950.

What he presented, in the form of a business reconstruction model, was so effective that in the next twenty years it propelled Japanese business to the forefront of modern commerce. His model was almost the opposite of the traditional military business model popular in the U.S., it didn't focus on a hierarchy but instead, on the principle of individual workers and managers attaining "profound knowledge" and then using this enlightened awareness to concentrate on loftier business issues rather than taking a local focus work as just a "job".

Deming focused on the individual first, then on the organization. In his model, the first step was the transformation of the individual.

> *"This transformation is discontinuous. It comes from understanding of the system of profound knowledge. The individual, transformed, will perceive new meaning to his life, to events, to numbers, to interactions between people.*
>
> *"Once the individual understands the system of profound knowledge, he will apply its principles in every kind of relationship with other people. He will have a basis for judgment of his own decisions and for transformation of the organizations that he belongs to. "*
>
> *"The individual, once transformed, will:*
>
> - *Set an example*
> - *Be a good listener, but will not compromise*
> - *Continually teach other people*
> - *Help people to pull away from their current practice and beliefs and move into the new philosophy without a feeling of guilt about the past"*

It was on this basis, on the individual rising to a greater challenge and gaining a more encompassing view and appreciation of the impact that his or her work had upon the overall success or failure of a venture that led to the astounding development of Japanese quality and production capabilities during the 1960's and 1970's.

Deming's principles were the foundation for what would become known as the "WOW!" in the 1990's. The principles of corporate operation and his focus on the individual striving to attain "profound knowledge" have the essential ingredients for success in every business, at any time, under virtually all conditions.

His principles and purposes were fully defendable, inherently based in common sense, and indivisible – they could not be eroded. If you followed them, your business and your career would be crafted upon ethical function surrounded by true concern for doing what was right and good for the customer.

Deming considered a customer to be both external (someone who buys your products) and internal (employees). Although Deming did not stretch his theories and principals to the full extent that radical customer care delivers today, he certainly laid a solid foundation for its eventual development and growth.

WOW! must work within a win-win environment, or it will not succeed. This is, and always will remain, a difficult challenge. Anyone who writes or speaks on the "WOW!" or extreme customer satisfaction strategies must admit that it is not as simple as slashing the price in half; rather it is complicated, involves incredible effort, risk-taking and cooperation amongst employees and management, and truly requires a rebirth of the management and worker ethic platform.

Deming was also a strong Christian, as evidenced by his song writing and the very essence of his work: it was moral, ethical and servant-based.

THE ELEMENTS OF THE WOW!

I developed and began teaching the WOW! courses in Canada in the early 1990's. WOW! grew as a natural extension of DOUBLING, as a larger dimension of it, and as I researched more deeply into the extraordinary examples of the companies that could make WOW! happen every day, it became apparent that this was a philosophy of business that could indeed transform companies, their workforces and even entire business communities.

The basic principles of creating the "WOW!" are a blend of disciplines and theories. Some you will likely recognize, others seem to be just common sense, yet others are profoundly deep and require significant investigation and thought. If compared with Deming's 14 points, they are remarkably similar. Here's my list:

- **WOW! is dynamic**. It must be created afresh everyday.

- **WOW! demands that you find a different way to do business** so that problems and opportunities can be addressed completely without the need for committees, studies, or other risk-sharing mechanisms. WOW! is accomplished corporately through accountable individuals acting with authority and with the best of intentions for a win-win outcome.

- **WOW! depends upon integrity, honesty and commitment**: if you make a promise, you keep a promise.

- **WOW! begins with having the end result in mind** as your goal, just like Covey's Seven Habits of Highly Effective People. Other management theorists expound upon this point, but it is too obvious to avoid: understand what you are trying to achieve before you take action. Have the result, the goal, clearly defined in all dimensions before committing your effort. Once committed, don't let go until you've accomplished the result. In this case, the goal is to create customer delight.

- **Seek first to understand the customer's expectations** concerning the solution or performance and try to see it from their point of view before offering solutions. If no expectations are present, or if they are unformed, then help the customer develop and express them. To achieve the WOW!, you must meet or exceed the expectations that are held in the mind of the customer. Your solution must be perceived by the customer to be superior to that of the competition.

- **Under-promise and over-deliver**; this is the foundation of exceeding expectations. Set the expectation at a level you know you can meet or exceed. In DOUBLING, this represents the very heart of the sales strategy – it virtually eliminates objections.

- **Try to do things right the first time**. This means:
  - On time or sooner
  - At quote or under
  - Complete solution, not partial
  - No unpleasant surprises
  - No return visits required to do what should have been done initially
  - Fix it free if it fails.

- **Problem or opportunity ownership must be sought on an individual basis** by all employees. If you see a problem or opportunity, you immediately own the problem until the responsibility can be accepted by another. If it comes to you, it stays with you.

- **Act on the problem or opportunity immediately**; do not delay the solution.

- **Act on it until the solution is complete**.

- **Decide quickly, act immediately, resolve completely**

- **Focus on the 20% core customers that provide you with 80% of your repeat business**. Win them conclusively.

- **Promote your performance by deliberately leaving understated clues** for your customers to discover that will reinforce their decision to choose you and your product or service.

- **Listen to your customers daily.** Listen intensely. Make changes based on the customer's perception of you and your product or service. Fine tune your staff, your offerings, your actions so that the customer begins to widen the gap between you and your competition.

- **Always get the customer involved in the solution**. It's their expectations that are important.

- **Everyone in your business must be a customer satisfaction specialist.** Develop depth and capability by cross-training and mentoring so that everyone has primary customer satisfaction capabilities and that all staff share in the same WOW! attitudes and actions towards the customer. (How many times have delicate negotiations led to a hard-won sale only to have the accounting or shipping department destroy it by uncaring, even spiteful attitudes.

WOW!-based companies focus on every possible client contact avenue and ensure that the experience, if it occurs, will reinforce the customer's experience, not traumatize it.)

WOW! Orchestration

WOW! cannot be accomplished using traditional lines of authority and reporting. Everything must be rethought in terms of satisfying the customer. Here are the organizational axioms of WOW! arranged in a series of four concentric rings or "zones", with the customer at the heart of the bulls eye.

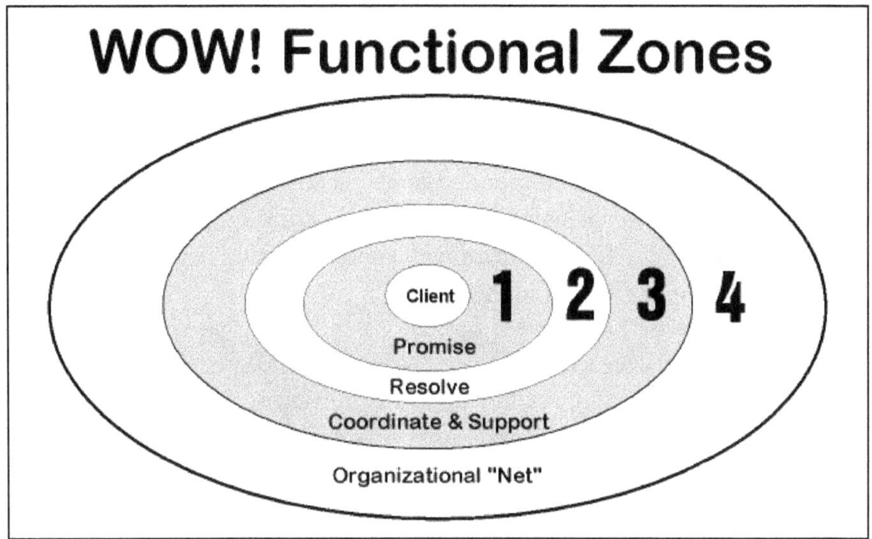

The customer is the focal point of the business. Make the client happy and he or she will return to do more business. Your cost per sale drops and your margins improve.

The employees who are closest to the customer are the most important in the company.

These are usually the sales and service teams, but includes any form of customer contact, including billing, product returns, phone enquiries, reception, product handling, etc. This is the innermost zone of the circles where promises are made and expectations set.

Those that provide support to the "front line" sales and service groups are the next most critical area, for they generally provide the actual product follow-through or service solutions. In an auto dealership, they are the mechanics and the business office that supplies financing; in a retail setting, the cashier; for commercial salespeople, the shipping department and the delivery drivers.

If these people do not have the tools to deliver the solution expected by the client, then a failure (an "OW!") looms on the horizon. This is the zone where resolution takes place, where solutions are crafted, and expectations are met or exceeded. It is also the area where most of the client trauma occurs.

The next zone involves mid-management and line management, poised to take extraordinary action for supply and decision to assist in the delivery of the solution. They manage by exception. They put out fires. They light fires. They constantly look at ways to improve delivery and remove obstacles for field performance success. Their performance failure could mean resolution failure.

The last zone involves support from the traditional business infrastructure resources: accounting, information technology services, warehousing, shipping, receiving, ordering, order processing, legal, etc.

This is the "glue" that exists to serve the first three rings. Vitally important that the employees in this zone work quickly and cooperatively with the first and second ring, the "administrative" ring is also the most likely to provide the source of inadvertent WOW! failure – the "OW!". If operated within the total customer care context, it can improve customer relations dramatically.

WOW! IN ACTION

Nordstrom, a major U.S.-based department store, abounds with WOW! stories, many of them as the result of customers telling their stories to the press. Here's one of my favorites:

A little old granny and her young granddaughter were buying something at a Nordstrom's store. While standing at the cash register, the salesperson overheard the granny mumble something as she rummaged around in her purse, "Oh, dear, I must have left the money for the movies on the dresser. Oh, I'm sorry, dear (as she turned to her granddaughter), but I guess we can't go to the movies this afternoon as I promised we would."

The sales clerk, obviously trained and supported in Nordstrom to take advantage of quality customer opportunities, took $20 from the cash register and handed it to the granny, and with a warm smile that only true giving can bring, said, "Have a movie on Nordstrom's".

Let that sink in for a moment or so. What management style, what infrastructure, what accounting process, what training, what hiring, and what philosophy enabled a sales clerk to give $20 of the company's money to a completely unknown person without having to go through any management approval processes – and to feel completely secure in her actions! When you can answer those questions to your satisfaction, then you will understand the WOW!

WOW! creates extraordinary loyalty amongst customers and amongst staff. Of course it has its failures and costs and abuses; but it also has its triumphs. Everyone does not get it right the first time, things don't always get fixed in one visit and the competition occasionally steals away a sale by over-promising and under-delivering. But in the overall context of doing business, it secures future sales by endearing the client base to your company (or to the salesperson). Repeat sales from loyal customers at a defendable profit margin is the goal. WOW! is the path.

Deming's Principles

Following are Deming's principles that made the economic reconstruction of Japan possible, and then became the foundation to the explosive boom in WOW!-based businesses around the globe. The underlying expectations that Deming had when he put this list together were:

- Change is always occurring; manage it through *leadership*, not programs.
- People must be given the chance to gain a sense of pride within their work that is genuine and not as a result of some external scheme
- Profound knowledge comes from understanding the greater purposes of life and commerce; workers with the understanding of how they influence the outcome on the larger scale create problem-free products and solutions.

- The people closest to a problem also tend to be those most capable of a practical and immediate solution.

- Leadership is a *character* quality made up of honesty, integrity, forthrightness, sincerity, compassion, determination, courage, experience, knowledge, commitment, responsibility and accountability.

- Leaders encourage, direct and get involved personally when required; they are natural mentors, not fearful of promoting others deserving of advancement.

- Leaders tend to be "meek" in the Biblical sense, meaning that they are not self-seeking and attention-drawing, but courageous, hard-working, committed to an ideal, supportive of the team – even the weakest member – and willing to take the heat of criticism.

- Leadership is more important than management.

Dr. Deming proposed his formula in a landmark book Out of the Crisis published by MIT Press in 1986. These are the principles that led to the explosive turnaround of Japanese industry following the Second World War when Japan was known for inexpensive and poorly-made items. In less than twenty years, the management process that was adopted created the most reliable automobiles and electronics in the world, and pushed Japan into the forefront of global industry.

- **Create constancy of purpose** toward improvement of product, sales and service, with the aim to become competitive and to stay in business, and to provide jobs.

- **Adopt the new philosophy**. We are always in a new economic age. Management must awaken to the challenge, must learn their responsibilities, and take on leadership for change.

- **Cease dependence on inspection to achieve quality**. Eliminate the need for inspection on a mass basis by building quality into the product and into the sale in the first place.

- **End the practice of awarding business solely on the basis of price.** Instead, minimize total cost. Move toward a single supplier for any one item, on a long-term relationship of loyalty and trust.

- **Improve constantly and forever the system of production**, sales and service, to improve quality and productivity, and thus constantly decrease costs.

- **Institute training on the job** and use the mentoring process to deepen worker capability.

- **Institute leadership**. The aim of supervision should be to help people and machines and gadgets and computers to do a better job.

- **Drive out fear**, so that everyone may work effectively for the company.

- **Break down barriers between departments**. People in research, design, sales, and production must work as a team, to foresee problems of production and in use that may be encountered with the product or service.

- **Eliminate slogans, exhortations, and targets for the work force asking for zero defects and new levels of productivity**. Such exhortations only create adversarial relationships, as the bulk of the causes of low quality and low productivity belong to the system and thus lie beyond the power of the work force.

- **Eliminate work standards** (quotas) on the factory floor. Substitute leadership.

- **Eliminate management by objectives**. Eliminate management by numbers, numerical goals. Substitute leadership.

- **Remove barriers that rob the hourly worker of his right to pride of workmanship.** The responsibility of supervisors must be changed from sheer numbers to quality.

- **Remove barriers that rob people in management and in engineering of their right to pride of workmanship**. This means abolishment of the annual or merit rating and of management by objective.

- **Institute a vigorous program of education and self-improvement**.

- **Put everybody in the company to work to accomplish the transformation**. The transformation is everybody's job.

THE CHRISTIAN CONNECTION

Every point in both WOW! and Deming's 14 points are worthy. They are ethical, moral and filled with common sense. They speak of leadership, not management titles. They require strong character to make the process work without injury or loss to the corporation or the client. They require strong commitment, courage and boldness to turn disasters into opportunities for creating the WOW! effect.

Spirit-led Christians are excellent candidates for orchestrating the WOW! Everything that Christ stands for is fundamental to making the WOW! happen, day after day. Christ led, first and foremost, by serving. He was not afraid to manage in the trenches, to show by example, to mentor and to trust, to seize the appropriate opportunity to WOW! the people.

But He was not a grandstander, he did not work His miracles to impress, but more to solve a problem, usually a very personal, irresolvable issue. Many times His work was in private; His "customers" became His strongest promotional force. Jesus was not autocratic; He was not flamboyant, He was not a boaster: He promised and He delivered. His was a demeanor of quiet resolve, of determination, of commitment, of tremendous passion.

So can be your life. If you want to be in a truly rewarding position, seek out organizations that believe in and practice the WOW!

philosophy, both externally and internally, for that is where your beliefs will be best positioned for use.

Rapport

Split Personalities · We Act for Reaction · Selling to the Visible · Selling to the Invisible · The Importance of Paying Attention · Preferential Communication Systems · Style Types · The Five Styles · Controlling Tension · More Rapport · RSVP · Selling to a Group · Altering Your Probes · Altering Your Responses · Altering Your Timing · The Hand Model · Your Doubling Strategy · Doubling

Split Personalities

When working as a conference planner and coordinator, it used to amaze me the way people changed when they were away from their normal environments. Most participants were well behaved during the seminars, but as soon as the program was finished for the day, a transformation began. Mild-mannered accountants became fluid and uninhibited and bank managers could be found drunk and skinny-dipping at 3 o'clock in the morning.

We all contain personality slants that suit us from time to time depending upon our needs. Behavioral changes can be extreme, like the straight-laced, no-risk, pin-striped accountant at one conference who turned into an unabashed, beer-guzzling lunatic who shinnied up a 30-foot flagpole in the dead of night to retrieve a tattered old weather-beaten hotel flag as a take-home trophy.

We change from minute to minute, hour to hour, day to day. Sometimes we change radically, like the mild-mannered soul above, and sometimes we change in a more subtle, less detectable manner.

These subtle changes are most difficult to observe, but also the most important to deal with in terms of selling. If you can catch the minute shifts in the way a person is behaving, then you can react to the change and either counteract it (if it hinders the sale) or encourage it (if it favors the sale).

We change our behavior because our needs change inside. These changes fall into defined categories. It is important for you, as a salesperson, to understand that every single person has a dominant, defined personality: their "comfort zone" personality. To some degree that dominant personality will either challenge you or embrace you.

It is your job, as a professional communicator, to interpret actions, inflections, surroundings and a myriad of other clues so you can affect rapport.

Rapport is simply defined as getting along with another person in a comfortable and cooperative manner. In terms of selling, it means developing a relationship where both parties are working towards a common goal: the sale or purchase of goods or services on terms that are satisfactory to both parties. Rapport can be warm and friendly or it can be digital, pin-striped and programmed. Depending upon the needs of your prospect, rapport takes on many faces. The establishment and maintenance of rapport is entirely your responsibility.

If rapport is established, the sale has a chance. If rapport is not established, there is little chance for a sale. There is a chance for a prospect-driven purchase, but little chance for a salesperson-driven sale.

We Act for Reaction

In terms of interpersonal communications, everything you do is intended to obtain a specific reaction from another person. We act to get a reaction from someone else. Your prospect does it and so do you; it is an intricate, continuous communication game. If you question and probe your prospect it is because you want the prospect to react in a specific manner: to divulge information, show buying signals, reveal expectations, etc.

If you understand that every person acts to obtain a personal benefit, be it expressed and obvious or deceptively subtle, then you are beginning to understand human communication. Prospects behave in certain ways because they need something: from you, your product or service or something else. They act to obtain. You act to obtain.

> ***If you can determine what your prospect's conversational needs are and then satisfy those needs you have established rapport and probably made a sale.***

An old axiom states, *"Selling is finding a need and filling it."* The essential truth of that statement hasn't changed. We know more about what "need" means today, but the basic need-fulfillment aspect of sales remains. Second Dimension Sellers and Third Dimension Sellers go beyond seeking the need. They create the need or the expectation.

SELLING TO THE VISIBLE

Bookstore shelves are overflowing with new discoveries in body language, the physical behaviors that reveal our inner feelings and desires. Some books look at romance-oriented tangents and others look at the business benefits of reading the customer.

Responding to the "visible" clues of a client is important. People do show you definite behavioral signs on which you can base certain assumptions. You then can take appropriate action to reinforce the exhibited behavior or to counteract or redirect the behavior towards a more productive position.

Any pilot who has done a considerable amount of instrument flying, as I have, knows the routine of instrument scanning. When I flew, we didn't have an "autopilot" that would keep the plane level and on course. Instead, it was all in the hands of the pilot. Scanning was the only method by which the pilot could maintain proper altitude, heading and speed when the pilot couldn't see past the clouds or darkness that envelops the aircraft. Every few seconds, the pilot's eyes sweep the entire array of gauges and dials, paying priority attention to those that report the attitude of the aircraft and then secondarily scanning the instruments that monitor the engines and radios. Certain gauges are more vital than others at specific times. This technique relates to "people scanning" as well. Some reactions are more important to monitor than others during specific situations.

If the aircraft experiences an engine failure in flight, then certain instruments, especially those pertaining to the remaining operational engines, receive increased priority in the scanning process. If the aircraft encounters severe turbulence or icing, then the instruments pertaining to airspeed and altitude become the most important. If on final approach into a major metropolitan airport, then the rate of descent, airspeed and the instrument landing system avionics are key. Changes in the situation affect monitoring priorities.

When selling, you must be aware that situational changes can bring about behavioral changes in your prospects. They will change their behaviors because their needs have changed. Changes in behavior are especially important to recognize when a buying decision is being considered or approached. When you notice that the behavior of your prospect changes, even slightly, then you know that your prospect's needs have also changed and that you must react accordingly. Behavioral changes come in many forms, but the basic areas to watch are:

- Physical stance (opening up or closing and protecting);
- Speed of movement or "pace" (slowing or increasing);
- Range of movement (restrained or flamboyant);
- Type of movement (becoming more purposeful or loosening up and becoming more expressive);
- Eye contact (indirect or direct);
- Voice volume (becoming louder or softer);
- Voice tone (becoming direct and curt or warm and understanding);
- Fidgeting or nervousness (becoming more obvious or stopping altogether);
- Language construction and choice of vocabulary (becoming tentative or concrete);

- Preferential communication system being used: visual, auditory, kinesthetic or intellectual;

- General demeanor (becoming friendlier or cooler).

As you will soon see, you can easily identify these changes and initiate a strategy to reinforce or redirect them.

The body communicates what the mind contemplates.

What you see is really what you've got. The studies that link physical behavior with mental or emotional condition are in agreement: the body shows it all.

If you feel sad, your countenance changes and displays "sad" for all to read. If you're happy, there's a spring in your step and a lift to your voice and your hands can't be stilled. If you're mad, the brow furls, the fists clench and the voice growls.

Even subtle changes can't be hidden from the trained observer. However, the degree to which these traits are observable may vary greatly: in a person who tends to be warm and emotional, a greater degree of physical change or expression can be seen; in an unexpressive person, the changes are much more difficult to detect.

Selling to the Invisible

The hardest part of understanding rapport involves the invisible: what the prospect is thinking or feeling. Hidden expectations can often make or break a sale without any outward signs. Selling to a prospect means dealing with the visible (actions and reactions) and selling to the invisible (their personal and corporate expectations).

How to do you sell to the invisible? It is actually simple. It is called *expectational selling*: exploring and exposing the customers' expectations and then making your presentation address those expectations. Salespeople who ignore a prospect's expectations are setting themselves up for a career confined by First Dimensional boundaries.

THE IMPORTANCE OF PAYING ATTENTION

Most Second Dimension and Third Dimension Sellers have something in common: focused attention. When with clients, nothing in the world matters except what goes on within ten feet of them. They watch for any clue that could give them insight into the expected behavior of their conversational partners. They observe the office: tidiness, charts on the walls, goals expressed, family portraits, corporate slogans, awards, type of furniture, color or lack of color, etc. A

ll these things express the individual. This why I prefer going to a prospect's business: to observe.

The eyes of the salesperson should scan the prospect constantly for little changes in behavior that might signal a decision breakthrough or a protective bunker being built. Are they accepting or are they rejecting? Are they compliant or are they defiant? Are they opening up or are they getting ready to defend themselves? Do they seek detail or do they enjoy dreaming and scheming?

These things are the salesperson's guideposts to successful communications and selling.

Look for the observable clues that tell you something about the individual, such as pictures, diplomas, trophies, crafts, hobbies, awards and unusual jewelry. I remember one time I was with a prospect and was making slow headway when I noticed tiny specks of paint on his watch. As I mentioned earlier, I am an amateur carpenter and house fixer-upper. I made a comment about renovations, and from then on rapport blossomed. It never would have happened if I hadn't observed and interpreted the meaning of those little flecks of paint.

To double your sales, double your observation and attention. Focus and block out all extraneous thought and activity while with your client. Picture yourself as a radar-controlled video camera that has locked onto its target and now follows it without fail, recording all that it sees.

Preferential Communication Systems

People tend to use one of four primary preferential communication systems to represent their personal communications preferences. The systems are: **visual, auditory, kinesthetic (feeling)** and **intellectual**.

We tend to choose one system when we communicate, and tend not to mix or change systems. When you are observing your prospect or client, listen intently for the type of preferential communications system being used.

> *"Bob, I **see** what you're trying to show me, but I can't imagine where we would use it." (Visual)*
>
> *"Bob, I **hear** what you're saying, but it just doesn't sound like a good project at this time." (Auditory)*
>
> *"Bob, I've got **a good grasp** on this subject, and I don't feel that it would be good for us right now." (Kinesthetic)*
>
> *"Bob, I **understand** your product but I don't think we could use it right now." (Neutral)*

The same objection stated using four different preferential communications systems. If you were Bob, your best strategy would be to match the preferential communications system used by the prospect.

> *"I can **picture** your position, Frank, and I'd like **to see** us work towards an imaginative solution." (Visual)*
>
> *"Frank, I know this **sounds** a bit farfetched, but after **listening** to our many satisfied clients **shout for joy** after finally deciding to buy, I think that you, too, might **hear** a positive report from your staff." (Auditory)*
>
> *"Frank, as you might be aware, most of your industry has already **picked up** on this technology and have got a **solid grip** on tomorrow." (Kinesthetic)*
>
> *"Frank, as **you know**, most of your industry uses this technology now." (Intellectual)*

What you want to avoid is to mismatch preferential systems. It's like one person speaking French and the other speaking Spanish: they are similar languages in construction, but not in sound. Your strategy is to match preferential systems. This lessens tension and paves the way for better, more intense communication.

STYLE TYPES

We have been categorizing and pigeon-holing each other for many centuries. Galen (first century AD) divided people into four categories: the sanguine, the choleric, the phlegmatic and the melancholy. In the 1920's, Karl Jung divided people into four groups, each subdivided into either introverted or extraverted characteristics. He called his groups thinkers, feelers, sensors and intuitors. Another theory dealing with stress describes us as Type A or Type B.

The social styles described by three different groups in the 1970's classify us as drivers, expressives, analytics or amiables.

Alessandra and Cathcart, in their milestone work, "Relationship Strategies" classify people according to their exhibited behaviors as thinkers, directors, socializers or relators. To a degree, all these classification schemes are correct. They all examine and describe the behavior traits of you and me.

I developed a program based on personality style types in a training program that I called *Radical Rapport.*[4] This program influences every single aspect of my sales training. It represents the basic, practical and yet sophisticated communication needs within the selling environment.

The sales environment has a significant contributing effect on behavior; someone who behaves in a particular way under normal circumstances acts differently under the influence of the sales environment. Thus, I have purposefully addressed the styles in the context of selling only. This is the primary difference between my style types and others.

---

4. *Radical Rapport* is available directly from the author as a workbook text that accompanies his course.

Radical Rapport continues to be the single most influential training program for salespeople because it helps salespeople to organize existing interpersonal skills into focused, practical, and powerful practical rapport strategies.

I call the four dominant client styles in this program the *Impulsive*, the *Examiner*, the *Victor* and the *Relater*. A fifth style, the *Flexive*, is the style that many salespeople strive to become.

These styles are based on the observable actions and changes in actions that your prospects and customers make. The style identification also considers the clues exhibited through a person's working environment, such as his or her office, dress and positional responsibilities. What people show you through actions and expressions are indications of their personal and corporate communication needs.

We each have a composite personality. We move around from style to style at a moment's notice, but we tend to have a dominant style for each area of our lives (work, leisure, family, romance, etc.). This suggests that we change our behavior because our inner needs change. If we require sympathy and cuddling, then we appear sad; if we need to blow off steam, then we appear wild, crazy or mad. If we seek control, then we exercise precise and determined mannerisms; if we want to laugh, then we loosen up and become expressive.

Each of us has a composite psyche that shows a different side to our personalities depending on how we feel inside and what we need to accomplish or defend, personally and corporately.

The five primary styles are formed by the combination of two main behavioral expressions: *demeanor* and *action*.

Each expression is shown as a graded scale: demeanor grades from social behavior towards business behavior; action grades from tentative action towards forceful action (see diagram).

The Demeanor Scale

Demeanor is used to describe the way people present themselves. It represents their mannerisms, their postures and their attitudes.

Demeanor is represented as a vertical scale with *social behavior* located at the bottom end and *business behavior* attributes found at the top. As you ascend from social behavior towards business behavior, you become more concerned with tasks and less concerned with peoples' feelings and opinions.

Demeanor also includes expressions of the individual through clothing, accessories, furnishings, grooming, and the office environment.

Social Behavior

Social behavior is the willingness to share one's feelings and to demonstrate emotions without undue hesitation or restraint.

People exhibiting this type of behavior tend to be touchers and sharers, intuitive and relaxed. In my observation, they tend to use word pictures and stories, explaining things in graphic and emotional terms. They express personal ideas and concepts rather than facts and well-constructed plans. They are more likely to express personal opinions rather than details and tangible results, and to talk in general rather than specific terms.

Time seems unimportant to the person exhibiting social behavior. If he or she says, "I'll be home around five," it could mean that the person will be home sometime in the late afternoon or early evening.

The person exhibiting social behavior uses his or her body as an active communication device, with animated facial expressions and gesturing arm and hand motions. The whole body becomes involved in getting an idea or thought across. Social behavior results in touching, hugging, closeness and a willingness to chat and share.

Business (Task) Behavior

The opposite of social behavior is *business* behavior. Business behavior (or *task-directed* behavior) shows few signs of personal emotion or feeling. People exhibiting business behavior tend to be factual, task oriented, punctual, businesslike and disciplined. They express themselves through data, facts, figures, objectives and deadlines.

Time seems to be of critical importance to people exhibiting business behavior and they tend to be punctual and time-organized. They do not generalize but rather speak in specific terms. They rarely use their body to express conversation except to make pointed, purposeful gestures in order to emphasize.

To people exhibiting business behavior, information is valuable, but feelings are not. Opinions have no place; facts do. They look for results and process, categories and specifics. They plan and then act according to their plans. Their tools include computers, machinery and efficiency studies, which they use to turn a profit or to ensure that a process is followed correctly. Their life blood is data, data, data.

The Action Scale

The other main expression of behavior that you can observe is exhibited actions. The action scale is graded from *tentative* to *forceful*. This is an easy scale with which to work, for action is either visible or, by default, it is absent.

Thus, if you see body or vocal "action", generally the individual is showing some form of forcefulness.

If you see little or no action, then the individual is showing tentative behavior.

Action is a very important rapport quality to observe when establishing rapport, for this is where the most dramatic changes in behavior take place. To encourage rapport, pace or mirror the customers' actions closely.

Tentative Behavior

Tentative behavior shows a reluctance to step out and lead or to take action. When people exhibit tentative behavior they tend to be withdrawn, methodical and quiet. They are usually excellent listeners and observers. Tentative behavior is quite easily spotted through the lack of eye contact, a softer handshake, a quiet and steady monotone voice and the cautious way in which all things are done.

Look for a slower pace, methodical activities, personal cautiousness, lack of decision-making abilities and an affinity for detail.

People demonstrating tentative behavior seldom initiate conversation, but they do tend to ask a lot of focused questions intended to uncover specific information. They seldom accept anything at face value.

Forceful Behavior

Forceful behavior shows a desire to be in control, to take action, to lead others and to make things happen.

People exhibiting forceful behavior tend to make bold statements, to be action-oriented and to be decisive. They also work at a much faster pace, exhibiting this speed in their speech, in their hand and body motions and even in their writing. Memos from forceful people are usually short and to the point, using "bullets" instead of narrative.

These people tend to exhibit a strong affinity for personal and business goals. Forceful behavior is the one of the prime assets of the achievers of the world.

Look for a strong handshake, a loud and fast-paced voice and quick, determined actions.

THE FIVE STYLES

By crossing the *Action* and *Demeanor* scales at a right angle, the four primary behavioral styles (Impulsive, Victor, Examiner and Relater) and the complex Flexive style are formed.

The styles are identified by the combination of demeanor and action exhibited during a conversation. Remember that each of us is a composite of all four primary styles and our behavior towards others represents our efforts to manipulate rapport. Since needs periodically change during any given conversation, exhibited behavior changes to reflect these needs. By reading your customers' behaviors, you can interpret their needs *at that time.*

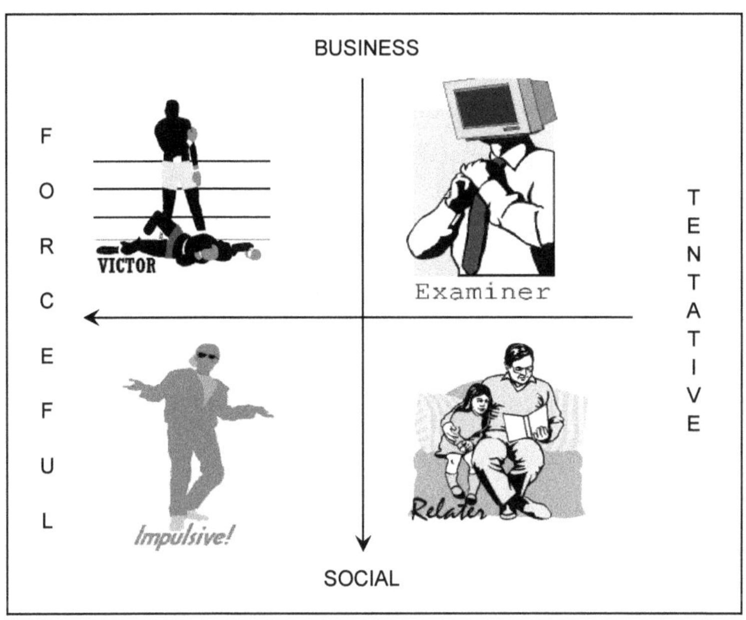

The Impulsive

The Impulsive is a combination of *forceful action* and *social demeanor*. Impulsives are usually boisterous, fun to be with and happy, with a strong sense of humor and a quick, reckless style. They tend to be touchers, jokers, and risk takers, and are usually overly animated in their expressions. They tend to use visual and kinesthetic communications. As you might expect, many go into sales and entertainment.

Picture your stereotype of the old-time used-car salesman, with colorful, expressive clothing and gaudy accessories. He's always got a deal cooking and is always glad to see you.

The Impulsives are animated, show plenty of expression and cannot talk without using their hands. Their voices are emotional and modulated and are used as one of their top tools for communication. In fact, the Impulsive might also be termed the Communicator if most of their conversation weren't aimed at discussing themselves.

Impulsives are dreamers and schemers; they suffer from perpetual "big dream-itis." Sometimes they make it; many times they don't. Look for strong personal opinions on just about everything. They tend to describe things using vivid, emotional word pictures. They are persuaders, actors, con men and cut-ups. They deal with stress by using humor to diffuse tension.

Recognize Impulsives by their attention-getting dress and accessories. Their hair tends to be cut in a popular style and they generally have large wardrobes. They seldom wear the same clothes twice in the same week. *They enjoy being the center of attention.*

They are fast-paced, vibrant and vivacious individuals who love to get involved on the spur of the moment. Impetuous and risk-taking, they can bounce from one idea to the next with abandon. If let loose, they turn into children.

As salespeople, they usually are dynamic, daring and fearless. They tend to be easy to motivate but hard to manage, with wide mood swings and a tendency to improvise rather than to prepare purposefully for the sales encounter.

As customers, you should appeal to their personal desires and dreams. Boost their egos whenever you can. You must sell to them personally, not to the corporate interests alone. Build dreams and futures, paint vivid word pictures and get them emotionally involved.

Go for a quick decision, but make sure it is a manageable one. Also, ensure that all promises and commitments are in writing. Impulsives have a great tendency to express ideas before they are fully developed or authorized. They hate red tape and procedure, and usually find some way to avoid the details of life.

Their greatest need is *to be recognized.*

The Relater

A combination of *tentative actions* and *social demeanor* results in the Relater style. Relaters are excellent listeners who observe carefully.

They are interested in the whole person as they talk, not just listening to the words but trying to interpret what lies behind the words. They are warm, friendly and sincere and will give their all for a worthy cause.

They shy away from personal and business risk (except for human causes) and many gravitate towards the helping professions: nurses, social workers, teachers and secretaries. Relaters want to become friends and to know you better and more intimately.

They are concerned for your well-being and the well-being of others and of the community. These are the whole-earth people and the animal rights defenders. They are people who care and are not afraid to express their innermost opinions and ideas. They generally sacrifice their self-esteem and ego in favor of a worthy cause, person or product.

Recognize a Relater by a warm and sincere greeting, a slightly limp handshake and indirect eye contact, and he or she tends to use kinesthetic communications.

A Relater's voice is comforting. The Relater's dress is relaxed: usually loose-fitting clothes, a sweater and a pair of comfortable slacks or jeans. In the past, many male Relaters were pipe smokers as opposed to cigarette smokers. Slippered feet, a cardigan sweater and a wing chair complete the scene.

In their offices, you'll notice furniture that welcomes you to converse on an equal basis. You may talk around a coffee table. You'll notice the office walls and desk covered with pictures of family and friends, and the office colors are often warm and inviting, un-intimidating.

As salespeople, they tend to dwell on client *relationships* rather than on sales productivity. To the Relater, a good client relationship is sales productivity, even though the numbers might be lower than average.

They are excellent listeners and work well with clients who require a personal touch. They tend to be motivated by principles and causes and not by personal material gain.

Easy to manage and steady, dependable workers, they tend to lack personal enthusiasm and "guts," preferring routine, safe, salaried selling situations where they can get to know the clients personally. They also tend to exhibit a high degree of sympathy, as opposed to empathy, taking on their clients' causes as their own.

As customers, take the time to get to know them personally and allow them to help you with minor tasks or troubles. When encountering Relaters, I usually lay my cards on the table and explain to them that I don't know how to sell to their particular businesses or corporations and maybe, if they wouldn't mind, they could help me through the process the first time. You won't have to do much more selling once they adopt you. Unfortunately, Relaters are rarely found in corporate purchasing positions.

Their greatest need is *to be accepted.*

The Examiner

Having *tentative actions* and a *business demeanor*, Examiners are usually found doing complex, detail work. Adverse to taking risks, they tend to hide in the process and rules of business; usually they work in institutions, banks, governments and the process departments of industry (accounting, data processing, legal, engineering, technical services, etc.).

They generally act withdrawn and contemplative and are usually poor social conversationalists, neither adding to nor initiating conversation on a personal level. They tend to rely on intellectual and auditory preferential systems for communication. If asked questions, they tend to respond with correct answers and offer little else to embellish the response, being careful not to divulge their personal positions or thoughts. They are excellent at doing support work and taking care of the details of life and business, but they lack the active and decisive qualities of the more forceful styles. Their checkbooks always balance.

Examiners are probably the most difficult style for the average sales person because they have "opposite" behavioral actions. In other words, the Examiner is tentative and businesslike; most salespeople are forceful and personal. If you look at the diagram of the five styles, you'll notice that they are diagonally opposed, meaning that each style has to adjust towards the other in order to achieve comfortable rapport.

Examiner

Examiners have a strong desire to be correct and efficient, even if they are not effective.

They will use corporate policies and procedures as their defense. The Examiner does not rise to a challenge directly, but rather waits and carefully plans his or her attack for the optimum time.

Identify them by their out-of-date clothing, conservative style and lack of color in dress: browns, grays, three-piece suits, thick-soled shoes, white shirts, clean fingernails, conservative and restrictive hair styles, monotone voices and indirect eye contact. They prefer glasses to contact lenses.

They do not physically touch as the Impulsives or Relaters do, nor do they tend to express personal opinions. They seldom decide on anything unless it is first fully researched and documented.

As salespeople, they are excellent for detailed portfolios (technical, financial, etc.) where a high degree of accuracy is required. They tend to work and plan their sales as a matter of procedure, fully documenting, keeping appointments and remaining in scheduled communication.

Examiners react skeptically towards externally applied motivation and rely on satisfying the customer by being correct in their documentation and their opinions. They are excellent when dealing with other Examiner-style purchasers. They tend to be easy to manage and resistant to change and motivation, but they are steady, reliable and dependable in their daily work. They seldom make employment changes unless a considerable amount of analysis and thought has preceded their decisions. They seldom fail because they seldom risk. *Everything* is planned.

As customers, Examiners tend to act in partnership with others, usually in committee, so that the risk concerning any pending decision is spread around. They seldom risk quick decisions and will retreat when pushed to close too soon. They must digest facts and figures, compare, analyze and conclude a decision in due time. They tend to be skeptical about any claim not supported by complete documentation or proof.

The key to selling them is to take advantage of the business evaluation process that they use, and simply to supply them with the required information as requested or suggested.

Let the process (policies and procedures) of their business work to make the buying decision rather than depending upon the individual for a decision. Examiners, in most cases, are only the custodians of business procedures, not the creators of them. They insure that the procedures are followed correctly.

It is important for you to let them know that you expect the process to deliver a *decision.* In meeting with them, be careful to manage your pace and your voice so as not to alarm or upset their cautious manner.

Their greatest need is *to be correct.*

The Victor
With *forceful action* and a *business demeanor*, the Victor is noticed immediately. The Victor takes charge quickly and lets everyone know that he or she is in charge. They are task- and goal-oriented and seem to have little time for the human side of life during business hours. Business *is* his or her life: getting the job done, organizing others, being the Victor. Bottom-line facts and figures are important; feelings are not. They tend to use intellectual, auditory and visual Preferential Communications systems.

The Victor has the unique ability to do many tasks at the same time, or so it appears. They are highly efficient and effective, tend to use the telephone constantly and always seem to dodge the punches just at the right time. Their egos are immense and probably well-deserved, or at least so they think.

Most Victors are on their "next" marriages and suffer from chronic workaholic syndrome. Do or die!

The Victor's pace is fast; the voice is purposeful and sometimes loud but not as modulated as the Impulsive's. The Victor exhibits control in everything. The Victor runs things and people, many times to successful conclusions. They tend to be visionary but temper their visions with plans and budgets.

Identify Victors by their handsome dress, high-quality clothes, polished shoes and top-of-the-line accessories. Their offices show power and control. The Victor sits in the big chair and you get to sit in the "sinker" chair.

The Victor has a firm handshake and a steady, penetrating stare that looks for any sign of submissiveness. The Victor has to know where he or she stands in the pecking order. As a salesperson you cannot sell to the Victor by being a bigger Victor. You can be equal, but not bigger.

Actions are deliberate; gestures, if any, are purposeful, such as a pointed finger. Look for an unexpressive poker face, a factual, results-oriented vocabulary and expectations for a crisp, bottom-line sales presentation.

As salespeople, Victors tend to rise rapidly to the top, learning the important skills quickly and thoroughly. They like to take control of the selling situation and sometimes can overpower their clients without knowing it. They sift through motivational materials to locate what works for them rather than being blindly sent on an emotional journey. They tend to read the important books on selling and personal success and to plan career paths that might be different than what their employers have in mind. Depending upon the extent of their egos, Victors may be difficult to control and manage only because they think they can do the manager's job better, and they probably can.

They are excellent for tough, tension-filled selling situations, and they tend to want to work longer hours than their peers. As a manager, you must watch them carefully to make sure they don't take on too much at once; if they do, help them reorganize quickly to get back on track. They tend to be the superstar performers.

You must sell to Victor clients by being fully and totally prepared. Know your information, competition, pricing and options inside out. Be prepared to cut a deal now: pre-arrange the authority to do so and let the Victor client know that you have the authority to finalize the sale. Authority figures respect other authority figures.

Victors like to make decisions and like to get on with business. If you sell to them and they trust you, then they will come back to you again and again.

The Victor is best equipped to start and build new companies or pilot new projects. They enjoy the "hunt" and always play to win! A strong observable ego is usually part of the package.

Their greatest needs are *to control and to win.*

The Flexive

The fifth personality style is flexible with other people. In one sense, they exhibit none of the dominant observable behaviors of the other four styles; in another sense, they exhibit all the traits. This is because they "mirror" their conversational partners. They "flex" to make others feel comfortable.

The Flexive is identified by his or her ability to change conversational posture without stress and by the lack of overly strong or overly weak behavioral traits. They generally take a wait-and-see approach rather than boldly indicating their personal conversational intentions. They adjust their behavior to suit you.

As salespeople, the Flexive is the ideal, all-round choice. They tend to be easier to manage than Impulsives or Victors and yet are more enthusiastic and risk-oriented than Relaters or Examiners.

They have the ability to make clients feel at ease quickly without losing sight of their sales goal in terms of production. Flexives tend to be empathetic, not sympathetic. By this, I mean that they tend to recognize and understand the position that a customer might be in but they do not adopt or join the customer in emotionally or physically sharing that position. Empathy means understanding philosophically; sympathy means joining in.

Generally, Flexives are adequate planners and good strategists. They learn to adapt to situations without undue stress or tension and usually make excellent management candidates.

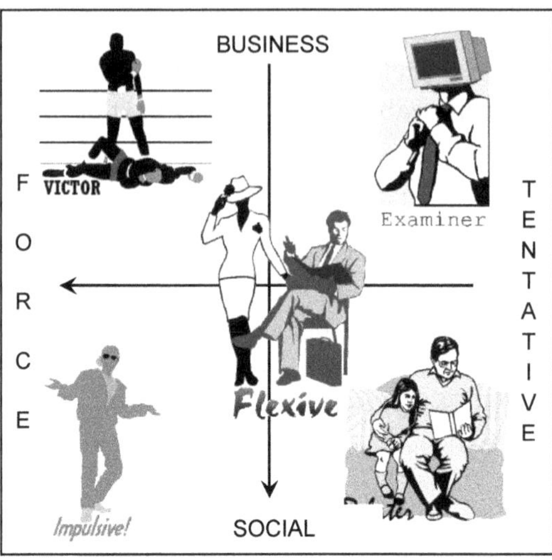

In selling to Flexives, remember that they are anxious to follow your lead. They readily get excited when you get excited or can settle down for a serious discussion of financial details. These are the easiest of all customers to sell to because they tend to be cooperative and open.

They tend to use intellectual preferential communications systems unless your language prompts them to change. Their flexible behavior tends to show you their cooperative sides, but they, too, have a dominant style that is hidden from view. Look carefully for the accessory clues of wardrobe, office furnishings, pace and voice intonations, furniture arrangements, color and textures, pictures and charts to gather additional information concerning this person. Sell to what you see, but remember there lurks a dominant "home-base" style somewhere.

Imagine the four styles as the bases in a baseball diamond and the pitcher's mound as the Flexive. The Flexive originally was trained to be a first baseman, second baseman, third baseman and a catcher before learning how to pitch. He or she has latent attributes that don't show when they are "on the mound."

Controlling Tension

The natural result of conflicting styles is tension. By learning to modify and control your behavior, you can lessen the tension between you and your prospect. With low levels of tension, there are high levels of information exchange. With high levels of tension, there are low levels of information exchange.

Reducing Tension

To reduce conversational tension, change your actions to reflect the same style as your conversational partner. Use the same Preferential

Communications system (auditory for auditory, visual for visual, kinesthetic for kinesthetic, intellectual for intellectual).

Increasing Tension
To increase conversational tension, act in the opposite style to the person. Use a conflicting Preferential Communications system (visual for auditory, kinesthetic for visual, auditory for kinesthetic, etc.). This is sometimes necessary when a decision is required and the prospect requires some tension to help promote a buying decision.

Low-Tension Situations
When people who share similar characteristics of demeanor and action get together, the situation results in the best form of communication with the lowest tension and the quickest and most intense transfer of information. When two similar styles communicate, they share a high degree of understandable information. Combinations of styles that result in low-tension situations are

- Relater with Relater;
- Impulsive with Impulsive;
- Examiner with Examiner;
- Victor with Victor;
- Flexive with Flexive.

Medium-Tension Situations
When people share one common behavioral attribute (action or demeanor), the situation is manageable, with a medium level of tension. With a slight alteration of your social behavior, you can create a low-tension, highly-effective conversation. Move gradually towards the prospect's behavioral style to reduce tension. Combinations of styles that result in medium-tension situations are

- Relater with Impulsive or Examiner;
- Impulsive with Relater or Victor;
- Victor with Impulsive or Examiner;
- Examiner with Victor or Relater;
- Flexive with any style.

High-Tension Situations
High-tension is likely to be the result among people who share neither similar demeanor nor similar action characteristics. In these situations, one style tends to dominate or intimidate another. This is when people tend to exhibit defensive behavior. In this situations, each style naturally intensifies its dominant traits.

In other words, an Examiner gets more businesslike, more tentative and more withdrawn; an Impulsive gets more animated and excited; a Victor gets brutally forceful and harsh; and a Relater gives his or her last dime to the cause.

With high tension, little or no information can be exchanged; the sale is going nowhere and unless some change in the seller's behavior is made immediately, the relationship is over. As a seller, you should move immediately towards your prospect's personality style to lessen tension and establish rapport. Combinations that result in high-tension situations are

- Impulsive with Examiner;
- Examiner with Impulsive;
- Victor with Relater;
- Relater with Victor.

More Rapport

In addition to the style flexing already described, there are other supplemental strategies that you can employ to strengthen initial rapport.

Common Ground
Use a statement that identifies a common area of interest that you share with the prospect:

> *"I see you're wearing a Rotarian pin. I've been a Rotarian for ten years. Which chapter are you with?"*

Referral
A referral from a colleague is a powerful way to introduce yourself. It opens all kinds of doors if used properly:

> *"Mr. Lundie of Overload Electric suggested that I see you in regards to saving your firm a considerable amount of time and money handling minor power failures and late night emergencies."*

Current Event
Use a current event, such as the weather or a business-oriented article, to help establish rapport:

> *"Carolyn, I couldn't help but notice that your firm uses the same type of filters that the Financial Examiner featured in its Consumer Watch column last week."*

Benefit Statement
Benefit statements start the conversation on a positive note. Get your customer thinking about solutions right away:

> *"Mr. Gray, we've cut losses of tools and equipment at Atomic Energy of Mellonville by* ***70%*** *last year. That represented a net savings of over* ***$100,000*** *in their annual tool budget. I'd like to see your firm do even better."*

Probing Approach
Use a question to get your prospect talking right away. Set the tone for the meeting. This approach is excellent to use with talkative styles, such as the Relater or Impulsive:

> *"Mr. Kolke, you, like all of our clients, have specific sales goals and targets that you are committed to meet. As you are aware, Herb, our firm specializes in helping sales managers like yourself see these targets achieved. Now, what improvements would you like to see in individual sales productivity and long-term account management, and why?"*

Personal Compliment
Complimenting a person may appear to be patronizing and a cheap way to gain confidence. Make sure that the compliment is sincere and has a basis in fact. Victors and Examiners are somewhat suspicious about personal compliments. Impulsives have egos that accept compliments readily if they are presented in the proper manner:

> *"Jim, you seem to keep this company hopping and, from what I hear, people throughout this industry really say impressive things about you. Let me say that it is a sincere pleasure to work with you."*

SELLING TO A GROUP

Interesting rapport problems and opportunities arise when selling to a group, be it a board of directors or 1,000 buyers in a conference setting. In dealing with small, controlled groups, such as a purchasing committee, you must do the following to establish the strongest rapport possible:

- Determine overall group and communication styles;
- Identify main product players;
- Satisfy the key 20%;
- Follow through.

1. Determine Overall Group Style
Determine the general overall style of the group (Examiner, Relater, Impulsive or Victor), and gear your presentation to this global style. This is not difficult to do if you take the time to find out from your meeting contact who the people in the group are and what positions or jobs they perform. With this information, you can profile the group.

For instance, imagine you were selling to a local community college, and your contact, the director of purchasing, informed you that there were three professors and two teaching assistants from the sociology department on the evaluation committee. You would expect the overall presentation to reflect a Relater tone and structure. You would prepare a low-key, human-issue approach that dealt with the impact on individuals or the community.

Prepare a lot of word pictures and graphic images to tell your story. You must use detail and figures to satisfy the director of purchasing and other Victor or Examiner styles in the meeting, but the support for the decision likely will come from the Relater style committee.

If, on the other hand, the director of purchasing had informed you that you were meeting with the director of security, the head of internal discipline and the campus police chief, then you would set your sights on a more factual, logical and precise presentation with lots of supporting data, bottom-line numbers, graphs and a strong implementation plan. You would come fully prepared to meet all challenges and to appear as strong and self-assured as you could.

It is unlikely that the group will have a common preferential communication system, so use the one that is best for the key members.

You may have to switch preferential systems when addressing different parts of your proposal that involve dealing with a specific member of the group only, such as the controller or the director of security. Focus your language to accomplish each specific task.

2. Identify the Main Product Players

Every group has members that are interested personally in your product. These are usually the actual users of your product. Identify these people and go out of your way to satisfy them. Sometimes it is necessary to deal with these individuals separately to satisfy their needs, especially when the person is of the opposite style from that of the overall group.

The product players are all-important to the purchase recommendation. They might not have the authority for making the actual purchasing decision, but, in most cases, they are the people who cause the purchasing decision to be made.

3. Satisfy the Key 20%

The 20/80 rule applies to most situations and it applies here as well. Even if the group is composed entirely of influencers and decision makers, there still will be a 20% dominant faction within the group that sways the remaining 80%.

Keep on the lookout for these key individuals, because if you can convince them, they will convince the remainder of the group. I've been in presentations where I knew if I could persuade one key individual in the group then the rest would fall in line. 80% support the decisions made by 20%.

4. Follow Through
If you make promises or suggestions during a group presentation, that you follow through with the right kind of information to the group members. In other words, you should prepare and send your product information in the form best suited for the individual. Information includes details for the Examiner, results and plans for the Victor, emotional "people" information for the Relater and exciting, opportunistic information for the Impulsive. Many times, if the purchasing agent is involved as part of an evaluation committee, he or she must be supplied detailed, factual information that actually might hinder your presentation to the rest of the group.

ALTERING YOUR PROBES

There are still some important things you should know about developing and maintaining rapport. The first involves a deep probing skill. How you ask questions and why you ask questions has a tremendous impact upon rapport.

The emotional personalities of Relaters and Impulsives react well to personal, opinion-based questions that involve their personal views. Structure your questions to draw out their thoughts and concerns, their hopes and their dreams. Many of your questions should begin with *"who,"* or *"what if."*

The Examiner and the Victor react better to factual, data-based questions that deal with the when, what and how of your proposal. Stay away from personal involvement unless it enhances the ego of the Victor.

Always try to match Preferential Communications systems for best rapport.

Altering Your Responses

Likewise, your responses should vary depending upon the style exhibited by your prospect. The social demeanor styles of Relater and Impulsive should receive a more animated response with word pictures or stories used to illustrate and emphasize.

The business demeanor styles of Victor and Examiner should be given more concise, factual and to-the-point responses that don't involve extensive word pictures or stories. They should concentrate on the results, the tasks and the plan.

The forceful action styles of the Victor and Impulsive should be given quick, enthusiastic presentations while the tentative action styles of the Relater and Examiner require low-key, slower presentations that give them time to digest, collate and contemplate. They *like* to think.

Altering Your Timing

Depending on the personality style exhibited by your prospect, adjust your personal timing and expectations to meet theirs. A fast-paced forceful individual expects results quickly and does not like to waste time. A tentative individual prefers to mull things over and to evaluate before coming to a tentative decision.

Your behavior must change to reflect the needs of your prospect. Some people require a week to think things over (or a year!) while others make decisions within seconds.

People are different, and you must plan to obtain the desired result. In one business I operated, the average selling cycle was two years. In another, it was two minutes. If you can't adjust your timing and your personal expectations, you will frustrate your prospect and yourself. In Cycle Shortening Strategies, however, you will discover ways to tighten up the longer selling cycles.

THE "HAND" MODEL

Remembering the Styles

There is an easy method of remembering the five styles – it's found on the fingers of your left hand. If you hold your hand up, palm facing you, the entire personality style program is visually and dynamically laid out for you to see and use.

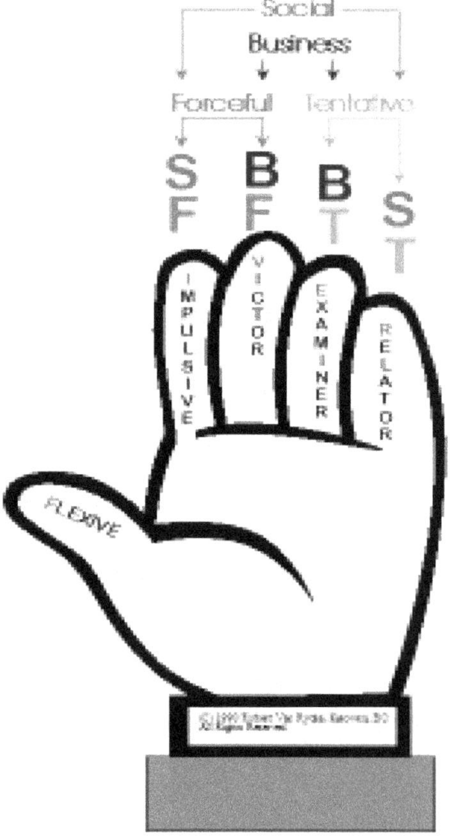

Each one of the four upright fingers represents one of the styles.

The thumb represents the **Flexive**, capable of touching each of the other fingertips at will. It is what the Flexive does: meets the communication expectations and needs of other styles before considering their own needs.

The index finger represents the **Impulsive**. Notice when you move the finger in relation to the other fingers, it has more freedom of motion, tends to be quicker and usually is the finger to get into trouble more often (testing the coffee to see if it is hot enough; pointing to some interest-grabbing event, etc.).

The next finger is the **Victor**. It stands the tallest on the hand, as if on a podium, signifying it wants the gold medal, not silver or bronze.

It is the most powerful of the four fingers, easily lifting a full pail of water by looping itself tightly around the pail's handle.

It also sits between two style types that it most often uses to make its plans succeed: the Impulsive and the Examiner. When you wiggle the Victor finger, it is not as flexible as the Impulsive, but it is still determined and fast.

The "ring" finger represents the **Examiner** profile. Of all the fingers, it is the least flexible, much like the Examiner style is in life. The significance of the "ring" is symbolic as well, for the Examiner is mainly concerned with contract and covenant; with obligation and rule, with correctness and with right and wrong. It stands also between two styles with which it tends to be most often associated: the Victor and the Relater. It is a finger, a style, that is most protected from outside blows.

The **Relater** is associated with the "pinkie". Being the smallest and most delicate of the fingers, it represents a personality style that is accommodating, protective and non-confrontational. It is almost purely social, with little threat of aggression towards others.

Using the fingers as a communications tool, simply by holding on to a particular finger with the other hand or placing the appropriate finger say, on your temple, you can relay immediate information to the person next in line to deal with your client, such as a business manager or "closer". This information can instantly result in a productive communications strategy.

Your Doubling Strategy

In this chapter we have briefly explored the ways you can use different personality styles and behavior to develop rapport. This discussion has been simply an introduction to techniques that require further study and trial before they can be fully useful. Rapport is essential to a sale, especially if you are involved in long-term sales cycles and customer relations. I stress that *you* must make the effort to establish and maintain rapport. Your customer is too lazy. Winners act, so you act!

DOUBLING

1. Invest in a copy of *Radical Rapport* and study its contents thoroughly (see appendix). Review and learn the styles. Each week, pick a style and develop strategies to deal with it. Learn the protective modes and the cooperative modes of the style. Reorganize your sales presentation and your questions to reflect the needs of each style. Practice adjusting your personal behavior to reduce the tension between you and each style or to achieve cooperation and acceptance. Ask others to help analyze your weaknesses and your strengths.

2. Look at yourself and determine what your selling style would be in relation to the five styles described. Decide what traits you might have to modify to improve the relationship with each of your customers and prospects. Create a strategic plan for altering your conversation for each one of your customers and prospects. Develop a personal rapport plan for one client each week. Use your plan as a guide only, because your client may change styles on you. The foremost strategy is to remain flexible.

3. People's actions reflect their needs. Make a concerted effort to meet your prospect's needs by taking full responsibility for developing and maintaining sales rapport within the sales meeting. Make a log of your sales visits each day and record how the client reacted to you or how you were able to develop a stronger rapport with your client. Look for change and look for areas of bonding.

4. Expectations are the invisible clues to selling success. Explore expectations and expose them through leading questions and direct probes. Before seeing each client, make a list of possible client expectations that reflect the client's position towards your company, products and you personally.

5. Pay 100% attention while with your client. Notice everything. Especially look for changes in behavior or in personal accessories that might indicate a change in style. Practice this each and every time you enter someone's office, car or house. Become a detective. Every day, pick one new location. After visiting it, make a list of all the clues you could pick up from the environment. Make it a game; make it fun.

This is one excellent way to take the "bite" out of visiting clients who might not be pleasant to call upon.

6. To reduce tension you must exhibit behavior that reflects your prospect's behavior. Practice moving towards your client's behavior by reflecting what you see. This skill is called pacing. Do this consciously with at least one client each day, and then increase it to more and more clients until you feel comfortable with pacing.

7. When selling to a group, seek out the influencers and leaders; concentrate on the 20% who dominate the 80%. Follow through on all promises. Be prepared to deliver three types of information: executive summary, general overview or proposal, and full detail. Each week review in advance for your group sales by preparing a group profile and selecting the information relevant to each group member. Personalize all material with the group members' names (correctly spelled) if possible.

8. Study your vocabulary to see whether you use visual, auditory, kinesthetic or intellectual Preferential Communications. Most likely, your sales presentation is either saturated with one channel or it is a mix of multiple systems. Begin now to separate and construct four separate sales languages: one for the visual communicator, one for the auditory client, one for the client who expresses himself or herself through feelings and one for the client who uses intellectual or “thinking” language.

9. Identify the expected sales cycles of each of your customers or prospects based on their individual personality style types. Adjust your timing expectations to reflect the differences in the way people and businesses make decisions: longer cycles for Relaters and Examiners, shorter cycles for Victors and Impulsives.

THE PROBE

GIGO · Quality Demands Questions · Probe Focus · Probe Architecture · Low-Stress Probes · Moderate-Stress Probes · High-Stress Probes · Converting Selling Statements · Responses · Building, Breaking or Stimulating · Getting Past the Common Response · How Now, Brown Cow? · Who Are the Players? · Your Real Goals · Customer Profile · Dancing · Defining the Essentials · Quick Qualify · Two-Minute Warning · Fish or Cut Bait · Always a Sale · Your Doubling Strategy Doubling

GIGO

When I graduated from college with a major in computer programming, it was the age of the mainframe business computer and I was riding on the leading edge as a programmer-analyst. Early in my training, the instructor explained that age-old axiom of computer programmers everywhere:

"GIGO" Garbage In = Garbage Out.

Simple, sometimes overused, yet astoundingly accurate: what goes <u>in</u> is what comes <u>out</u>. It surely was evident as soon as I began building my programs. Whatever I did in terms of structuring the "intelligence" of the programs was evident in the final result. As well, whatever was fed into the computer in the form of data was what would come out the other end.

There were only two ways that superior information could come out of the computer:

- by having superior data going in, in which case the computer just threw up what it ate and the result was superior data coming out,

- by having the program (the set of instructions designed to manipulate the data once it went into the computer) work the data to form new, more interesting results. This second possibility is much like taking raw sales figures and turning them into various profit and activity reports and graphs.

In selling, you are the programmer. You can obtain average information from your customers and, without a lot of work, turn out average results. Average results mean average sales. Welcome to First Dimension Selling.

Average Information In = Average Information Out

Or, you can take average information and work on it, massage it, embellish it, enhance it and present it in a more interesting and superior way. The result is better and more interesting output from average information. This is still First Dimension, but you are starting to think and act more strategically. However, it takes a lot of work.

Average Information In + Work = Better Information Out

Another method is to seek superior information. With superior information, superior results are almost a natural occurrence. To get superior information, you must ask superior questions. Welcome to the beginning of Second Dimension Selling.

Superior Information In = Superior Information Out

The combination of getting superior information and working hard to massage and manipulate the information into an unforgettable presentation is an operation that will assure increased sales, bigger sales and more frequent sales. This is Second and Third Dimension Selling at its best!

Superior Information In + Work = Unbeatable Information Out

The effort you spend in developing and using quality techniques to uncover information that is not normally supplied to a salesperson will pay off. Sometimes I have spent an entire day concentrating on what questions to pose and what information to get from my prospect. This process firmly set a particular event as a goal in my mind and, nine out of ten times, I'd come away with the extra information I sought.

Prospects divulge as little as possible to salespeople most of the time. You have to prepare carefully, then persevere with your probing so that you get superior information from your prospect. You want the equation to also read,

"Quality In = Quality Out."

Quality Demands Questions

The average prospect will give you average information. Average information leads to average sales and average income. To start building quality sales, you must seek superior information. The way to do this is to ask more intelligent questions.

Ask questions that uncover the specifics about the possible sale. Don't waste selling time with generalities or safe questions. Get down to business. When I'm with a client, I've learned that by asking specific questions, you not only get the prospect's attention, but you also start earning his or her respect.

Anybody can ask average questions.

You have to start learning how to ask penetrating questions. Ask questions that your competition is afraid to pose. Get directly to the heart of the matter. Isolate the key decision components and explore each one.

Probe Focus

Each probe can be positioned to take advantage of the prospect's preferential communication system. This is a very important step in the construction of all questions. If your prospect is showing "visual" and you're probing using kinesthetic (feeling) probes, the mismatch in communication systems will encourage tension and misunderstanding. Once you have determined your prospect's preferential system, try to consciously insert similar terminology into your probe structure: feeling for feeling, sight for sight, sound for sound. This will help your probes to become penetrating and meaningful.

For intellectual communicators, use words like *think, believe, understand, know, sense* and *aware.* These are unspecified words with intellectual meaning. However, as soon as your prospect reveals his or her preferential communications system to one of the three "active" systems (auditory, visual, kinesthetic), then immediately match systems.

PROBE ARCHITECTURE

Probes can be phrased in one of three ways: **open, closed** or **conditional**. Each one of these probes has a different probe architecture, and your prospect's response depends upon which of the architectures you chose to use.

Open Probes

Most quality questions start with ***who, what, why, where*** or ***when***. As a result, they get the prospect to divulge information: they get the prospect to explain. These questions are known as “open” probes.

When you ask a question using one of the "five W's," you likely will receive an answer that contains useful information. In addition to the five W's, there are also ***how, tell me, explain, describe, clarify, detail, educate me*** and a host of other synonyms that get the prospect to talk.

Open probes result in information. The better you structure your question the better your response will be. Ask a stupid question, get a stupid answer. Ask a superior question, get superior information.

> *"Where do you see using the new piping systems, Mr. Anthony?"*
>
> *"How do you feel the increased flow will be of most benefit?"*
>
> *"Why would your company be interested in looking at a review at this time, Mr. Gray?"*

"As you see it, who would be driving the new car most of the time, Ms. Kaufman?"

"When would be the most effective time to show the new re-treading system to your engineers, Heather?"

Closed Probes

Closed probes have a primary goal of getting the prospect to ***agree*** or ***disagree*** with the subject of your question.

Closed probes are used to restrict conversation by limiting response to yes, no or specific information. These questions are as valuable to use as the open probes, but they require caution due to their uncanny ability to increase tension. The closed probes begin with such words as do, have, are, will, won't, aren't, can, can't and shall. To certain personality styles, they can be intimidating.

The biggest danger with closed probes is that once the answer is received, you have to start the conversation over again. Closed probes restrict communication whereas open probes encourage conversation. The job of the closed probe is to verify or insert information or expectations.

"Am I correct in assuming that your company wants to see this unit installed as quickly as possible?"

"It sounds like this product must conform with the new consumer protection laws?"

"I get the feeling that you are going to be making your decision before the end of the month, correct?"

All of these questions result in specific information being obtained, usually in the form a confirmation. The prospect doesn't really get too deeply involved. Closed probes are used for effectively committing the prospect to specifics. They are used for commitment, closing or verification.

Conditional Probes

One of the most useful questions is the conditional or leading probe. They always contain an "if" and are designed to remove the intimidation from the question.

> *"If you were to try the tri-axial valve, where would you like to see its installation?"*
>
> *"If the project were to be seriously considered, then what budget range would we be looking at?"*
>
> *"If you were to consider competitive products, then which features or benefits would you feel are important that are not available with our product?"*

The conditional probe is one of the best methods of uncovering delicate information, such as budget, decision-making capacities, influencers, and process. They are very good to use with the tentative action styles of Relater and Examiner.

Low-Stress Probes

Probes can also be divided into stress intensities: ***low, moderate*** and ***high***. Depending upon your objectives, your strategies and your prospect's style, it is wise to select probes that will deliver important information without developing undue stress.

The first intensity level, the low-stress probes, can be used with all of the architectures (open, closed or conditional). These probes are structured or designed to be un-intimidating. They are not to be used for backing someone into a corner, but for drawing out background information and personal feelings.

The low-stress probes are broken into four subgroups: ***Conversational, Opinion, Tentative*** and ***Fantasy*** probes. These subgroups vary in their intent and their design but they all tend to be non-threatening to prospects.

Conversational Probes

Conversational probes relate to the development of general rapport. They include talking about the weather, the news, sports, fashion or anything else that is topical or even slightly personal. We are all familiar with these probes because most of us use them every day when we meet other people.

Closed Probe:
"Did you see how the Flames scored that overtime goal last night, Jim?"

Open Probe:
"I hear that you've a fine firm here, Mr. Morgan, with a good reputation around town. How long have you been in the trucking industry?"

Conditional Probe:
"If you were to head down south, where would you feel like going?"

Conversational probes are often used to start, maintain or encourage normal conversation. They are not powerful nor do they get unusual or important information unless by chance. Generally they are used by First Dimension Sellers as their sole means of rapport development. Conversational probes are used by Second and Third Dimension Sellers as just one of many ways to develop or maintain rapport.

Opinion Probes

Impulsives and Relaters react more positively to opinion-based probes than to fact-based probes. Opinion probes ask for an opinion or feeling on a subject rather than for a decision. Because of this, they tend to draw the personal side of the prospect into the sales arena.

Opinion probes are not very effective on Victors or Examiners because these styles tend to accept facts and figures more than opinions and feelings. Selling to Victors and Examiners using opinion probes might create tension and may produce an uncooperative selling atmosphere, unless your probe is aimed at supporting the ego of the Victor.

Opinion probes often include the words feel, opinion, perception, sensation, sense, experience, perceive, aware, belief, view or perspective.

Closed Probe:
In your opinion, do you see the claims made by this importer as valid?"

Open Probe:
"How do you feel about having the added power without the added cost?"

Conditional Probe:
"How would it sound to you if I could put together a package that would include both the options at no additional monthly cost to you?

Tentative Probes

Relaters and Examiners respond better when they are not directly challenged by a decision or a choice. For these personality types, structure your probes to be tentative rather than direct. This is easily done by phrasing your questions using tentative terminology, such as *might, per chance, possibly, tentatively, suggest, perhaps, maybe, could* and *should.*

Closed Probe:
"It may be possible to save money by using two rather than three cross-link modulators. This sounds like a better route, don't you think, Miss Winsor?"

Open Probe:
"How would you feel about building a tentative proposal that would look at a test application of the fertilizer should the conditions change?"

Conditional Probe:
"If your department could see itself in a position to afford our services, how and where would you suggest that we could help you the most?"

Fantasy Probes

Relaters and Examiners have difficulty with facing direct decisions. Because of this, it is worthwhile to pose questions in a manner that takes the prospect away from the active decision-making process. Also, if you feel that the advancements that your product represents are too radical or severe for your prospect to absorb or accommodate, then you will more than likely have to do some fantasy work. Fantasy probes explore the future. They are the "what if?" questions that take people from their present realities to new realities.

Closed Probe:
"To be able to purr down that country road in the autumn with the wind rushing through your hair and the smell of fallen leaves slowly smoldering in roadside fires; sounds great, doesn't it, Bill?"

Open Probe:
"What if we could find a way that you could afford to own a Blitsfire 16, Norm? What if we could find a way to put you where you really feel you belong? How would you feel about that, Norm?"

Conditional Probe:
"If you could imagine for a minute that all your conventional drive trains have been replaced with our incredibly advanced Magna Train, what sort of impact and advantages would you see for your fleet operations?

Fantasy probes use imagination-stimulating words such as *imagine, suppose, hypothesize, presume, speculate, propose, suggest, theorize, conceive, project, create, visualize* and *think.* Use them in conjunction with the key verbs, adverbs and adjectives of the Preferential Communications system that the prospect uses.

Practice creating word pictures about how a prospect might use your product and how the product's advantages and benefits come to the forefront.

MODERATE-STRESS PROBES

Moderate-stress probes are the primary information-revealing and retrieving tools used by the professional salesperson. You'll notice right away that these probes look for hard information, for choices and for detail. They focus 100% on the sale. They directly involve the prospect. They take work to use them but they get results when used properly. The moderate-stress probes are categorized into the following sub-groups: ***pointed probes, expectational probes, set-up probes, alternative choice probes*** and ***factual probes***.

Pointed Probes

Pointed probes go right to the heart of your sales purpose: to explore or expose information that is critical to your selling success. To develop pointed probes, isolate the essential information you wish to address and then structure some questions directly addressing the issues involved. As issues arise within the selling interview, note them on a piece of paper (one of my favorite tactics) and then let your subconscious mull the issues over while you continue on. Come back in a few minutes to address each issue or point. Let's look at a few examples around the subject of budget:

Closed Probe:
*"I am assuming that you see your budget range for a purchase such as this is somewhere between **$8,000** and **$10,000**, is this correct?"*

Open Probe:
"What do you feel would be your expected budget range for this purchase, Ms. Burke?"

Conditional Probe:
"If you were to go ahead with the project as described, then what size budget would sound good on a yearly basis?"

Most of your good selling probes will be of the pointed probe variety. Ask yourself (before asking the prospect), *"Would I take notice if asked this question? Would I get involved? Could I sit and let it slide by?"* Subjecting yourself to each probe gives you insight as to how your prospect will feel. This technique is called role reversal. It is an excellent method of testing your questions for effectiveness.

Expectational Probes

Earlier in this book I mentioned that exposing and exploring expectations represents one of the key differences between First Dimension Sellers and their more successful counterparts. Every prospect and customer has expectations, and it is up to you to draw these expectations from the invisible realm into the visible. Your prospect has to hear his or her own expectations out loud. To draw out expectations, the best word to use is *expect,* but other words, such as *anticipate, hope, look forward to, wish, want, propose, estimate, think, require* and *demand* can draw out expectations as well.

Closed Probe:
"In looking at the information that you've provided, Mr. Kessler, I would say that you expect to purchase this system for between $4,000 and $5,000 per station, is that correct?"

Open Probe:
"What does it sound like you could expect in terms of daily fleet maintenance, Mr. Hawkins?"

Conditional Probe:
"If I were to arrange for a full demonstration, who do you feel would likely attend?"

Set-Up Probes

Set-up probes are preceded by a qualifying or limiting statement. These questions are leading so that the information returned is specific.

Closed Probe:
"I've noticed that you are using TypeFree word processing software with a Quadroptics laser mouse. There are several enhancements available in the newest version that greatly improve the speed of formatting. I'm sure that these speed features would be seen as beneficial by a power-user such as yourself, right Joan?"

Open Probe:
"You know, Ray, almost every day you hear of another chemical leaching into the water systems of our cities. I'm sure you've heard that we don't need any more chemicals in what we drink or eat, so what would you say if I told you that this filtration unit removes every known cancer-causing chemical from your household drinking water… Thoughts?"

Conditional Probe:
"Mutual funds have been a contentious issue during the last year, but in some isolated cases they have delivered an amazing return. If I could assure you with accredited documentation that there was a significant opportunity to double your investment within two years, how would you feel about that, Kathy?"

Set-up probes do exactly what they say: they set the prospect up for a pointed question. You control and limit the response by the way you pose the question. Quality in = Quality out.

Alternative Choice Probes

The favorite choice of most salespeople, especially to encourage commitment or decisions, are alternative choice questions. Alternative choice probes present two options for the prospect to choose between.

The prospect rarely notices that there is a third alternative: not to choose either one. You provide a choice between two positives.

The open architecture is most often used for this type of probe and usually the questions are intended to elicit an opinion. It always includes a phrase that offers two choices, such as the intellectual *"which would you prefer,"* or *"which sounds better to you"* (auditory), *"which one feels better"* (kinesthetic) or *"which looks better to you"* (visual).

Closed Probe:
"The decision as to whether you would prefer two or four doors has already been answered by your two children, wouldn't you say, Mrs. Leaver?"

Open Probe:
"Which would you feel more comfortable with, Jim, the 400-gig or the one terabyte system?"

Conditional Probe:
"If there was a chance that you could afford this model instead of the basic unit, then which would sound better to you, the red exterior with the matching red interior or the shocking green combination with the leather?"

Alternative choice probes are important because they provide you with the basic tool for getting positive customer decisions.

Factual Probes

In contrast to opinion probes, factual probes stick to the facts, the whole facts, and nothing but the facts. Factual probes are best used for Victors and Examiners and they can also be used to increase tension with Impulsives and Relaters. They include terminology such as *facts, figures, amounts, bottom line, results, analysis, plan, process, accounting, decisions, black and white* and other concrete terms that add a factual flavor to your probes.

Closed Probe:
"As you can see by the operational profile and expense forecast we have prepared, it is clear that the installation of all four switches would be seen as the best bottom-line decision, wouldn't you agree, Mr. Victor?"

Open Probe:
"In structuring an implementation plan, what would you say would be a good target completion date?"

Conditional Probe:
"If this project were to proceed on schedule, how soon do you feel a budget decision could be expected?"

HIGH-STRESS PROBES

High-stress probes are used for getting commitment or agreement when moderate-stress probes won't accomplish the task. They must be used with authority and confidence. The tactic of "ask and shut up" often forms an integral part of their use. The high stress probes come in two varieties: ***commitment probes*** and ***confrontational probes.***

From an integrity position, high-stress probes can put you in a difficult position. Be careful that you are not embarrassing or diminishing your client by using what is commonly seen as high-pressure. It is true that some customers actually need confrontation to help them make a decision. Please don't make is your first-line strategy.

Commitment Probes

Commitment probes come in many varieties and are used all the time by salespeople wishing to close a sale. In the chapter on engineering commitment, you'll read about how to seek commitment continuously throughout the selling process. Encouraging commitment is an integral part of everything you do with a prospect. However, the situation often requires an actual, *"Do you?"* or *"Don't you?"* question.

Many commitment questions are actually "set-up" statements with a little "agree" question tagged onto the end. In old selling terms, these "agree" questions used to be called "nail downs" because the salesman was seen as nailing his prospect into a coffin and driving each coffin lid nail down with a *"don't you agree?"* statement-question. It is a horrible image of the relationship between a salesperson and a client. I suppose that is where many of today's stereotypes of salespeople originated.

It is valuable to have your prospect accept incremental commitment during the selling process, and commitment probes seek to establish agreement during all phases of the sale. Small agreements add up to an overall conclusion of agreement. Commitment probes are used to gather feedback from your prospect: to see if the prospect understands and agrees with your presentation as you proceed. Waiting to seek agreement to the very end of a sale could be intimidating for the prospect and it could waste a lot of your selling time.

Closed Probe:
"The first date would sound more suitable for the new product line launch, wouldn't you agree, Greg?"

Open Probe:
"Christopher, when do you feel you would be in a position to finalize the purchase on the particle beam neutralizer?"

Conditional Probe:
"If you were to decide to introduce the Dingbat Double Duty Duct System to your fleet this year, where would you see its initial deployment, Mrs. Friend?"

Confrontational Probes

Every now and then a salesperson should be prepared to call a prospect's bluff. This is when the confrontational probes are used. Confrontational probes leave no room for compromise: they demand a straight answer and they demand it now.

There are times when you just want to cut through the fog and get down to doing business. Having done business in the Republic of Texas, I've run into a few "good ol' boys" who use confrontational probes when you're least expecting it. Confrontational probes go for the throat, so be prepared for unexpected responses when you use them.

First, set the stage, then pop the question. Top-notch journalists often use them to press their subjects past factual responses into emotional responses.

Closed Probe:
"Mr. Dickey, we've looked at this point several times, and each time we see the same conclusion emerge. I think we can agree that you've said that you could see how and why this product would be valuable to your firm immediately and in the future. So, is there anything else that needs to be examined before we see to the final paperwork?"

Open Probe:
"Al, I've been dealing with you for six months now, much longer than I think either you or I expected to be involved in this process. I have to know your real position on this, Al. Are you going to purchase the system now, and if not now, then when – or tell me why not?"

Conditional Probe:
"Al, I think it would be good for us if we could conclude this transaction right now. If you're ready, I'd like to hear your final cash offer."

Converting Selling Statements

Most First Dimension Sellers sell by using product statements. These statements are usually in the form of product-oriented phrases but sometimes are in more powerful, user-oriented phrases.

Product-Oriented Statement:
"This new by-pass valve is made with titanium and chrome alloy steel, and carries a five-year unconditional guarantee."

User-Oriented Statement:
"This new valve will assist your piping system engineers by allowing a faster and more efficient delivery of fluids with fewer maintenance requirements."

These statements certainly help to explain your product but they do little to *involve* the prospect. By converting each statement into a question or series of questions, the prospect becomes involved and interested.

*"Mr. Martin, what improvements for your piping system would you expect to see from a valve that could deliver **20%** more fluids with **50%** less maintenance?"*

The prospect has to feel, hear or visualize the system and product in use. He or she has to analyze and formulate a response, and verbalize the result. In short, the prospect has to work, has to become involved and has to get in touch with your solution and his or her problem. In terms of selling power, the probe approach requires more effort on your part and on your prospect's part, but the added energy builds a better sale. Again, in your statements, utilize the preferential communications system of the prospect and slant your statements visually, audibly, kinesthetically or maintain an intellectual style.

Responses

The first aspect you want to watch for in a prospect's response is the preferential communication system used. Listen for feelings, facts, visual words, auditory responses or intellectual, sterilized words. Match your probes and replies to the prospect's Preferential Communications system.

Responses or answers come in three basic forms: ***positive, negative*** or ***not at all.*** We need not get more complicated than this. Either the prospect responds by giving you good information, by giving you bad information or by giving you no information or feedback.

When you receive a good response (the prospect agrees to or supports your sales presentation), then you will want to build upon the prospect's opinions, feelings and decisions.

When you receive a negative response (the prospect disagrees or objects to your sales presentation), then you will want to break the prospect's response and reorganize it into a more positive response.

When you receive no response, then you must stimulate the prospect into giving you feedback.

It is always important to have a selling "game plan" so that when you get a bad response you can take a planned course of action that will get your prospect back on track.

If you use closed probes, you will likely get answers that stop the conversation. It is up to you to get it going again, so be ready immediately with another probe. Use too many short, closed probes and you'll raise your prospect's blood pressure.

However, you must also learn how to handle the prospect that gives you too much information. The response is your goal; how you use that response will determine how far you go in selling.

BUILDING, BREAKING OR STIMULATING

If you get no response from your prospect, you must first stimulate the prospect into providing a response, negative or positive, so that you understand how well your prospect is understanding your presentation and if the prospect agrees or disagrees. Use opinion probes to stimulate conversation and to gain feedback. Without feedback, you're taking a chance that the prospect is either accepting or rejecting your presentation. You don't know, so ask. Without feedback, you're selling blind.

Once you've obtained a response from your prospect, you're faced with the decision to build upon a positive response or break down a negative response. Build or break, a simple decision: but if you are aware that you consciously must make the decision and then take appropriate action, you will soon be able to take command of any selling situation.

You *build* by reinforcing the answer with additional supportive information and by using additional similar probes.

You <u>*break*</u> a response by redirecting, proving, explaining, reversing or refocusing the prospect's response.

If your prospect hands you a response that doesn't make sense, which is often the case in selling, simply ask another question to clarify the response or use the word *"Oh?"* with a questioning tone. Many times prospects will tell you one thing when they mean something else entirely. The strategy of *Ask, Listen,* and *Interpret* should be used in every conversation.

> **Ask:** Probe for good information. Wait for a response.
>
> **Listen:** Carefully pay attention and listen to the whole response: interpret the body language, the tone, the inflections, the eyes and the message.
>
> **Interpret:** If you are not crystal clear on what the prospect is saying, then clarify by asking another question or by using the word *"Oh?"* Or, repeat the last few words of the prospect's statement, *"Too expensive???"*

When you are satisfied with the answer, stimulate by asking another question. Keep this up until all the prospect's expectations have been explored and all the parameters have been covered.

GETTING PAST THE COMMON RESPONSE

To get past common responses, ask uncommon questions. Decide what information you really require from your prospect to encourage a quick sale and then build specific probes to get to that information. Use the preferential system to your advantage. Let's say you need to know who actually makes the final purchasing decision for your product. It is critical that you get a name. Your goal is clear.

> *"Mr. Lougheed, I clearly see that you are my primary contact concerning the evaluation of this product. For my personal understanding, however, I am having trouble seeing just who, aside from yourself, is involved in*

> *making the final decision and how that decision is made. Would you please explain or show this to me?"*
>
> *"Mr. McKay, I am assuming that you make the final decision on this product. If I am hearing you incorrectly, then could you tell me who does make the final decision?"*
>
> *"Aside from yourself, Mr. Duckworth, who else do you feel might be involved in the final decision?"*

Average questions get average responses. Specific questions get specific responses.

How Now, Brown Cow?

Finding out what the evaluation and purchasing process is within a new prospect's firm is sometimes a bit tricky. The professionals never leave this stone unturned. Your effort in selling can be amazingly reduced by having your prospect provide a complete road map for your selling success. All you have to do is ask.

List all the information about the purchasing process that is critical to getting the sale completed: who is involved, what is the expected timing, how is the final decision made, what paperwork is required, etc. Then develop questions that will extract that information from your prospect. Let them tell you how to sell!

This little strategy is so overlooked and yet so simple to use and so effective that it alone can easily double your sales.

> *"Mrs. Finch, I haven't dealt with your firm in the past and I wondered if you would be so kind as to help me picture the evaluation and purchasing process involved here. Maybe we could start by looking at how new products are evaluated and selected."*
>
> *"Terry, if after our meeting today you should feel like testing our product, then what steps do you feel we should consider next?"*

> *"If I am hearing you correctly, it sounds like the next step should be a field trial, right?"*

Think beforehand what you need to know, especially what you didn't think you would be privileged to know, and design questions to draw out the answers you seek.

WHO ARE THE PLAYERS?

One of the most important area of sales is to determine who is involved in evaluating, recommending and deciding upon your product.

You must always proceed with caution, because you don't want to step on toes or bruise egos. The simple rule here is always to *include* the person with whom you are talking.

> *"Mr. Esco, aside from yourself and Gail, who else would be seen as being involved in the decision-making process and how?"*
>
> *"Ms. Burke, aside from yourself, who else do you feel would like to be involved in presenting the trophy for the event-winning 1970 Dodge Charger?"*
>
> *"It sounds like there might be a number of different departments involved in hearing the proposal and sounding out a decision. Aside from yourself, Phyllis, who else would be involved in hearing our presentation and what would their roles be?"*

This simple technique, "*aside from yourself*", will get you through more tight spots than you could ever imagine.

YOUR REAL GOALS

Have you thought about your selling responsibilities? Being entirely selfish for just a moment, think about what you need to accomplish in selling: to sell the most, to the most, for the most. Now of course, this goal doesn't take into account all the intricacies of market pricing and competitive pressure, but it states in maximum terms what you should seek for yourself and your company. Maximize profit margins, maximize sales volume and maximize your client base. Sell to as many qualified people as you can. It seems simple enough as a philosophy, but if enacted, it will keep you hopping for the rest of your selling career.

If you take on these "maximize" goals, then it becomes ultimately important for you to develop some strategies that will start maximizing your selling efforts.

There are three basic ways to increase your current product sales: sell *harder*, sell *smarter* or sell *harder and smarter*. If you realize that your ability to sell harder cannot be radically expanded (you might be able to work 50% longer than you do right now), then the obvious thing left to do is to make better use of the time you have: *sell smarter*.

One of the first things to recognize about selling smarter is that you must spend your selling time with people who exhibit or express a high potential to become a customer. It only makes sense: spend time with those who want to buy and can afford to buy. I don't know how many *years* I've spent talking to the right people at the wrong time, the wrong people at the right time and the wrong people at the wrong time. What you want is the right people at the right time!

Of course, an ideal combination is to sell harder (leave your "job switch" on longer each day) and learn to sell smarter as well.

The first step in maximizing your selling potential is to determine who is worthy of your selling time.

Customer Profile

Have a good look at who buys now. Get out your current customer list and start drawing up a profile of what your average customer looks like. Create a picture of your prospects. Look at some of the obvious parameters:

- Type of business, industry or institution;
- Job position of purchaser (decision making or evaluating and recommending);

- Age or experience of purchaser;
- Size of business (number of employees, locations, etc.);
- Type of equipment, product or service previously used;
- Age of equipment or product being replaced;
- Location of business (or home, office, cottage, etc.);
- Viability of prospect (cash-rich, stable or debt-ridden);
- Length of time for purchase transaction from first call to sale;
- Size of purchase in dollars or in units.

When you analyze your current customers, you get a glimpse of what your future customers will be like if you continue to do the same job of selling that you have done in the past. However, look at the potential in your current customers as well. Modify the profile to reflect a balance between what works now and what you would like to see in the immediate future. The modified profile is what you build your strategies upon:

- How can you sell more to the same type of customer?
- How can you sell faster to the same type of customer?
- How can you get better profit margins from the same type of customer?
- How can you find more of the same type of customer?
- How can you find customers who will buy more with the same effort as you currently use with your present clients?
- How can you find customers who will buy faster with the same effort you currently use with your present customers?
- How can you find customers who will buy at higher margins than your current customers?
- How can you expand your current prospecting scope into virgin territories or industries?
- How can you modify your own personal selling skills to shorten the sales cycle, identify buyers from non-buyers and increase the size of the individual sale?

The essence of profile development is finding the customer who buys the most volume, at the highest profit margin, in the shortest space of time. This takes careful thinking and investigation.

One of the first strategies you should employ is the **Quick Qualify** strategy.

It implies that you can quickly weed the prospecting field of undesirables and leave it with just those worth nurturing. To do this, you must have some form of qualification profile to qualify (or weed) against. I use this term because I am the world's most uneducated gardener, and I couldn't tell an orchid from a dandelion in their incipient growth stages. I would either leave them both in the garden or pull them both from the garden. In prospecting, you must know who to leave, water and nurture and who to pull up and discard. To do this, you must have an appreciation of who represents good potential and who does not. Is the prospect a dandelion or an orchid? Your customer profile helps you recognize and identify what you are weeding.

DANCING

I used to have a sweatshirt with a picture of Snoopy wound up in a dancing twirl. Beneath the ecstatic dog was the caption, *"To Dance is to Live and to Live is to Dance"*. I enjoy dancing. I enjoy dancing most of all when my partner enjoys dancing too. From the simple mechanical process of feet properly placed in time with the music, an emotionally charged relationship on the floor emerges. Two people acting in unison, each taking and each giving so that the result is seemingly greater than the individual parts. Much like a nuclear reaction, you get more than you expect. But try dancing with a klutz. The results are strained and awkward; better for both if you don't stick with it. The music's over: look for a new partner or head for home to soak your toes.

What's this got to do with selling? Just about everything. Just about all the important aspects of selling are found in dancing.

To Get the Most Out of Dancing You Must First Go to the Dance

You can't sell if you aren't where people are buying. Go to the client or get the client to come to you. The more often you're in front of your prospect (personally or in other ways) the more influence you exert.

To Dance Well You Must Practice and Develop Dancing Skills

Certainly I used to practice dancing as most teenagers did, but it had no effect unless I could try it out with somebody on the dance floor. Similarly, if you practice selling skills alone and never integrate your practice with actual selling to your prospects, no one benefits from your efforts. But if you learn to sell well, everybody benefits, especially your selling partner: your prospect.

Learn to Dance to Different Beats, Rhythms and Sounds
Versatility is the trademark of a true dancer. When the music changes, the dance changes. Sales professionals are the same; when the prospects change, the seller changes. Never out of step, the sales pro goes right from a waltz into a watusi.

To Get the Most Out of Dancing, Choose the Right Partner
Dancing with a dud is no pleasure. Dancing with someone who enjoys, follows and adds is a sheer delight. Selling to a dud is no fun. Selling to someone who recognizes and appreciates your skills and is ready, willing and able to buy is also a sheer delight. The difference is extreme: not only can you dance longer, harder, more intensely and with a certain degree of passion with a good partner, but you can do it night after night after night. The same goes for good selling partners (your clients).

Your job is to sell. Selling only happens with clients who are ready, willing and able to buy. Qualifying your prospect is necessary just to find out if they came prepared to dance or if they just want to watch. You'll have more fun dancing with a dancer. You don't have to dance with a dud.

DEFINING THE ESSENTIALS

To find out if your prospect can dance, define some of the essential information that you must discover. Here are eight essential **Quick Qualify** categories:

1. **Performance**: What are your prospects expecting in terms of primary product or service performance requirements?
2. **Budget Range**: How much do they expect to spend? What is their budget range and do they have funds available now?
3. **Timing**: When do they expect to make a purchasing commitment? When do they require the product or service?
4. **Decision Makers and Influencers**: Aside from the prospect personally, who else would be involved in the decision to purchase and how?
5. **Purpose**: Why are they considering a purchase now?
6. **Location:** Where would they expect the sales negotiations to take place? Where would they expect the product or service to be used?
7. **Competition:** What competitive products or services are they considering? What particular benefits of competitive products do they most like?
8. **Priority:** What is their highest priority within the purchase?

You might have *more* essential categories depending upon your type of business but generally they will fall into the who, what, why, where, when and how categories. Eight questions known as the **Quick Qualify**. You may think it straightforward and abrupt, but I assure you that you will find out who wants to dance and who just wants to sit and listen to the music. Your job is to sell.

QUICK QUALIFY

For each of the personality styles, probes can be slanted differently to extract the same essential information without jeopardizing rapport.

As a matter of practice, if probes are used properly, they tend to strengthen rapport.

For instance, your probes to the Victor should be factual and bottom-line direct questions. The following represents a salesperson probing for the eight Quick Qualify categories to a **Victor** prospect, Ms. Mead, who is exhibiting visual communication signs.

1. *"Ms. Mead, aside from yourself, can you see anyone else here who should be considered in the buying or evaluation process?"*
2. *"From information supplied to me through your inquiry, you indicated that you picture your firm replacing the **4551** transfer switch system, is this correct? Why do you see this occurring at this time, Ms. Mead?"*
3. *"What do you see as your expected budget range, low to high, for the replacement project?"*
4. *"When do you want to see all the new switches operating, Ms. Mead?"*
5. *"When do you expect to see a purchasing commitment made?"*
6. *"If you are looking at competitive equipment, then what features or benefits most impressed you and how would you see us addressing these areas?"*
7. *"I noticed that the valves are destined for your Alaskan operations. Do you see the sales negotiations remaining here or being transferred to the actual installation site?"*
8. *"What do you see as the most important priority for you or your company in this purchase, Ms. Mead?"*

Relaters would require a different approach because they are less decision-oriented and more people-oriented. Your questions should be more personal and emotional. Again, the eight Quick Qualify questions as they would be posed to a **Relater** prospect, Mr. Frank Friendly, who is exhibiting a kinesthetic communication style.

1. *"Frank, I am so glad that we could get together today. I appreciate you taking the time to share some of your thoughts and feelings on this important matter. I hope you feel that I am not rushing you by getting quickly to the point of my visit, but unfortunately my personal schedule is just jam-packed with interviews today. I hope you don't mind. Before we get started, Frank, is there anyone else, aside from yourself of course, who you feel should be involved in the evaluation and decision concerning our product presentation today?"*

2. *"Frank, according to our conversation earlier on the phone, you felt that you had a concern about the viability of the transfer switches in your Alaskan operations. What sort of problems have you been experiencing?"*

3. *"Frank, what kind of budget range do you feel your department would have available for this type of purchase?"*

4. *"Assuming that you feel everything can be arranged to meet your budget and performance expectations, when would you expect to begin the switch replacement process?"*

5. *"Frank, if the evaluation committee were to accept our products, when would you feel that the purchasing department might issue an acquisition notice?"*

6. *"Frank, you've seen lots of products similar to ours. Can you tell me what you like most about the products that you've seen? Is there something you haven't seen that you feel you would like to see?"*

7. *"Even though these switches are destined for your Alaskan operations, do you feel that there are other sites that might consider a similar switch replacement project?"*

8. *"Frank, in your estimation, what do you feel is the highest priority involved with this project?"*

You can see how the questions are slanted and posed in an entirely different manner than those for the Victor. They are softer, more tentative, more personal. If you developed a battery of four questions for each Quick Qualify category slanted towards each style and Preferential Communications system, imagine how powerful and productive your selling could become.

Two-Minute Countdown

In many of my sales training programs, we seek to get all the essential Quick Qualify information within two minutes from Impulsives and Victors. For Examiners and Relaters, we allow six minutes. Try it. Role play with a friend or fellow salesperson and try to get the essentials within a set time. You'll be amazed at how much can be accomplished in so little time. I've seen six-month selling cycles cut to six minutes, usually because the salesperson expected longer selling cycles. Don't accept current standards. Find out who's going to dance and find out fast.

Fish or Cut Bait

If the prospect meets your criteria for a good potential customer, then continue on in the selling process. Determine all the needs, desires and parameters. Develop and present the solutions. Negotiate a commitment and follow through on service and delivery. Ask for new leads and referrals. Sell additional products and services once a selling relationship has been established. Expand your horizons.

If the prospect does not fit your profile of a potential customer, then cut bait. Fishing is fun when they're biting, but it's a bore when they're not. No fish biting, no dinner to cook. If they aren't going to buy, move on.

I had a sales manager that worked for one of my companies. Rene would train our sales agents to prompt a response by using a simple but effective phrase:

"Sir, a Yes is as good as a No."

This works very well to take the pressure OFF the client. It allows him or her to "approve" the next phase of the sales process or to gracefully bow out and end the sales process. When you don't know where a prospect is positioned in the sale, and you think the prospect is not being serious about the sales, or if you just need to know if the prospect is planning to waste your time by being polite and not "honest" – then try this question.

ALWAYS A SALE

After deciding that a prospect doesn't warrant your selling time right now, consider the other selling possibilities. These possibilities could include a future appointment (right prospect at the wrong time), a referral (wrong prospect at the right time) or developing a relationship that might be useful in later years. Never throw a business card away, but file it for future reference.

In short, if you can't sell your product or service, sell the person on the *idea* of your product or service. Extract something: a lead, a referral, a plant tour or just a handshake. But most of all, sell yourself as a person who is pleasant to be with in the sales environment. And then, move on.

YOUR DOUBLING STRATEGY

Doubling your sales is easy if you can talk to better qualified people. Determine today that you will not leave your sales conversations to chance but will orchestrate your contacts so that you can be with the people and businesses most likely to buy.

Replace statement selling by asking questions, primarily open probes. You'll find out that your prospects become involved and interested and generally sell themselves when you are through. By asking quality questions, you'll get the prospect to reveal or establish personal and corporate expectations. This is critical, as you'll read in later chapters.

DOUBLING

1. Commit yourself to mastering the probe. Make this a 90-day goal, and begin setting aside time for your daily exercises now. Spend 20 minutes per day for the next three months learning the intricacies and architecture of the probe, and then watch your sales career zoom. Build a battery of prospect-related probes to uncover unusual, uncommon and useful information.

Start a Probe Book. I prefer a small spiral-bound lined notebook that I can carry with me in one of my briefcase pockets. When you use a new question or think of one, *write it down*! Your Probe Book will, in time, be one of the most valuable skill development tools that you could ever have. Seek superior information so that you can massage and manipulate it into an outstanding result. Write down what type of information you are seeking and begin to structure probes that can uncover that information. Develop questions that get the prospect involved, generally open or conditional probes. For every category of information you require, develop at least 20 different types of questions that can do the job. Out of your 20, ten will likely be ridiculous or ineffective and ten will likely work. Conditional or leading probes are amazingly versatile in their ability to uncover critical and sometimes sensitive information. Identify these areas, and start building your conditional probe portfolio. Record all your questions in your Probe Book.

2. Fully acquaint yourself with probe architecture. Practice rephrasing your product statements into user-oriented questions by using all three types of probe architecture for each statement. Start building a variety of probes that you can use to draw your prospect into the sale. Probe intensities must also be fully understood before true selling flexibility can be achieved. Focus each probe to reflect the preferential communication systems (visual, auditory, kinesthetic and intellectual).

3. Finally, there's a good reason to watch television. Isolate several good news interview shows weekly, and study how the interviewer extracts information. Try to discover just how the interviewer gets to the information that matters most. Watch particularly for strategies and probes used to gain conversational control. You'll probably notice that an interviewer seldom answers a question with anything other than another question. Study and work hard at converting yourself from statement selling to question selling. Be committed to going beyond the norm.

4. Answer a question with a question if you can. When a customer responds, either build or break the response. Make a conscious effort to listen and interpret what the prospect says to you. If it's not clear, ask another question to clarify. Ask, listen, interpret. Practice one day each week by responding with questions to all the questions asked of you during the day by anyone.

5. Slant all your probes to reflect each style's communication strengths or dislikes. Work hard on this area. Use your Probe Book to record your statements and your questions. This point alone can double your sales quickly.

6. In your sales presentation or interview, determine what specific items are good areas upon which to seek agreement. Develop a series of closed and conditional probes to begin engineering commitment on these areas. What processes are important to the sale and how are these processes handled? Note them in your Probe Book, and then develop at least five conditional probes for each area. Make a determined effort to find out the how, when and why.

7. Look at your current sales presentation. Does it include intimidating or conversation-killing closed probes that could be converted into open probes? Each day, write down all the current dead-end questions you find yourself using and start the conversion process to conditional probes or to open probes.

8. Who are the influencers and decision makers? Again, structure open and conditional probes using the phrase *"aside from yourself"* to

determine and discover where the shortcuts and the decisions actually lie. Develop one new decision-maker question each week.

9. Find out who wants to dance. Decide early and decide quickly if your sales partner is there to dance or just to listen to the music. The art of Quick Qualify doesn't wait for the second song to start playing. Define the essential information elements that distinguish a dancer from a listener. Each week, build at least one new question for each of the essential eight areas and then modify these questions for each of the four style categories and each of the four Preferential Communications systems. Remember, good user-oriented questioning tends to strengthen rapport.

10. The essential eight quick qualify questions should be practiced over and over in all style formats until they are second nature. Do it every day. Never stop reviewing and rebuilding. You'll be sick of them, but you'll know them by heart. Practice until you can Quick Qualify in two minutes for Victors and Impulsives and six minutes for Relaters and Examiners. Practice until you can do it. Watch out for the intimidating effects of speed in your voice and in your movements. Make a decision early either to continue or to move on. Commit to your decision and take action accordingly. Always leave your prospects with the feeling that your meeting has been profitable for them.

Expectational Selling

Expectational Selling

In the Duty section of this book, I refer to *"Doubling"*, frequently. My original manuscript from 1991 was entitled *Doubling, More Than 100 Strategies for Doubling Your Sales – A Guide for the Professional Salesperson*, and many training courses were delivered under this title. The training was very effective and proved that the skills and strategies work and work very well. So the Duty section of *Sellegrity* is called *Doubling*, and it has been updated for this edition (2018).

For years salespeople have been taught to present their products using a *"find the need and fill it"* approach. The need sought was primarily based on function and use; the product presentation was oriented towards explaining the features of a product in terms of their related functions, advantages and benefits. Most sales training today still follows these lines.

Doubling expands this concept. You see, need is a condition brought on by desiring something or lacking something. It is a state of being, a state of desire. This state of need doesn't always exist within a prospect and, even when it does, it is separated from the salesperson by a layer of expectations. Most sales training ignores the expectational layer and attempts to deal directly with the need. *Doubling* does not. It pays particular attention to expectations because I believe that expectations are the pipeline to the need.

Expectations are the actions of mental and physical anticipation associated with events. Actions are much closer to selling than a state of being, for we tend to react to observed actions rather than to inner emotional states. *Doubling* is completely focused on the expectations that a prospect has and develops, and through these expectations the needs can be addressed. For this reason, *Doubling* is, by definition, practical.

A good sale only occurs when most or all of the prospect's expectations have been explored, explained and satisfied. It's no good selling a widget to a person who expects the widget to do more than it can do. It creates a poor sales relationship: the customer will return no more and your widget sales will suffer from a lack of repeat business.

Expectational selling places the responsibility on you to draw out, explain, set and reset the prospect's expectations. Only then can you proceed with presenting the capabilities of your product or service in a fashion that your prospect will appreciate and understand.

Develop the expectations and you'll develop the need.

Satisfy the expectations and you'll satisfy the need.

After all, if you keep track of the prospect's expressed expectations and you meet or exceed those expectations, how can he or she say no? It is the most powerful and permanent method of selling. The result is a sales relationship that will grow far beyond the original purchase.

WHY EXPECTATIONAL SELLING WORKS

When my children were very young, they had, like most children, an undeniable appreciation for ice cream. I could count on this desire for at least one serious confrontation should we happen to be in the local mall where there was a flagrant display of at least 31 "delicious" flavors of ice cream. It's not so much that they thought they wanted ice cream, it's that they convinced themselves that they needed ice cream. In this case, I was trying to get rid of a need, for the need was already firmly established. The cries and pleas would rise towards my awaiting ears, *"Oh, p-l-e a-s-e, Daddy. Just this o-n-c-e???"*

My kids were predictable, like most. Pam liked milk chocolate with sprinkles, and Daniel liked sherbets, especially grape. They *expected* to get their favorites. One time, the scooper made a horrible mistake and managed to get the bulging blob of frozen whatever-it-was directly into the hands of my daughter without first going through the mandatory paternal scrutiny. My daughter wound up with something that was obviously not chocolate, and the look on her face told all. Expectation: chocolate with rainbow sprinkles. Reality: something swirly without *any* sprinkles at all. Would she eat it? Not in your lifetime nor mine, and everyone within earshot soon knew about her disappointment. Kids let you know right away when their expectations are not fully met. If the cone is too short or the ice cream too "melty," if the sprinkles are the wrong kind or if her glob is smaller than his, they let you know.

(Cosmic note: my daughter, Pam, is now a mother of three and they all act exactly like she did – it seems that there is little new under the sun!)

Doubling focuses heavily upon uncovering, exploring, setting, resetting and introducing expectations so that you can meet or exceed them through your product or service completely. The difference between kids and customers is that kids are up front and customers generally are not. Kids do all the interpretation work for you. With customers, however, *you* have to do all the interpretation work. The result is still the same: satisfy or exceed the expectations and you please the customer...or the kid.

All Prospects Have Expectations

Anytime you plan to do anything, you have expectations concerning the upcoming experience. Some of the expectations are visible, some are hiding just under the surface and some are deep and unexplored. But they are always there for everything you do.

The more you repeat an experience, the more familiar you become with its effects upon you and the easier it is to deal with the expectations that arise. For instance, if you should take up flying, as I did, your first few hours will be filled with mixed emotions because the experience is new and different. Your hands are cold and sweaty, your heart rate soars, and if it weren't for the comforting presence of the flight instructor, you'd probably slip into mild panic or hysteria. It is a combination of elation and terror brought on by the unknown. Years later, after having logged many thousands of hours in the air, the same activity is controllable, non-threatening and easy on the nerves. You've been there before.

This scene tells a story about expectations. Our emotions, our reactions and our perceptions are all influenced by the familiarity of the experience. Repeat the experience and our expectations alter.

We all have expectations: expressed, unexpressed and undeveloped. You have them as a salesperson and all of your prospects and clients have them. The more familiar we become with a particular situation, the better we become at understanding it, anticipating it and controlling it.

Professional buyers and purchasing agents know a lot more about selling than you do, primarily because they see it from many different angles all day long. They have expectations concerning how you will behave and react and how they will react. Their reactions tend to be factual and businesslike.

If your product or service is new and not presently used by your prospect or the prospect's industry, you and your prospect must address many unexplored and undeveloped purchasing expectations.

If, on the other hand, your prospect is familiar with your type of product or service and has made similar purchasing decisions before, then the expectations tend to be fixed, usually on price, and few surprises await either the purchaser or the salesperson.

Generally, someone who is not used to purchasing your product may become emotional about the purchasing process. Examples are a couple buying their first home or a business investing in its first computer system. In cases where the prospect is new to your product, you must take care to explain what is happening and to explore the prospect's future with your product. You must work hard at uncovering, explaining and setting expectations before the sale can be completed.

The effect of having a prospect purchase before his or her expectations are fully satisfied or explored is called **buyer's remorse.** We've all had that feeling of, *"Oh no, what have I done???"* It happens when you step into uncharted territory, making uncommon decisions in unfamiliar surroundings. Buyer's remorse is nothing more than unfulfilled expectations kicking at your stomach because they were neglected during the sale. Pay attention to the hidden expectations and buyer's remorse will be greatly reduced or eliminated. Generally, the bigger the price tag, the more severe the remorse.

Decision-Making Experience

Some people are professional decision makers, others dabble in making decisions and some avoid decisions altogether. The effect of a prospect's decision-making capabilities upon a sale can be quite startling. People always have a comfort zone surrounding their decision-making abilities.

Understand that purchasers have two primary sensitivities to decision making: personal and corporate.

I know corporate buyers and executives who routinely make million dollar decisions but have difficulty with personal decisions of a couple hundred dollars.

If your prospect is a junior accounting clerk trying to make his or her first corporate buying decision on a new computer software program, then you can bet there are unforeseen expectations lurking around somewhere. If the prospect is the head of the Management Information Services Department, then the route has been well traveled before. Decision-making experience and the dollar values associated with the decision-making experience greatly influence the way that you should approach and present your product and service.

For instance, if your prospect makes $100 decisions routinely but makes $1,000 decisions rarely, then you can expect some decision resistance if you are selling at the $1,000 level or above. Almost without exception, managers enjoy purchasing restrictions ($500 personal limit, $1,000 departmental signing authority, etc.) and if you exceed these authority amounts, a new approval procedure must come into play. Generally, the decision is transferred to a higher management level or it goes to a committee for approval.

Your expectations concerning the ability of your prospect to make decisions concerning your type of product and the price of your product will influence your selling procedure. If your customer understands your product and makes similar decisions routinely, then you are looking for an average selling process or even a shortened selling process. If they are uncomfortable with your product or your price, you must explore and educate before you attempt to close.

Style Types

The effect of personality style upon expectations is considerable. For instance, direct decision making is much more prevalent among the forceful-action Victors and Impulsives, and indirect decision making is almost always the domain of the tentative-action Relaters and Examiners.

Relaters and Impulsives, with their social demeanors, have expectations that are more feeling-oriented than fact-oriented. They will be more concerned with their personal involvement and personal use of a product or service than they will be about the corporate or financial impacts. Victors and Examiners deal only with the facts.

The differences between business and social demeanor can be seen when a typical couple is buying a house: the husband (a Victor) checks for structural soundness, electrical service, plumbing, insulation ratings and other practical things. The wife (a Relater) is concerned with the colors, the brightness, the cleanliness, the smell and the comfort. Both people are interested in the same house, just from different perspectives. Different perspectives yield different expectations. The smart real estate agent recognizes and addresses both sets of expectations.

Because the different styles will look at your product and presentation from different perspectives, it is a good idea to prepare your presentation to address directly your prospects' individual expectational slants. Always match preferential communication systems to ease tension and encourage understanding.

The Relater
If asked, Relaters usually express expectations openly and in human terms. The Relater may wish to hear and see the emotional side of your product or service and will want to understand how it might affect others. The price can be rationalized if the proper human effect can be achieved. Be careful to ensure that the budget is fully explored but not overemphasized. Expectations concerning direct decision making must be handled diplomatically.

The Impulsive
Impulsives like to be included personally and to get fully involved with their purchases. Their expectations tend to be self-centered and they will generally rationalize *any* decision as long as the personal benefit is strong enough. Be careful to address the more practical parts of the sale (budget, authority, etc.) thoroughly but light-heartedly. Impulsives are prone to buyer's remorse because of a tendency to make rushed decisions. Expectations are clearly personal.

The Examiner
Examiners have their expectations surrounded by logic and reasoning. If the purchase is corporate, there will be no personal involvement. If the purchase is personal, there will be no corporate involvement. It's black and white to them. Address each expectation in a logical, sequential manner without hoopla or fanfare. The decision will be made more quickly if all the points are covered and supporting data supplied for scrutiny. Do not press for decisions, for they come after the evaluation process. If you have the best value and provide the most complete, logic-ally organized information, you win. Someone exhibiting strong Examiner behavior will not be unduly influenced by opinions or feelings, so stick to the facts.

The Victor
Direct and factual, controlling and businesslike, Victors immediately expect distilled information and the best value. Then they'll work to improve the value, usually by getting you to lower your price. Expectations are corporate but with a touch of ego-centered personal feelings as well. Cover the important bases because Victors tend to have *absolute* expectations instead of flexible expectations. Remember, opinions and feelings are not important; facts and results are. Do your homework!

EXPRESSED EXPECTATIONS

When your prospect expresses a purchasing parameter or a personal opinion, weigh it against his or her exhibited style before acting upon the information. Facts and feelings expressed as product expectations are valuable because they give you insight into the prospect's value appreciation. If an opinion is expressed by an Examiner or Victor, it probably has limited meaning to the sale. But if an opinion is expressed by a Relater or Impulsive, it has greater meaning to the sale.

Opinions can also indicate misleading or incorrect information, hearsay, or rumor. It is important that you recognize whether a prospect is expressing correct or nearly correct expectations concerning your product in your initial meetings. If the prospect is expressing a position that is wrong or is considerably misleading, then you must take steps to reset the prospect's expectations by providing correct information or proof.

Listen for your prospect's verbal clues:

> *"I was really expecting a more competitive price."*
>
> *"It seems to me that it should be a little faster than this."*
>
> *"It would be really nice if we could get it by Friday."*
>
> *"I'd feel more comfortable in blue or green."*
>
> *"We weren't expecting to move on this until spring."*
>
> *"We have too many different types now."*

"If the figures seem OK, then we can move on."

"I want it on the floor by noon and no later!"

"I've seen the competition and it really impressed me."

The prospect is always giving clues to his or her personal and corporate expectations. Ask, listen, interpret. Clarify the expectation and rephrase it into terminology that you both clearly understand. Verify that the expectation is valid and find out whether it is a rigid or flexible expectation.

UNEXPRESSED EXPECTATIONS

Prospects hide things from salespeople, especially if they have some hidden agenda or purpose. Once, many years ago, I had a small manufacturing firm and I needed a photocopier. I could not afford one, but I decided I'd have a look at the bottom-of-the-line "personal" copier.

I made my call to the local copier equipment company and within a day there was a personal copier on my desk to try for a few days. I thought this was great, but after using it for a number of copies I felt that it was a bit slow. The salesperson returned and inquired how the new machine was working. I promptly revealed my concern. Ten minutes later, a bigger personal copier was on my desk, and it stayed for a week.

An expectation that had not occurred to me previously suddenly made itself apparent: all I had to do was to keep raising the expectations and a bigger unit would be sent on trial.

I had now developed a hidden expectation. I would state my new performance requirements, not to see if the equipment would meet them, but to see how long I could keep the copier on a "try it, you'll like it" basis. I could not afford even the smallest of copiers at the time but no one ever asked me if I could afford to buy it. They just kept bringing more copiers.

I was elated, but at the same time I knew that eventually I would have to end the charade and either stop my compulsive copying or buy a unit. Eventually I did buy a rather sophisticated machine that was far advanced from the initial desktop unit, but not until I had been through eight or nine copier distributors' entire lines. The bigger the machines, the more copies they expected me to make. So I did. Half of the salespeople even supplied me with paper! I didn't want to disappoint them and they didn't want to disappoint me.

I had a hidden expectation that wasted a lot of salespeople's time. But no one ever *asked.*

To this day, I feel somewhat ashamed about this ploy: it was not very ethical, and I sincerely apologize to the copier salesmen that were involved. I guess they should have probed more effectively.

Prospects will rarely expose their hidden ploys or expectations; you must observe and act when appropriate. The salesperson who finally sold me a copier was the one who caught on and did something constructive about the situation. He realized what was going on, brought it to my attention (called my bluff), and together we designed a plan so that he could win and I could win. It took guts and good selling to do it.

If you suspect a hidden motive, you have a choice of either confronting it, ignoring it or playing into it. By confronting it, you risk expulsion or you may, like the salesperson above, work out a solution so that both win. By ignoring it, you will be played and discarded as the prospect sees fit. By playing into it, you can give and take as you see fit and, at the appropriate time, you can confront the prospect.

UNDEVELOPED EXPECTATIONS

An unusual situation occurred when we introduced our security marking "paint" into Canada. The paint carried rare-earth trace metals that formed a chemical identification code and could be designed and assigned to each customer on a unique basis. It was daubed on computers, tools, equipment, raw materials and even on documents to declare permanent ownership.

The whole focus was to deter theft because you couldn't remove the chemical identification no matter how hard you tried. It worked. But my prospects, who were generally plant managers or security directors, had never seen or heard of such a product, nor were they familiar with its effects upon theft. They had undeveloped expectations.

I spent most of my time explaining how firms could expect lower equipment and tool loss rates and increased productivity, even though it seemed pretty self-explanatory. The expectations were there, but they were empty. I had to fill them up with something useful, something of value, something corporate, something safe, something understandable.

If you know or suspect that the product or service that you represent carries with it a degree of the unknown, then you must take the time to explore and explain so that you can firmly set expectations. Do not be afraid to *implant* expectations.

> *"Ed, as you can see by the survey results among our current users of* ***KT70*** *products, you should expect to save between* ***30*** *and 35% on your tool expenditures next year and each year following."*

Personal Expectations

Prospects have personal expectations that should be addressed during the sale. Style types have an influence on how much effort and what type of effort should be put into satisfying these expectations.

Generally, personal expectations tend to vary with the product or service being purchased. Obviously, there is less personal involvement in a corporate sale but again, depending upon the type of product or service, a significant degree of personal use might be involved. For instance, selling grease and oil to a trucking firm has little personal appeal, but selling a new computer system or software package to a small business might have an enormous personal impact. Selling a new roof to a homeowner has limited personal involvement, but selling a new bedroom suite is totally different.

Personal expectations vary with the product and the person. If you suspect that your product carries with it a strong opportunity for personal use or involvement, then you must explore the prospect's anxieties, feelings, opinions and potentials on a personal-use basis.

> *"Jenny, I'm sure that you feel confident using the system as it is now, but what sort of things do you feel you might need help with during the next few weeks as you're learning and integrating the new graphics program?"*

Personal expectations tend to be associated with personal-use products. Do not neglect these expectations. Draw them out and get your prospect to physically, mentally and emotionally explore the use of your product.

Corporate Expectations

All corporations have expectations that surround even the smallest of purchases. In general, these expectations fall into the following categories:

- Safe buying habits;
- Financial parameters;
- Performance specifications;
- Decision-making process;
- Timing;
- Delivery and installation;
- Training;
- Support and maintenance;
- Competition;
- Benefits;
- Emotional Expectations;
- Relationship Expectations.

Safe Buying Habits

Prospects who are required to purchase on behalf of a company have specific expectations that are important to the corporation *and* to themselves. For instance, if your prospect were a purchasing agent who made improper or poor buying decisions, then his or her job would be in jeopardy. This is important to understand. The professional buyer will make safe decisions.

If your product or service is either side of the norm, then expect that your prospect will have a great deal of difficulty deciding whether to risk a decision to purchase your product. Also, if a competitive product exists that is recognized as being a safe buy, then you will have to work against the prospect's existing comfort zone.

Generally, company buyers tend to play not to lose. Few people risk their careers over poor buying decisions. If you represent a product or service that is nationally recognized as being a safe buy, then this is a strong corporate selling point and should be emphasized through drawing out the purchaser's expectations concerning buying safety.

> *"Mr. Crocker, we both can see that it's important the decisions your company makes be sound, and it's comforting to know that our products are recognized world-wide for their outstanding quality. As they say, no one ever got raked over the coals for buying IBN. What do you see as your firm's position on buying quality, Rod?"*

Financial Expectations

All prospects, be they corporate or personal, have financial expectations. These can be expressed through examining a budget range, an expected purchase price, a monthly payment, a yearly amortization figure, a long-term return on investment, an interest rate and any other form of financial involvement. Financial expectations are closely tied to value relationships. Value is the relationship between goods or services received for money rendered. The better the value, the better chance you have at getting a sale.

You must find out the prospect's value expectations and then work with what you've received. If you know that you can deliver a higher value than expected, your sale will be easier. If you know your prospect seeks a better value than you can offer, your selling task will be more difficult.

Keep your eyes and ears open for clues that tell you if your prospect can handle the financial terms that you express. For instance, if a couple is looking at buying a house that has a price tag of $500,000 and they appear to be intimidated by this figure, convert it into something more palatable, such as monthly mortgage payments. This way, the value can be enhanced because the prospects feel they get so much for so little.

When exploring financial expectations, seek a budget range from your prospects, not an absolute figure. This is extremely important because it establishes an expectation of *pricing flexibility*.

> *"Mr. Harris, what sort of budget range, low to high, do you see for your new car?"*
>
> *"Are these low and high figures fixed, or can you see some flexibility if we find an exceptional value?"*

Keeping in mind that value is essentially goods received for money paid, if you do not explore the financial parameters and expectations with your prospect, at least one-half of the value relationship remains unexplored.

PERFORMANCE EXPECTATIONS

Product performance and product features make up the other half of the basic value relationship. It is what you *get* for what you spend. In terms of technical and mechanical product or service sales, performance is a high priority, perhaps the highest priority in the expectational mix.

For every key element in the performance areas of your product or service, you must develop probes to draw out the prospect's expectations. These areas could include product features, functions and advantages.

> *"Mr. Robson, how often would you expect your fleet to require new tires?"*

> *"Lois, how many people would you see using our training facilities during the next six months?"*

> *"David, how many branch locations do you feel require the new computers?"*

It's up to you to explore every area of performance and every positive feature or advantage should the prospect expect or warrant it. Obviously, if the prospect is fully conversant and familiar with your product or service, it is not necessary to explore these areas in detail unless it is critical to establish your product as being in the running with other products. In this case, you must explore areas that make your product stand apart from the competition and add to its overall value.

Decision-Making Expectations

Decisions can be made in one of three ways: (1) personally by the prospect or by a purchasing committee, (2) through an evaluative or bidding process, or (3) through avoiding a "no" decision (by default it becomes "yes").

Your job is to determine how the decision is made, who makes it and when it will be made.

Most Victors and Impulsives make their own decisions. Just to be sure, ask the simple but effective question:

> *"Aside from yourself, who else do you see being involved in making the decision, and how?"*

For Examiners, decisions are almost invariably made through process or by committee. The system dictates what gets purchased and how. Ask Examiners these questions:

> *"Mr. Davis, could you please show me the process by which products such as this are evaluated and purchased by your organization?"*

"Sir, how would you recommend I proceed to the next stage in having these products evaluated for use in your company?"

Your job is to find out how the decision is made, and who or what is involved in the process.

TIMING EXPECTATIONS

When is the prospect expecting to use or install your product? Many times this can be the primary motivator for the sale. Let's say you are driving to an important meeting and suddenly you notice that your car's temperature gauge needle has moved into the red and steam is beginning to escape from beneath your hood. You must pull over within a matter of seconds if you are to avoid permanent damage to your engine.

Inspection reveals a split radiator hose and just down the street you spot four gas stations opposite one another at the corners of an intersection. Nursing your car to the first station, you inquire about immediate repairs. They say you'll have to leave the car overnight. Station number two reports the same. Station number three indicates they could do the repairs and have you on your way in a couple of hours. Station number four says they'll have it fixed within 20 minutes. The prices are about the same, give or take a few dollars. Who do you choose? Obviously the one that most closely matches your timing expectations: station number four. Your prospect might have a similar urgency. Explore this with a probe:

"How soon would you like to see the pool installed, Mrs. Meredith?"

"I am assuming by your responses that there is an urgency to your purchase, Mr. Lee. Exactly how soon do you need the pumps installed at the plant site?"

Even in personal sales, timing can be a great motivator, especially if you see a significant emotional attachment to the product:

"Tom and Sandy, I know that you are going to feel really happy with your new Invader 7, and I have a little surprise for you. Normally, you know, it takes about three days to process and prepare your new car for delivery, but I can make special arrangements, if you feel like, to have it ready for this afternoon at four.

If we can settle on the color, you can drive it home tonight. What do you think, folks, which color do you think you'd feel more comfortable with, the green, gold or the shocking pink?"

Delivery and Installation Expectations

Delivery and installation are closely related to timing, but if they can offer an advantage over the competition then you should build an expectation around them. For instance, if you were selling carpet and you offered free installation and free delivery, develop probes to explore the prospect's expectations concerning these areas:

"Mrs. Willets, I'm sure that you can see that it takes a considerable amount of time and expertise to install wall-to-wall carpeting, and I'm sure you were expecting to pay the going rate of $4.00 a square yard for installation. However, I am going to see if I can include professional delivery and installation at no extra charge. How does that look to you?"

Of course the prospect is going to say it's all right. Now, if she goes to a competitor, they will have to meet or exceed the expectation firmly set by you. For corporate clients, meeting delivery and installation expectations are often a part of the purchasing agreement. Draw this expectation out and have it fully visible to both yourself and the prospect.

"Jill, what do you see as your requirements for delivery and installation if we were to proceed with the purchase?"

Training Expectations

With technical and mechanical products especially, there is a good chance that some training may be required to bring operators or users up to speed quickly. Training shortens the period required to get to payback for most purchases, and the sooner operators can learn how to make new equipment profitable, the better it is for you and the client. Set expectations by exploring them through probes.

> *"Mr. Vopni, most of our clients are elated about our product because we see to it that the operator is completely trained even before we install the new systems.*
>
> *I don't know if you have fully looked at the training aspect of your purchase, but now might be a good time. What do you see as your expectations concerning operator training?"*

Explore not only how much training is expected, but what type, for how many, where and when it should take place, any extraordinary skills or parameters involved, what the budget range is for training, training for subsequent users, internal training versus external training, etc.

Support and Maintenance Expectations

It is typical for a First Dimension Seller to conclude the sale as soon as the prospect has agreed to the product or service. Second and Third Dimension Sellers look for the long-term relationship with the client and realize that support and maintenance are as much a part of the sale as the main product is. Support and maintenance expectations exist in many prospects, and, depending upon the industry, these can be either fully developed or totally embryonic. In either case, an opportunity exists for a more complete and solid sale.

> *"Mr. Goldberg, what are your feelings concerning maintenance and parts service for the upcoming year?"*
>
> *"Sarah, as you know, most people feel that service is a big part of the computer package these days and I'd like to get a reading as to how you perceive the service function working throughout your company's operations."*

Competitive Expectations

Competitive expectations are one of my favorite areas because they reveal how serious prospects are about buying and what motivates them in terms of product features and functions.

Always assume that your prospects are evaluating a number of alternative products or services. If they haven't already, you can bet they will before they buy, especially if they are corporate buyers. Unless you are on a preferred suppliers list, they must look for the most competitive prices. This regulation can sometimes be carried to absurd extremes. To illustrate a weird twist to the requirement for competitive pricing, the following little story might serve as a reminder to always ask about competitive pricing policies.

When we were selling the chemical security marking products to Ford Motor Company in Detroit, there were no other suppliers of the product anywhere. After months of trial and testing, Ford decided to purchase our product for one of its computer facilities in Dearborn. Months went by but no purchase order materialized. After much poking and prodding, we found out that Ford's purchasing policy stated that there had to be a minimum of two suppliers before any product would be entered onto the purchasing system. Since we were the product's sole manufacturer, there simply were no other suppliers. In effect, we were causing our own delay. *We* had to create another firm to act as the secondary supplier before the system could complete the purchase. Always ask.

> *"Mr. Watson, I'm sure that you have seen other products such as this. Could you please describe to me what features or functions that you liked in the other products you've seen and perhaps what you would like to see that you haven't already seen?*
>
> *"John, you are probably aware that our firm is the exclusive supplier for this product and there are no other available sources. How do you see this affecting the purchasing procedures?"*

Find out about pricing, delivery, installation, value, training, timing and all the other corporate and personal expectations that already exist concerning your competition. This gives you a realistic view of where you stand in relation to your competition as expressed by your prospect.

BENEFIT EXPECTATIONS

What is in it for the customers? What are your customers' expected personal and corporate benefits? If you can find out how they expect to benefit and then sell directly to those benefits, your selling will be a breeze. Go after both personal and corporate benefits:

> *"Mrs. Anthony, what do you personally see in purchasing a new sound system? What benefits are there for you?"*
>
> *"Cindy, could you please tell me what benefits and advantages your firm expects by going to a full-service contract?"*

EMOTIONAL EXPECTATIONS

Emotional expectations come in the form of feelings and opinions. They are most commonly found in Impulsives and Relaters. To these style types, emotional expectations are as real and as important as factual expectations are to Victors and Examiners. Draw out the emotional expectations with probes that address the personal issues:

> *"Mary, how do you feel about this project and its impact upon the resources of the North?"*
>
> *"Pat, what opinions might you have concerning the new management format?"*
>
> *"Judie, how do you personally feel about these colors?"*

RELATIONSHIP EXPECTATIONS

Most commercial and corporate prospects will be establishing a long-term sales relationship with you and your company if they buy. Find out about their expectations concerning the corporate relationship:

> *"Mr. Keys, if your firm were to go ahead with this contract, how do you see our companies dealing with one another in the future?"*

> *"Jill, you know that if we conclude this deal, it sounds like we'll be working closely together during the next few weeks. Is there any way you would like to expedite our meetings so that we can get the system in place and running as quickly and as smoothly as possible?"*

Relationships can grow naturally or you can design them. In most cases, it is better if you can control the relationship in an unobtrusive way. You spend the extra effort and time.

EXPECTATIONAL PRIORITIES

The old selling books called them "dominant buying motives." I call them expectational priorities. Of the many expectations surrounding a purchase, some have higher degrees of importance than others. If you can locate the ones with a high degree of importance and concentrate on satisfying these, then the sale will stand a greater chance of completion success.

How do you find out? First, listen and observe the intensity levels and the details that surround your prospect's responses to your expectational probing. The responses that have added color, emotion or factual detail are generally the more important replies. Also, if the prospect expresses an expectation without being asked, then it is a good bet that it is a high priority item.

> *"Harry, we've discussed a lot of personal and corporate objectives this morning. I'd like to see if we could take a minute and summarize these objectives and expectations so that we both clearly view the purchasing and operational priorities. Which would you see as the most significant of your priorities, Harry?"*

Unrealistic Expectations

Sometimes people get in their minds that your product or competitive products can do things they can't or that they can't do things they can. These are called unrealistic expectations. They are dangerous and can lead to misunderstandings and emotionally destructive feelings. No one likes that.

If you suspect that your client has unrealistic expectations concerning your product, then address the problem with examples and proof to overcome the existing expectation. You have to replace the expectation with a better, firmer, more solid one.

If you suspect that your client has misinformation concerning a competitive product (usually an inflated expectation), then you must tread more carefully. The old adage in sales that says, "Never knock the competition," still holds true in an ethical sense. However, if you have proof that the prospect's expectations are inflated due to false claims, you may suggest that your prospect contact a third party to obtain the correct information.

If you have watchdog agencies within the industry to which you can direct your prospect, then gently and politely guide your prospect to these sources. You may use newspaper or magazine articles that factually explore both sides of the story, if available. But do not, under any circumstances, directly or personally attack your competition.

> *"Mr. Wesley, I've been in this business for many years and I've seen all the products on the market and I've seen their capabilities. I only want to see that you make an appropriate decision for your firm. Please, take this as a constructive remark.*
>
> *I believe you have been shown incorrect or misleading information. At this point, I would not wish to continue until you have fully satisfied yourself with correct information and therefore I am recommending that you contact Mr. Bill Bolton at the Industrial Watchdog Society.*

He will show you unbiased, correct information concerning this matter. I would give you proof myself, but I would rather see you obtain it from an independent source."

UNCOVER, INTRODUCE, AGREE AND ACCEPT

The basic technique for setting expectations is to uncover expectations, introduce new product-specific expectations, have your prospect agree that the expectations are valid and useful, and then have the prospect accept the expectations as part of the selling mix.

In most cases, you will use a set-up statement with a closed probe to obtain both agreement and acceptance.

> *"Mr. Cunningham, you felt a few minutes ago that you would be satisfied with a **10%** return on your investment on an annual basis."*
>
> *"So if we could find a program that would include at least a **10%** return rate, would you feel comfortable pursuing the details?"*

SATISFYING THE KEY EXPECTATIONS

Your primary goal in any selling situation is to satisfy or exceed the key purchasing expectations.

In many selling courses, this is referred to as seeking the buying motives and then selling to these motives. I always found this a difficult thing to do, because I never could quite determine what the real motives might be. If I could, great. But when it comes down to it, who really cares why the guy wants to buy a funeral plot for his three cats? As long as he states his expectations and you can meet or exceed them, then the sale is ultimately concluded.

Motives are only truly revealed when a closeness is established, and this is a rarity in selling today. However, expectations come from motives. They are the outward expressions of inner motives, just as movements, inflection, vocal strength and pace are the outward expressions of personality style. What you feel or need is what you show. Your prospect's expectations *are* his or her motives, for all intents and purposes.

By isolating the key 20% of expectations as top priority and then putting all your efforts into exceeding these, you can expect to close roughly 80% of all your sales if you can meet or exceed these key expectations.

The reason I suggest that you focus on these key areas is that it is virtually impossible to meet or exceed all the prospect's expectations. In cases where you can get a higher rate, by all means do so. But what you must avoid is dwelling on an expectation that you cannot meet or reset, especially if it is minor or insignificant. If at all possible, you must turn any expectational disappointment into a positive opportunity for your prospect.

The Power of the Quote

To attack someone usually results in an immediate reaction: fight or flight. However, there are times when you must confront and change a person's way of thinking. This is where the power of the quote comes in.

Let's say you have a client who just refuses to listen to good sense. Instead of attacking him, you use a quote to illustrate the situation.

> *"Peter, you know just the other day I had to deal with a circumstance where my client just didn't quite understand the long-term benefits of providing his staff with free chocolate milk. I had to say to her, `Cindy, it's been absolutely proven that production rises by over 5% when your staff has free chocolate milk, while your added cost remains insignificant.' This is what I had to say. And you know...she finally caught on."*

The use of quotations in conversation is excellent in that it isolates your message from directly involving the prospect. It explains things in a method that is gentler, kinder and more effective than if you had demanded that the prospect take the action personally.

RESETTING CURRENT EXPECTATIONS

When you encounter or uncover expectations that you know you cannot meet, you have several choices:

> **Ignore** it and hope that it is a low-priority or unessential expectation that will not unduly affect the perceived value.
>
> **Restate** it as a lower priority. It might be expressed as a high-priority expectation (price is often like this), but it can be reduced to a lower status by several methods. The key strategy is to remove it from being a contentious or decision-killing item. It remains as the same expectation, but it is seen in a different light.
>
> **Reset** the expectation if it is to remain a high-priority item. It usually takes some quick thinking or a lot of preparatory work to get around a sticky expectation or purchasing parameter. Resetting means getting the prospect to agree to a different expectation than originally expressed.

The key ingredient in expectational selling is to be able not only to meet but to exceed the key 20%. If you are unsuccessful in lining up the key 20% in your product's favor, then the sale will likely not occur.

INTRODUCING NEW EXPECTATIONS

When you have reached a point where you feel the prospect has revealed most of the critical expectations and has agreed to them or has accepted them during your sales interview, then comes the time for adding new expectations that specifically address your product's strong points (features, functions, advantages, benefits, etc.). By introducing these new expectations (and meeting them), your product's value relationship increases.

> *"Mr. Wiley, I believe we have a pretty good picture of what your company requires in terms of a reverse-flushing siphon system. There is one other area that is uncommon in the siphon industry, however, that we haven't discussed.*

*That is the recent and somewhat revolutionary inclusion of an automatic fume sensor, which has proven to cut siphon downtime by over **50** hours per year per valve.*

This type of maintenance saving is of significant interest to most commercial users, especially users in your industry.

Let's have a quick look at how many siphon installations your plant currently has, Ian, and what potential savings the new siphons might provide if all the old units were replaced."

The item referred to above is either a special feature of this salesperson's product or it is unique to a new class of products. In any event, the salesperson is introducing the advantage after all other specifications and expectations have been exposed. In this manner, the fume sensor becomes an integral part of the expectational portfolio and the competition must either have the same system, have a better system or be prepared to talk the prospect out of his newly developed expectation.

INTRODUCING KEY SPEC EXPECTATIONS

I once helped a businessman try to market one of his new inventions. It was a personal emergency strobe light designed for boaters and hunters that could send a visual signal for up to 20 miles. One restriction: the product had to have Coast Guard approval if it was to be sold as a safety device in marinas and sporting goods stores or to the Navy. To get this approval, it had to pass a series of tests according to it's MIL SPEC. It exceeded every test but one: it didn't have a 4.9 volt battery!

The only competition for the product was an existing light developed prior to World War II for the U.S. Navy in case a sailor was thrown overboard. The now-wet sailor could switch on his emergency flashing light and rescue boats could then spot him in the water at night. The only problem was that the darn thing wasn't much brighter than an ordinary flashlight and if it became physically detached from the man it would sink like a stone. This new light would float, gave off a powerful blue-white strobe that could be seen for many miles even in daylight, automatically activated itself when it became wet and ran on regular "C" size batteries which were available everywhere in the civilized world. So why wasn't it accepted? Because it didn't have a 4.9 volt battery.

You see, when the first light, the competition, was originally accepted, the manufacturer was clever enough to devise, propose and have accepted a "key spec". A key spec is something that only your product has and it is written into the purchasing specifications of the customer firm, in this case, the U.S. government.

Although the new light could run circles around the old one, cost half as much and did ten times as much, it didn't have a 4.9 volt battery, which was called for in the original, unchanged purchasing specifications – the MIL SPEC. In fact, the only thing that ever did have a 4.9 volt battery was the old, existing light. The battery was made to specifications by a major battery firm and sold only to the manufacturer of the original light. Dirty pool? Yes. Smart selling? Yes. To this day, as far as I know, the inventor's light has found only a smidgen of success, mainly because it doesn't have a 4.9 volt battery.

If you really want to make it hard on the next salesperson coming through the door, get involved in writing the purchasing specifications for your products. This opportunity does not often occur, but when or if it does, *get involved.* If you can isolate some key operational element that your product or service offers but the competition does not, then develop, set and get agreement on your key spec features. Then get these features included as key specs in the customer's purchasing specifications.

We set the key specs for our security marking products with a number of major multinational companies. They should be using that darn paint for decades to come simply because the specs are so unusual and un-releasable. In a twist on the key spec strategy, when finalizing the sale of the security marking paints, we agreed to release the chemical codes to the firms only if they would specify the particular code number and only if they would keep the chemical code specifics totally confidential. This meant that only we would get to see the bid request. Talk about a difficult competitive situation for the next security paint salesperson! Not only is the salesperson up against a hidden key spec, but he or she isn't even allowed to see the spec!

ADDED VALUE EXPECTATIONS

Added value means enhancing the existing value. It may be a tangible enhancement, such as "two burgers for the price of one," or it may be a *perceived* enhancement for added value, such as "get a chance to win a free trip to Cut Bank, Montana." The main strategy to increase the value relationship is to

> Establish an acceptable, normal expectational portfolio for the sale and have your customer agree to it and accept it as good value;
>
> Enhance the portfolio by adding extra features or subtracting expense (cutting the accepted price).

Added value truly cements your prospect's commitment to the purchase and helps to rationalize any doubt or unsatisfied minor expectations. But don't use it unless you have to and don't use it except at the appropriate time. Use it to enhance accepted value. Before you can enhance accepted value, you must have accepted value. Generally, I save added value for the product presentation stages or the proposal stages where it will have more impact. If you introduce it too early, as many First Dimension Sellers do, then it gets lost in the rest of the selling mix and doesn't have nearly as much impact as it would if you held it for a special inclusion once the acceptable value had been established.

SELLING TO EXPECTATIONS

After you have uncovered and explored the prospect's purchasing expectations, it is time to organize and present your product to meet or exceed these expectations. Most of your product influencing is done through the sales presentation or proposal (covered in depth in the next chapter), so let it be said that the only effective presentation method relies upon satisfying the agreed upon objectives and expectations. These can be a combination of the prospect's original expectations and your added value expectations, which are introduced after the primary value relationship is established. Key spec's may or may not be an integral part of the original expectational mix. The method used to sell to expectations is fairly simple:

Set the expectations through probing and uncovering the needs of the customer;

Isolate and agree upon the key 20% of the customer's expectations;

Formulate a solution that exceeds the key 20% and meets as many of the remaining customer expectations as possible;

Determine what features, functions, advantages and benefits could be considered added value;

Make your presentation based upon exceeding the key 20%, satisfying the remaining 80% and adding the added value expectations at the end to increase the overall value perception.

Most Objections Come from Expectations

A lot of trouble comes from not understanding customer concerns and objections. As customers, we feel uneasy about purchasing something when we haven't dealt with all of our expectations, voiced or unvoiced. If whatever we intend to purchase falls short of what we expect, an uneasiness is triggered in us that results in an objection to the salesperson.

Notice the heading to this section says *most* objections, because there are some concerns and objections that don't come from unmet expectations. Some come from a prospect's inability to make a decision, some come from prejudices and some come from political areas, but most come from unsatisfied personal or corporate expectations.

Some objections are valid, but most are not. Second and Third Dimension Sellers tend to treat all objections as invalid until proven to the contrary.

Objections are strange things, seldom meaning what is spoken. But this is the nature of actions that stem from uneasiness about a product or service purchase. It's like when you get the flu: sometimes it lets you know you've got it by a sore throat, other times by aching muscles, yet other times nausea and a bad case of the trots. However it shows up, it is still the same thing: a virus. The effects are different but the cause is the same.

Thus it is with objections. The cause is the same: unsatisfied expectations. However, the effects are different. Excuses such as "like to look around," "have to talk to my wife," "got to get another quote," "have to investigate the budget guidelines," abound from customers feeling uneasy about you, your product or a host of other things. All these excuses are the result of the same cause: an uneasiness brought on by unsatisfied or undeveloped expectations.

Remove the cause (unsatisfied or undeveloped expectations) and you will remove the effect (objections).

In other words, if you spend your time carefully covering all the primary expectations of your prospect, the objections normally encountered with your product or service should virtually disappear.

You may still be left with several other concerns to deal with, and that is where a process called forestalling is handy.

Forestalling and Eliminating Objections

I don't deal a lot with objections in this book. During the last ten years in which I have been personally using expectational selling techniques, I have found that objections seem to fade away and are no longer an issue. In fact, it is my personal observation that most Second and Third Dimension Sellers have little trouble with handling objections simply because they don't get them that often.

One reason is that they practice the strategy of forestalling. This simply means that if you know of a potential negative or an area of concern that your prospect might use as a personal defense or objection, then expose it and eliminate it as a potential problem early.

> *"Mr. Juriet, many people are under the impression that a house brand product is inferior to the brand name competition. In some cases, this is absolutely true. However, in this case, the reverse is true: the house brand is actually superior in construction, application and durability to all of the brand names. Here, let me show you this consumer's report."*

The idea is to remove the detonators now so that if the "objection bombs" are dropped later, they won't explode and blow up the sale. Work with your prospects, helping them to understand your products.

The simple and easy to use formula for forestalling:

> ***State*** the objection *before* the prospect brings it up;
>
> ***Bridge*** from the objection to the solution using *"but"* or *"however"*;
>
> ***Restate*** the objection in positive terms, offering the beneficial advantages by looking at the problem from a different perspective or by offering documentation or providing a demonstration to offset the objection.

YOUR DOUBLING STRATEGY

Your strategy is clear: *to uncover, explore, explain* and *set* as many expectations as you can. If you control the expectations you control the sale. Every expectation that lies hidden or unexpressed is a potential objection, concern or trap. Dig them out and then sell them back.

Satisfy the expectations and you satisfy the prospect.

By exploring, explaining, including and resetting expectations you have set the stage for a powerful selling show. The prospect has virtually told you exactly what to do to satisfy his or her needs. All you need to do now is to follow through.

DOUBLING

1. The basic technique for dealing with all expectations is to *uncover, introduce, agree* and *accept.* Do this for every expectational area important to your sale. Practice the structure of expectational probing and planting.

2. All prospects have unexpressed and undeveloped expectations. Listen carefully for *expressed* opinions and parameters, for these are likely to be the key expectations that must be met. Some expectations will never be revealed; others require that you dig them out. Don't leave any expectational stone unturned. Make a list of expectations that *should* be addressed in your normal sale, and make it your job to explore each of them.

Expectations are expressed motives. Determine the prospect's expectational priorities and put most of your presentation and solution effort into addressing the key priorities. Work on the 20/80 guideline: meet the key 20% of expectations and you will close 80% of the prospects. Meet or exceed as many of the remaining expectations as possible.

3. Prospects have two distinct decision areas: personal and corporate. Don't confuse the two. Deal with the one that is dominant in the sale. Personal expectations are as important as corporate ones and should be examined and included in your selling strategies. Make it a point to find out how your prospect fits into the sale personally.

4. Take your list of corporate and personal expectations and then develop a series of probes that will uncover and explore each expectation on your list for each one of the personality style types. Expand your probes to incorporate each of the four Preferential Communications systems.

5. Make a list of common unrealistic expectations concerning your product, your competition and your industry. Develop strategies and probes that will flush out all unrealistic expectations and remove, reset or replace them with proper expectations. Avoid setting expectations that cannot be met or exceeded under normal circumstances.

6. Practice introducing new expectations that are linked specifically to unusual or unique features, functions, advantages or benefits of your product or service. If possible, introduce key spec expectations into your purchasing description or purchase order. For each of your products, isolate something that makes it unique and could be used as a key spec.

7. After establishing current and accepted value, then begin to enhance the value relationship by either adding to the product/service side or by reducing the expense side. Develop a portfolio of added value specifics concerning your product. Develop and practice methods by which these added value areas may be introduced.

8. Most common objections stem from the uneasiness brought on by unmet expectations. Expectational influenza is caused by not uncovering, exploring and explaining expectations. Other specific concerns and objections that are common to your product, service, industry, price or whatever may be dealt with through the simple strategy of forestalling. You bring it up before they do.

Develop a portfolio of forestalling probes and scenarios addressing all of your common and many of your uncommon objections. Look at addressing each area as an expectation that needs to be set and met. Practice using quotes as a forestalling mechanism.

9. Venture into the area of competitive hot spots by asking about competitive expectations. Never personally knock the competition. Always inquire about benefit expectations, why these benefits are important and whether the benefits are sufficient to cause a decision. Develop a full battery of competitive probes.

10. As with everything in selling, strategy depends upon the style exhibited by your prospect. Different style types have different expectations and intensities. Address the prospect's particular style. Listen to the language of expression and return your expectational solution in kind: feeling for feelings, facts for facts, details for details, generalities for generalities.

Adjust your behavior to the needs of the personality style.

PROFESSIONAL PRESENTATIONS

Traditional Feature-Benefit Presentations · Expectational Presentations · Reorganizing Your Product · Planning for Impact · Documentation · Proposals · Group Presentations · Two Birds with One Stone · Delivery · Presence and Practice · Next Step Commitment · Your Doubling Strategy · Doubling

TRADITIONAL FEATURE-BENEFIT PRESENTATIONS

Traditionally, there are two methods of presenting a product. The first method, which is used by most First Dimension Sellers, presents only the features and functions of a product to the prospect and puts the onus on the prospect to interpret those features and functions into personal advantages or benefits. This is called a features presentation, and it is weak and ineffective.

The second method, which is used mainly by Second Dimension Sellers, involves presenting the features and functions that make a product attractive, unique or interesting to a prospect, and then expressing the advantages and benefits that those features and functions represent to the prospect.

In addition, they provide proof in the form of documentation, testimonials or personal use. The salesperson does a lot more work but it results in a lot more sales. This is called the *feature-function-advantage-benefit-proof* formula, or *interpretive presentation.* It represents a great step past the First Dimension's feature-only presentations.

As an illustration, let's take a product with which most of us are familiar, a TV set, and see how we can present it using these two traditional methods.

Features Presentation:

*"Well, this set has a **56"** LCD screen, remote control and stereo sound. It lists at **$999** and has a three-year, unconditional parts and labor warranty."*

This is the typical presentation you hear in department stores around the world: straight feature selling, no interpretation into advantages or benefits. The prospect does not have to get involved and the salesperson relies on the prospect's product knowledge to interpret the benefits on a personal level. It is, of course, a dangerous method of selling. It is also a lazy way of selling. Strictly amateur.

The next salesperson is a Second Dimension Seller who has learned the skills and strategies involved with feature interpretation. The salesperson presents the product within the framework of the *feature-function-advantage-benefit-proof* relationship.

Interpretive Presentation:

*"Ms. DeWitt, this set has a **56"** LCD – or liquid crystal - screen, which affords comfortable viewing from almost anywhere in your living room. While the screen is large enough to give you this extra viewing dimension, at the same time it is engineered to retain clarity and excellent "true" color.*

"As well, this set features a deluxe remote control that can actually be linked to your cell phone by Bluetooth, so if you ever misplace your remote, you can always use your cell phone.

This also means, because it's Bluetooth, you can access your TV from literally anywhere, allowing you to set PVR recording at anytime from anywhere. You can read all about it in this consumer's report.

"Another interesting feature of this set is that it is equipped with high definition stereo surround sound, allowing you to fully appreciate the depth and fullness that surround sound offers. We've had many satisfied

customers stop by to say how much they enjoy this particular feature.

"One thing you'll be glad to have is a manufacturer's full, unconditional three-year warranty on all parts and labor, thereby giving you the peace of mind that if anything should unexpectedly fail, the set will be repaired promptly, correctly and at no cost to you whatsoever. As you might imagine, this is a big plus for those concerned about future maintenance costs. You can find a copy of the warranty right inside the owner's manual."

As you can see, the interpretive presentation style is far superior to the feature-only style because the salesperson is taking the time to examine and explain each feature or function in terms of the customer's eventual benefit. In some cases, proof was offered to back up the claims so as to remove any doubt. This type of presentation approach is powerful and skillful and, if used in place of the feature-only method, will easily double your sales.

However, there is even a better way to present your product. It can be used only after you and your prospect have explored, explained, agreed to and accepted expectations as the basis of the sale.

It is called the expectational presentation.

Whereas the interpretive feature-benefit-proof formula is fairly rigid and easy to learn (you must first present the feature or function, then interpret it into a benefit or advantage and lastly provide proof), expectational presentations are far more flexible, allowing a number of different combinations of format and therefore requiring increased skill by the salesperson.

Expectational Presentations

Expectational presentations require that you have already explored and developed a set of accepted expectations with your prospect. Once having set expectations, all you have to do is to meet them in order to sell the product. In effect, the prospect tells you everything you need to do to make a sale, if you have asked the right questions.

Instead of using the interpretive presentation, expectational presentations use four primary components, which can be arranged in a number of ways. The four components:

1. The expressed expectation of your prospect;
2. The benefit or advantage expected by the prospect;
3. The proof that the benefit or advantage exists;
4. The feature or function that allows the expectation to be fulfilled.

The four components can be stated in almost any sequence, but the feature/function component generally is left to last or next to last. These are just 10 of the 24 possible combinations:

Expectation - benefit - feature - proof;

Expectation - proof - benefit - feature;

Expectation - benefit - proof - feature;

Expectation - feature - benefit - proof;

Benefit - expectation - feature - proof;

Benefit - proof - expectation - feature;

Benefit - expectation - proof - feature;

Proof - expectation - benefit - feature;

Proof - benefit - expectation - feature;

Proof - feature - benefit - expectation.

The usual sequence is *expectation, benefit, feature* and *proof*. This sequence expresses the accepted expectations of the prospect, links them with the benefits or the advantages that the prospect hopes to receive, then links these benefits to the actual features or functions that bring about these benefits and finally binds the relationship with proof in the form of demonstration, testimonials, documentation, etc.

One advantage of presenting products or services in this fashion is that you tend to have features, functions, benefits and advantages that are *left over*. They are left over because you present only those features and functions required to meet or exceed your prospect's expectations. Your prospect might want to explore just one or two key expectational areas and not bother with the rest. Don't waste time trying to get all the key features and functions of your product on the sales table. It's all right to have some left over.

These surplus attributes can be used for added value if necessary. One of the major advantages of expectational presentations is that they don't tie you up trying to explain and demonstrate unessential features or functions and they leave you with "extra ammunition" should you need it.

Let's return to the TV salesperson, who has now learned to probe for expectations and then present the product in light of these expectations. Through the salesperson's expectational probing, she has discovered that you expect to purchase a large-screen, wall-mounted model with remote Blue Tooth control and stereo surround sound. You also expect to be able to connect the set to your sophisticated stereo sound system, PVR and satellite dish. Also, the salesperson has determined that you express yourself visually.

> *"Liz, I'd like to show you a model that I think will comfortably meet all of your expectations, including price, and probably even exceed many of them. It's our SS-700 model, right here.*
>
> *"Liz, you said that you wanted to look at an ultra-high resolution set with at least a56 inch LED screen, and that you wanted the best clarity and color definition possible.*
>
> *Because you watch a lot of movies and lower resolution usually found with large screens is tiresome to your eyes, I can see where this is a valid concern. By examining the SS-700, you'll notice that it has a larger, 65 inch screen and, according to every major consumer's report, has shown the best resolution and definition for its screen size, as you can plainly see. The resolution is actually*

*comparable to a much more expensive screen, yet it is a true **65** inch system. As you can imagine, the SS-**700** uses remarkable tech-nology, (wouldn't you agree?)*

(expectation - benefit - feature - proof)

"You also mentioned that a Blue Tooth option for the remote control was an operational essential. As you can see from this recent edition of The Video Picture, this particular set's Blue Tooth-enabled remote control is rated at the top of its class for operational ease and completeness, allowing you to set all of your PVR recordings from anywhere, anytime.

I think that you can see that all your expectations will be fully met if not exceeded in this quality system, (don't you?)

(expectation - benefit - proof - feature)

*"Liz, you mentioned how much you enjoyed listening to your friend's TV because the sound just seemed to surround you, and that surround sound capability was mandatory in whatever new set you were considering and that it had to be able to connect with your TX-**90** sound surround system, PVR and satellite components.*

*The SS-**700** was especially designed for this purpose, with the connections already in place on the special interconnect panel located right here, as you can see. No fussing or special harnesses required. You just plug the components into the panel. All the interconnect instructions are included in the owners manual, as shown right here on page **12**, to help take the guesswork out and make it easier, faster and safer for you. I'm sure you'll see to it to have everything working with total harmony in no time.*

(benefit - expectation - feature - proof)

*"As you can see, the SS-**700** truly does meet or exceed all these special requirements plus a few extras that you weren't expecting, such as..."*

This is the essence of expectational presentation: restating the expectation; identifying and linking the benefits and advantages, features and functions; and then proving your claims. To lock it in, get the prospect physically involved (touching or using the feature) or provide documentary or testimonial proof.

This technique is entering the realm of Third Dimension Selling. It totally controls the sales process by exploring and then presenting to expectations. It is faster because you deal with only those aspects of your product or service that are important to your client; it is more powerful because it deals directly with agreed and accepted expectations rather than suspected motives; it allows for better value relationships because it allows you to keep a sizable reserve of features, functions, advantages and benefits for added value should they be needed; it follows naturally upon the probing nature of consultative selling and therefore feels more natural to the client.

Reorganizing Your Product

Many years ago I designed and facilitated a workshop series for a major national computer reseller that implemented the expectational selling process within its customer service department.

As an intricate part of a new service offering, we spent six weeks service reorganizing their "product" so that the expectational sales program could take full effect. Once completed, however, their sales rose 400% in less than three months, without adding additional salespeople!

You, too, may be faced with reorganizing your product so that you can directly promote product features, functions and advantages through an expectational presentation. In the case of the computer service department, a single, ineffective brochure that described all of their service and support offerings was replaced with a series of modular marketing pieces that could be quickly culled into a custom presentation depending upon the needs and expectations of each customer.

As well, each basic expectational category could be further expanded by giving higher levels of detail (each getting more technically, functionally or financially descriptive) to suit the company's primary buyer type, the Examiner.

Carefully examine your product's advertising and support materials and be prepared to augment or reorganize the material to reflect expecta-tional selling formats better. I suggest that you look at your product or service in reverse...the way the customer would prefer to look at it:

> Define customer expectations into broad categories, such as financial expectations, performance expectations, productivity expectations, etc. Follow the expectational areas set out in the previous chapter or define your own. These categories become the foundation for the "entry" marketing pieces.
>
> Link each of the expectational areas with benefits and advantages that your product or service can deliver. This further expands each expectational area.
>
> Further link the benefits or advantages to the actual features or functions that deliver the performance.
>
> Add industry or customer proof to solidify the marketing claims.
>
> Slant your marketing pieces, sale presentation materials and personal presentations towards the target market style type.

PLANNING FOR IMPACT

If you have the opportunity to prepare for a presentation, even if it is only a minute or so, then organize your presentation so that it has the most positive and competitive impact possible.

Key 20%

Your primary objective is to give the key 20% of prospect expectations 80% of your attention and care. If you can meet or exceed these high priority expectations then you stand an excellent chance of success, even if you might not be able to meet the remaining lower priority expectations. You want to make your biggest impact in the key 20%.

Let's say your prospect stated five expectations and conceded to you that the financial one was the most important. You would spend most of your presentation time in satisfying this crucial expectation, perhaps offering alternative financial arrangements, such as payment plans, lease plans, creative financing, balloon payments, extended terms or whatever it took to make the prospect feel totally satisfied and comfortable with your solution to this objective. You would then balance out the rest of your proposal or presentation by quickly meeting the remaining expectations.

Sensory Involvement

People interpret and understand in different ways. For instance, some people understand better when they see things, others understand better when they hear things, others better when they touch things, others when they smell things and yet others understand better when they taste things. This reference is in addition to the preferential communications systems that we've been looking at in terms of language.

Notice the words *"understand better."* Most of the time a combination of the senses gives us our understanding and perception because one sense is rarely enough. By using many senses, it gives us a more complete understanding of a given situation or product. But all of us have dominant senses that give us stronger understanding in situations where they can be used. Conversely, these same dominant senses may actually hinder our understanding in situations where they cannot be used.

If you can get your prospect involved with the senses that he or she uses to increase and enhance understanding, the dominant senses, then you will create a deeper and more impressionable impact. Look not only for expression through verbal communication, but also through the way people act and respond to their physical surroundings.

Imagine using this technique if you were selling your home. If you were having a showing at a certain time, then wouldn't it be wise to try to make the impact of that showing as powerful as possible? Sure it would. Make it memorable. The most memorable of all the senses is smell. If I were selling my home and there was an open house scheduled for Saturday, I'd get the aroma flowing throughout the house of freshly baked pies or bread. I'd make sure that every picture hung straight and every basin, tub, tiled floor and countertop gleaned. I'd have warm, happy music gently in the background. If it was winter or a rainy day, I'd have the fire roaring and cinnamon-spiced cider cooking on the stove. Do something *better* to get more of the senses involved. It can make the difference.

If your client is a toucher (Relater or Impulsive), then get him to examine and feel your product. If she is an Examiner, then get her to explore the paperwork, the financial details and the warranty. If he is an Impulsive, paint a dream picture with words or use visuals or videos. Get the idea?

Why do you think the salesperson asks you to slide inside a new car? It's to *feel* the leather seats and to *inhale* that new car smell. When I sold aircraft and had the opportunity to order a new aircraft from the factory on speculation, I would invariably order the leather seat option because of the *smell*. I sold more aircraft with leather seats than any other kind, likely because they smelled good. The sense of smell is closely aligned with the sense of touch and taste, the kinesthetic senses.

To improve impact, develop a presentation that includes the senses that most closely match your client's Preferential Communications system.

Sight: videos, slides, graphics, magazines, tour plant

Sound: video and audio recordings, music, tour

Taste: coffee, your product (?), lunch, dinner, snacks

Touch: samples, proposals, models, photos, operation

Smell: fresh coffee, freshly baked rolls, newness, leather

Word Pictures

One of the keys to unlocking the mind's ability to interpret and understand is the word picture. By painting a mental image of your communication, your client understands better. Use the language that most closely matches your client's communication system and style.

Next to an actual experience, word imagery is the most powerful method of influencing another person. It provides a visual understanding expressed through a story. Interestingly, it is the method most often used to explain and teach complex and astounding truths and principles in the New Testament. Time-tested and effective, it is one of the salesperson's most valuable communication tools.

I constantly draw analogies through the use of word pictures when in a seminar or when with a client. It is a powerful method for creating understanding. I highly recommend a book on mental imagery called *The Language of Love* by Gary Smalley and Dr. John Trent [5].

Visuals

I am a believer in strong visuals. If you have access to visual arts equipment or software to make graphs and other forms of storyboard illustrations to assist you in getting your presentation across, then use them. If you do a group presentation where you are presenting projection visuals, especially graphs, have the graphic images reproduced as handouts.

I prefer to have my proposals follow the order of my presentation so that all the relevant graphics are in sequence with each participant's proposal as we proceed. Use color whenever possible.

The general rule for good projected visuals is to have no more than six lines of type and no more than six words per line. There's an old saying in the visual merchandising profession that "less is more". Don't complicate your visuals by jamming too much onto one graphic. Make them clear, concise and simple.

---

[5]. Gary Smalley and Dr. John Trent, *The Language of Love* (Pomona, CA:1989) Distributed by World Books, Waco, Texas.

I am absolutely intrigued with the capability of "PowerPoint™" and can easily spend days on developing incredible presentations with sound and motion and "neat stuff" – but beware, for sometimes complexity can work against you.

The bottom line: simplicity wins. When working with a prospect or a group, and a visual presentation is a must, then make sure that it adheres to the basic presentation rules: **six lines of type and no more than six words per line.** Graphics should stand on their own. Resist from having the automatic timing feature: advance your slides or text – control it using your mouse button or assistant.

Personalization

It's often been said that the most important sound to your ears is someone calling your name. Visually, I guess you could say that the most important thing to you is seeing your own name in print. Personalized proposals are big attention-getters. Whenever you can, include your prospect's name, title and firm on the cover and on each of the pages of your proposal. Your prospects will react more favorably when they see their names in print, and, interestingly, will be much more reluctant to throw away materials and proposals that are personalized.

Capitalize on your prospect's natural self-attention by personalizing everything about your presentation. Make proposals separately for each decision maker and each influencer. If you're setting up a conference room and you're expecting a number of people, have name badges (nice ones) and place markers with their names and titles on the table. This is especially critical when you are introducing new people or support members to an existing group.

Added Value

As mentioned earlier, added value is accomplished by either adding product and services or reducing cost. But added value is only perceived as positive once an established value relationship exists. For instance, if you buy a starter set of golf clubs and you are satisfied that you are getting fair value (goods received for money paid), then you recognize this as established or accepted value. If, the salesperson then announces that a golf bag is also included in the sale (free), the value now rises. Throw in an umbrella, a bag of tees or a dozen balls and the value becomes even more enjoyable. The key is to establish fair value first and then to add value to the package to create value feelings and appreciation.

Always try to provide strategically for added value. Hold it back until you feel it will have the most significant impact. Don't give away the entire store on the first encounter.

Selective Language

I once saw a commercial that made me laugh because it was so obvious in its use of what I call "selective double-talk." It was beautiful! The husband marches through the front door holding a number of large packages and exclaims to his beaming wife, *"Look at all the savings I came home with!"* After a brief discussion on the "savings" involved in his purchases, the wife grabs hubby by the sleeve and heads towards the door, announcing, *"Let's go out and have dinner with all the money we've saved!"* It's classic double-talk. They haven't saved anything. They've *spent.* And now they're going to spend even more on dinner! But to the consumer, the image of shopping at this department store carried with it ideas of great bargains and the bonus of a meal for two to boot!

What has happened? The ad used selectively misleading language to change a possible negative situation into a totally positive one. They forgot to tell you that you must spend to save. Spending money is purposefully missing because it is negative. Savings are positive. Dinner is positive. Happiness in the family is positive. This ad is an example of how selective language can add impact to a sale.

As well, you too can use selective language in your presentations by concentrating on savings, benefits, advantages, bonuses and all the other positive aspects while minimizing the negative aspects. In commercial proposals and presentations, you simply focus and build on the positives and minimize the negatives. Strategically plan your presentation to take advantage of positive language. It has been suggested that the following words are among the most emotional in a sales environment:

Guarantee	Health	Results
Proven	Safe	Advantage
Safety	Money	Savings
You	Benefits	Security
Family	Easy	Now
Positive	Love	Discovery
Investment	Reward	New

When you design your presentation, include positive, motivating words to talk about your product or service, the prospect's expectations and the benefits or advantages your product brings.

DOCUMENTATION

What you sell and to whom you sell will determine the amount and type of documentation required during the selling process. Personality styles also greatly affect the documentation requirements. For instance, if you are selling a pair of shoes to the average person, he or she is interested in the looks, the price and the fit. No documentation is needed. If you are selling a pair of athletic shoes to a professional sports figure, you have to prove that your shoes are the best available. This will take more than fit and figures; it will take test documentation and testimonials.

Similarly, if you're selling soap to restaurants for their kitchens and bathrooms, you need little documentation. But if you are selling fluids for cleaning the control instruments on a nuclear reactor, you require a truckload of endorsements, test results, environmental studies, regulating body approvals and who knows what else.

Documentation is important to purchasers, but in varying degrees. The Examiner wants every piece of information you've got available and will thoroughly analyze it all in due time. The Victor wants a summary of the important details. The Impulsive wants to be assured that the image fits and the Relater looks for the human and environmental impact. The documentation must reflect the needs and expectations of the customer. Arrange your documentation according to depth and locate additional supportive information that might better be found in magazine articles, trade publications and customer testimonials.

In many sales, purchase decision influencers are lurking about to ensure that you and your firm know what you're talking about. They're the Credential Checkers. Be prepared to supply the names and telephone numbers of people in your firm who can communicate with these documentation dogs. I learned long ago that likes talk to likes, and if I anticipate or run into an assault upon my technical or industry credibility, I always carry a "soother's" phone number. What or who is a soother? It's a person who can talk the same business language as the Credential Checker, someone who is a peer.

I ran into a lot of Credential Checkers in the computer industry and at the executive levels of the international security industry. I don't know how many times my name has been through the FBI, RCMP and Interpol computers, but I know it's more than a few. Be prepared to provide personal documentation when required.

PROPOSALS

Building good proposals is not an art, it's a formula. Once you know and understand the client's expectations, you simply build the proposal to meet or exceed the expectations wherever possible. The proposals address the key expectations in depth and lesser expectations as added value. I use a simple format and seldom vary from it:

1. Personalized cover;
2. Title page;
3. Table of contents;
4. Executive summary;
5. Proposal background;
6. Client objectives;
7. Resolution (product presentation);
8. Financial summary;
9. Implementation schedule;
10. Sample agreement;

11. Appendix and supporting documentation.

I highly recommend investing in good word processing software and printer that can deliver state-of-the-art proposals. Your client judges you by your personal and corporate appearance. This perceived appearance will either encourage the client to deal with you or discourage the client from dealing with you. You have an opportunity to influence the client through the preparation and the presentation of your proposal: make it match or exceed their expectations.

However, this can have a negative effect on clients who think that your services might be too expensive because you overindulged in fancy brochures and proposals. Match the proposal to the client in terms of style and Preferential Communications system. Choose your words carefully, because if you send a visual, opinion-oriented proposal to an auditory Victor, it will likely wind up in the circular file near the door. Likes deal with likes.

You might want to prepare several different proposal formats to deal with different types of clients. For instance, I have clients to whom I always send materials on expensive bond paper stock. I have others who just receive an e-mail.

Group Presentations

Prepare for your presentation well in advance by having plenty of materials, extra proposals, white-board markers, chalk, colored flip-chart markers, a collapsible pointer, extra projector bulb if you are using a projector, an extension cord (25 feet) and power bar, a bottle of dry-cleaning fluid or "Tide" pen for your clothes, a damp rag and some headache tablets. Get a "rollie" case to lug it all around neatly. Better yet, have an assistant be responsible for set up and removal.

The solution is to assemble your materials and the presentation at least a full hour before it is scheduled. Ask permission to set up, then you will not look like the mad professor trying to get everything underway while six or eight board members sit un-amused. If you are presenting in your own facility, you have the upper hand in terms of preparation and familiarity with the situation.

If you are presenting at your client's location, then be sure to be there early so that you can get grounded. Try not to look like the mad professor, drawing last-minute graphs and charts, scribbling name cards and sorting a stack of loose papers into proposals at the last minute. You must appear calm, organized and prepared.

If you anticipate technical questions, or questions that you cannot (or should not) answer personally, bring your team of company experts. Advise them that you are controlling the meeting and work out a signal system to limit or cut off their responses. I personally like ear pulling, tie straightening or neck rubbing as signals. Rehearse with your experts and demand that they follow your lead. One of the most disastrous occurrences in any group presentation is to allow the experts to start nit-picking and looking for discrepancies and areas of fault or disagreement. You must assume that most experts are Examiners (nerds) who have a natural leaning towards finding potential errors and fault. Give them enough time and they will.

One of the worst selling experiences I ever had was when our chief scientist accompanied me on a venture capital presentation to a government screening board. The government board also had a scientist. The two scientists got into a heated disagreement about some insignificant detail and the result was a lost opportunity for badly needed capital. Scientists *seldom* agree. To avoid this type of incident, prepare your group by using forestalling techniques.

> *"There will probably be some areas of our presentation that some of you may wish to explore in more depth, but in the interest of making the best use of the time available, may I please suggest some simple guidelines:*
>
> *"As we proceed, please note any points of detail that you would like to explore further. I will be glad to work with you at the end of the meeting on each point individually rather than discuss it during the limited group time.*
>
> *"There are several technical areas that we must discuss in depth and to help us all understand I have brought our Director of Technical Services, Jim Self, to present this section. Jim will also be available to help you with*

any of your unanswered questions at the end of the meeting.

"The specific purpose of this meeting is to (inform, conclude, present, etc.).

"The final objective of this meeting is to (make a decision, select the next course of action, evaluate and distribute the final proposal, select the technical training, etc.).

"Now, if we are all ready, let's begin."

This should discourage any detail-seeking participants from disrupting the meeting and challenging you in front of the influencers and decision makers. Unless the detail is vital to the group's understanding or evaluation, handle it off-line.

Two Birds with One Stone

Have as many of the decision makers and influencers attend your presentation as possible. In fact, insist upon it. You'll be surprised at what will occur if only you push a little to get what you need: all the influential players in one spot. Run down your list of players: the purchasing agent, the technical advisor, the purchasing department head, security, finance, etc. Whoever has impact on the decision should be there. All or nothing. This cycle-cutting strategy can take months off your sales cycle. Your task is to bring them all to one accord.

Have your client set a tentative date that will allow enough time to round up the group members. If you have to settle on a date a month or two away, it is probably worth the wait if you can get them all together. Indicate that you have had your much-in-demand experts rearrange their schedules specifically to attend this meeting and it would be difficult to reschedule. This is usually the case anyway. Don't ever lie, but stress the importance of meeting the committed date.

When your client is scheduling a meeting time, have him or her check with the most influential group member first for their availability and use the influential member's schedule as the group's schedule. Most employees respond to pecking order and if the boss says 7 o'clock on Saturday morning, the rest will usually accommodate.

Be sure to have your client draw up a participant list for you in advance and advise you on the type of individuals and their individual backgrounds before you prepare for the meeting. This way you can slant your delivery or materials for appropriate impact. This is also a good method of strengthening your rapport with your client, especially if they are Examiners or Relaters.

Produce an agenda for the meeting and clearly identify the time frame (start, duration, finish, question period) and the client's objectives for your meeting. Hand this agenda around to start the meeting or explain it on your first overhead or slide.

Depending upon the complexity and focus of your presentation, you might want to pass out your proposal or presentation materials as you proceed from topic to topic rather than all at once. I personally prefer to have my audience following me during the presentation rather than reading from a proposal.

DELIVERY

Delivering a group presentation is much like acting. You have butterflies in your stomach, your palms are sweaty and if you smoke you've already consumed a pack in the hour preceding the meeting. However, the show must go on, and you're the guest of honor. Adopt the role and take control.

Many people get paranoid when standing in front of a group; others love it. The way that I used to approach serious meetings was that I was the expert and the group really wanted to hear what I had to say.

Take the posture of a true meeting "pilot." You are the captain of this hour-long flight. Your "passengers" will speak highly of you if you can take off smoothly (and on time), cruise comfortably, warn them in advance of upcoming turbulence, feed them well (with information) and land without incident (and on time). Ensure that your support staff members are courteous, prepared and professional, for they are your flight attendants. The key to giving good presentations is that you place the responsibility for a good meeting where it belongs: YOU.

Y **You***:* You are the meeting pilot, the captain. You are in control of the meeting flight. You know the route and the destination. Learn to be a pro, don't scare your passengers by making risky or bold moves without warning or preparation. Jet jockeys don't get to fly for the major airlines until they learn to control their impulsive behavior.

O **Obligation to others**: It is your responsibility to ensure that all passengers are comfortable, are fed well with information during their flight and land safely, smoothly and on time, with no surprises.

U **Understanding**: It is your responsibility to encourage and provide understanding of how your product and service will benefit and affect each passenger. Sometimes you have to say the same thing five different ways before it is understood. Whatever you have to do, do it.

If you can, bring an assistant to the meeting. This allows you to maintain your presence at the head of the meeting while the meeting items are attended to, such as fixing coffee, passing out papers, hanging up flip-chart sheets, etc. It also provides a confidant for support and critique.

Presence and Practice

People attending group presentations paint your information with their personal impressions of you. Your material may be excellent, but if your appearance says "slob" your information is colored with hues of slob. You may have mediocre information but when a dynamic, enthusiastic, charismatic presentation enhances your material, it gets painted with "wow." Your presence is your appearance, your projection, and your personality.

Appearance

If you anticipate doing many meeting presentations, invest in your personal image and appearance as it would best be appreciated and accepted by your audience.

This could mean a top-quality business suit or outfit, expensive shirt or blouse, silk tie, silk socks and expensive shoes. Or it could mean ripped jeans and a sweatshirt – it all depends on the expectations of your audience. Dress to be accepted or to make a point.

Projection
This the ability to talk to everyone at the presentation, whether they are seated at the front or way, way in the back of an auditorium. In the case of a small group, to talk loud enough to comfortable reach each group member. Projection also means focus, meaning eye-contact and even body repositioning to move closer.

This is a practiced skill, one that becomes second-nature after many presentations, but one that must be learned nonetheless. Pay too much attention, come too close and you risk intimidation of your "target" and alienation of the remainder.

Personality
You can construct your meeting personality, much like an actor builds a character and remains in that character until the part has been played out. To understand what a meeting personality should be, go to some professional sales presentations. Trade shows are a good source of professional presentations, and they generally offer seminars and product presentations free of charge for attendees.

Another suggestion is to join Toastmasters or similar public speaking groups and begin to develop a structured speaking format. Through practice and polish, your confidence will build and your style will emerge.

As well, take some acting or drama courses to aid in your ability to draw upon emotions. Do not be alarmed if your meeting personality turns out to be something quite different from your business personality or your leisure personality. I am a totally different person when in front of a group than when I am at home with my wife and family.

You must also be able to slant your meeting personality to meet the needs of the dominant styles within each meeting group. You should build a stage personality flexible enough to meet the needs of your clients.

You should work hard on your diction and expression, paying careful attention to eliminate meaningless filler words, such as "OK", "you know", "right", “whatever” and "umm" unless they are used to gain commitment.

NEXT STEP COMMITMENT

At the end of every meeting, suggest a next step for the meeting members to adopt. Either get agreement to accept the material as presented and move to the next step, or isolate those elements that need correction or adjustment, agree to the adjustments, and then try to get the group as a whole to approve the project in principle.

Get the group to identify the next step. Get the group to commit to the next move (under your guidance). Do not leave the meeting without a commitment to something.

For personal one-on-one presentations, get your client to agree with your material, isolate the issues that are not meeting expectational levels, and obtain commitment to a next step that will address these issues.

YOUR DOUBLING STRATEGY

Preparing for a good presentation is the key to any salesperson's ultimate success. If you have been able to explore expectations and then sell directly to those expectations through your presentation, your client will have little to argue or complain about. Ensure that your presentation format follows your client's expectational priorities. Use other features and functions as added value items. Treat group presentations as a professional speaker would: prepare, take command and bring a strong personal presence into the meeting.

DOUBLING

1. Break all your products or services into features and functions. Then look at why a customer might buy your product: the benefits and advantages it provides. Link these benefits and advantages to specific expectations and then group the expectations into major categories (financial, functional, training, etc.). Organize your features, functions, benefits and advantages into a pyramid structure with a specific expectation at the top and the components spreading out to form the base. Prepare documentation and testimonials for each claim. Each week, explore a new aspect of your product in this fashion.

2. Develop dialog for delivering an expectational presentation. Link the expectations (objectives) with the benefits, the advantages, the functions and the features in a narrative that feels natural and is clearly and easily understood. Each week, develop and practice a new narrative that can illustrate your product in a slightly different way.

3. Practice delivering the expectational presentation in different component sequences. By becoming more flexible, you gain confidence and the ability to translate your product into language your customer understands and appreciates.

4. Every feature, function, benefit and advantage becomes added value when it can be described *after* the customer's key expectations have been met. Practice describing the added value areas of your product in narrative form. Use the same format that you used for describing your product above, but isolate the product as an "added benefit" or an "additional advantage."

5. Always focus on the client's key 20% of objectives or expectations. Address these first. Look over your past sales and try to isolate those things that tend to be the key 20% for your current clients. Write these down and concentrate on being able to present the expectational relationship without any flaws.

6. Begin to make a list of things you can do to draw in as many of the client's senses as possible into your presentation. List the five primary senses and decide how each one could be influenced during your presentation. This might seem silly, but all senses can be activated,

even if it is only through a word picture. Begin to practice and develop a powerful word imagery language. Practice by relating existing client stories or fictional analogies to make a point or expectation seem more clear and believable.

7. Start making a list of selective language phrases that concentrate on the benefits and positives of using your product or service. Change purchasing into saving, change downtime or maintenance into increased productivity, change training costs into increased abilities, etc. Start using this selective language purposefully within your sales presentations. Each week, take one of your products and surround it with selective, positive language.

8. Begin assembling your documentation and arranging it by levels of detail. Break out information to fit into the expectational format. Take one product each month and overhaul it into an expectational format. If there isn't existing documentation, then find it or make it.

9. Learn how to use sophisticated word-processing equipment yourself. Don't allow the sales support group to do all your work; insist on becoming involved in the creation and production of your proposals. Make it a year-long goal to master a competent word processing program. Then use it to personalize every proposal.

10. Determine that you will master the group presentation. Create a list of personal presentation weaknesses and set a deadline replacing them with positive counterparts. Invest in a wardrobe that puts you a cut above in appearance. Sign up for Toastmasters or some other program that encourages you to present in front of a group. Create a strong mental image of yourself as the consummate seminar leader and work towards that image. Explore and examine the world of professional speaking. Each month, take in at least one professional presentation from an outside group.

Engineering Commitment

Closing · Commitment · Engineered Commitment · A to Z · Control Strategies · They Can't Say No · Decision-Making Factors · Forestalling Objections and Concerns · Handling Unexpected Concerns · Quick Closing · Style Differences in Commitment · Negotiating a Decision · The Non-Decision Decision · Commitment Action · Your Doubling Strategy · Doubling

Closing

This chapter is about how sales are built so that the client buys as a matter of course, rather than as a result of some tricky manipulation or closing method. Strong-arm closing is for amateurs who don't understand the selling process. This is not to say that top professionals don't issue gutsy, tension-filled commitment challenges. Rather, I want to make a strong distinction between the salesperson who depends on "closing" as his or her primary selling skill in the sale, and the professional who uses many diversified "commitment" techniques as decision-making tools that are applied carefully and consistently throughout the sales cycle.

Commitment is the process of having a client or prospect agree with the concept of purchasing and then actually getting the prospect to take the action. It features many interlocking skills and strategies. It is the approach that Second and Third Dimension Sellers would use.

Closing, on the other hand, is the singular *act* of having a client make a decision to purchase. It refers to the probing technique that pressures a person into making a decision to purchase. It is most commonly associated with "high-pressure" selling techniques.

Most people today are well aware of pressure selling tactics and do a commendable job of defending themselves, as they should. Pressure closing techniques are generally applied only when a prospect can't decide, won't decide or doesn't even realize he or she must decide. Many industries have initially established themselves through high-pressure selling and, unfortunately, some continue to use these techniques today. Many areas have laws protecting consumers against high-pressure sales, and most reputable companies totally avoid this type of selling.

I mentioned earlier in this book that I did a sales training program for a chain of well-known health clubs. My objective was to change their style of selling from the old-fashioned, high-pressure techniques to a new form of consultative selling. When I was first contacted for the job, the area vice-president wanted me to experience the current sales process before I committed to the task. I did. I went as a prospective customer to the local club where I was given the usual tour and then taken to the "closing room" and handed over to the "closer."

The biggest immediate difference was the considerable contrast between the colors and textures of the closing room and those of the rest of the club. The club was in earth tones and featured abundant greenery and soft music. The lighting was indirect and warm. In contrast, the closing room was stark white with chrome and glass furniture, hard plastic seats, metallic etchings on the walls, no plants, no music and harsh cool white unfiltered fluorescent lights that buzzed continuously.

I was positioned against the wall with the "closer," a large, “beefcake” male, who sat between me and the closed door. There was no air movement in the room and I swear the temperature was much warmer than the rest of the club. This room was purposefully designed to increase the blood pressure of the incarcerated. It was a "closing chamber" and the techniques used were shocking.

Many months later, after I had completed the training program, one of the salespeople slipped me a copy of the club's old sales manual. It contained some of the most manipulative, embarrassing and downright dirty tricks that I have ever encountered in selling.

Closing, in many ways, still carries this connotation for many salespeople, and for many purchasers as well. Most books on selling refer to closing as the consummate skill among salespeople. I couldn't agree more, or disagree more. (There's a real politician's stand!)

I disagree in that using closing skills without the other selling skills in balance results in emotional decisions, buyer's remorse, cancelled sales, fist fights and a host of other nasties. Strong closers may squeeze out a decision, but they won't change the value relationship inherent in the sale. If someone gets pressured into buying something of questionable value, he or she is going to let others know. The customer might not come back and complain, but he or she will surely let anyone who lends an ear know of the experience.

Studies on word-of-mouth complaints indicate that, given enough time and opportunity, a disgruntled customer will negatively influence about 250 other people. There's an old saying that says "*what goes around comes around.*" It is applicable to high-pressure closing techniques.

However, I agree that closing is probably one the most important skills a salesperson can learn, because without commitment there is no sale. It's just that I, as do many other professional salespeople, look at closing as just a part of the overall development of the prospect's commitment posture. Usually you need a final yes or no decision, but if you have engineered the commitment throughout the entire selling process, then there is little or no resistance to the final decision. It happens as a matter of process, as a matter of course.

COMMITMENT

Sales are accomplished when the clients feel that their expectations have been met or exceeded. During the consultative selling process, commitment is built gradually, in increments, as information is sought and exchanged. Second and Third Dimension Sellers always build sales commitment in stages. They seek the clients' approval at every step, surrounding their clients with positives, approvals and agreements. Thus, there is no "close" per se. The final decision is executed as a matter of normal progression rather than as an exercise in arm twisting and brow beating.

In an earlier chapter, I presented many types of questioning techniques. You'll notice that most of the moderate- and high-intensity questions dealt with closing, while the lower-intensity probes dealt with exploring need and establishing commitment. Salespeople who use expectational selling will find little need for the high-intensity questions because they're just not required.

The whole purpose of developing an expectational selling style is so that you don't have to use the intense closing probes. Commitment develops as a natural effect of the expectational selling process.

ENGINEERED COMMITMENT

From the moment that you select a new prospect, start thinking of developing commitment. From the first approach right through to the ink on the dotted line, think about incrementally engineering commitment. Get commitment by design, not by demand.

Commitment occurs when expectations are met (or exceeded) and the client feels at ease with the function, fit and image of your product or service (and firm) in his or her business. To engineer commitment, you must examine everything that affects a positive buying decision. Everything you do, everything you say, every piece of information will either build commitment or erode it. To become a professional salesperson, you must become a commitment engineer.

To seek agreement in your sales conversation, use conditional or leading probes:

> *"Ms. Osterhout, it sounds like if you were to put an insurance rider on your home-owner's policy, your new computer would be adequately protected, right?"*
>
> *"Nancy, I can see that you have quite an interest in the auto-bagging feature of the KT25. What specific advantages do you see for your firm by installing the auto-bagger option?"*
>
> *"...wouldn't you agree? ....right? ....OK? ....this is suitable for you, isn't it?"*

These are all parts of phrases that help seek and build commitment verbally throughout your sales interview. Use them frequently to build incremental commitment as you proceed from expectation to expectation.

A TO Z

Analyze every facet of your product: service, sales approach, marketing materials, proposal materials, support documentation, support personnel, warranty, after-sales service programs, telephone support, communications accessibility and anything else that connects you and your company to your client. Analyze from A to Z. Then line these elements up in a full and total commitment strategy aimed at your target markets. Leave no obvious discrepancies, and arrange every possible facet to reflect positively in the customer's eyes.

This task might be difficult for the individual salesperson, but the salesperson is the one responsible for product representation to the client, so it is the salesperson who ultimately is responsible for developing or engineering commitment. It's great if you have everything working towards a sale, but if you don't, you must use your creative abilities and selling skills to gain commitment.

It may seem strange and absurd, but I would estimate that 80% of all businesses work against themselves in this area. Most of the organizations for whom I've had the pleasure consulting and training have spent a great deal of their resources to attract new clients only to have the whole relationship shudder and shake after the client's encounter with the accounting or service personnel. All the ducks must line up: every point of client contact must encourage a positive relationship between the client and your company.

CONTROL STRATEGIES

Control of the sale, especially of commitment, can be established in a number of ways. The first method is through style flexing, ensuring that you are maintaining a stress-free sales environment. Within a cooperative atmosphere, understanding and accomplishment are at their highest. In a tension-filled environment, you can make little or no headway.

Control is simply having others follow your plan. It does not mean that you have to order other people around or brow beat your clients into acceptance. It means that you know where you and your client are within the overall sales process. At any one time, your client or an influencer might seem to have control of the situation, but if you have a solid grasp of the selling process, the control will only be theirs for the moment. You must be able to steer yourself and others through the uncharted waters and come safely into port. By allowing the sales process and engineered commitment run its course, control will always ultimately remain with you.

- Control is gained when you *ask questions*. It is reduced or lost wholly when you defensively answer questions, especially if the questions are asked in a rapid-fire sequence.
- Control is gained when you have a technological advantage through training, experience or affiliation. It is reduced when your client has a better grasp of the situation than you do.
- Control tends to increase when you are selling on your premises. It is reduced when you are on your client's premises.
- Control is increased when you use focused selling skills. It is reduced when you sell through personality traits only.
- Control is increased when you have product, service and industry knowledge depth. It is reduced when you have only surface knowledge.
- Control is increased when you establish and maintain rapport. It is reduced when rapport is weak or broken.
- Control is increased when you initially agree with your prospect when an objection is raised. It is reduced when you defend or attack.
- Control is increased when you are prepared and practiced. It is reduced when you are spontaneous, unequipped and ill-informed.

Control is essential to developing a sale that features expectational selling and an engineered commitment. The commitment is engineered because you keep personal control; the reason you keep personal control is because commitment is engineered. Control and engineered commitment go hand in hand with expectational selling.

THEY CAN'T SAY "NO"

You are building a pyramid. With each expectation extracted, explored and resolved, you lay another foundation stone. With each agreement question you ask, another block is added and cemented in place with the mortar of rapport. With each benefit adopted, each feature and function linked to an expectation, each objective fulfilled, the structure grows higher, row by row. As the financial and budget parameters are concluded, the final row is added. With your closing questions, the cap stone is secured and the sale is completed. The final handshake turns the deed for the pyramid over to the new owner, your client.

Expectational selling builds a pyramid of commitment and agreement. Closing only caps the peak. If you haven't taken the time to ask and explore, to pause and explain, to get and maintain rapport, to understand and become involved, then when you try to close, you'll be putting the cap stone on too early: it won't fit right, it will feel awkward, it will look silly. Do your job completely, and the cap stone will fit as the architect intended.

Your goal is to build overwhelming evidence that purchasing your product or service is the proper decision, a decision made with confidence and made at the right time; a safe and risk-free action.

Your challenge is to build your selling case so convincingly and to engineer it so carefully that the cap stone will fit snugly when applied. The sale closes: no remorse, no regret, no anxiety. It's a good sale and a good purchase, a winning situation for both sides.

DECISION-MAKING FACTORS

Every client has his or her own comfort zone when it comes to making decisions. Anytime you exceed any one of these comfort zones, stress will build within the client. If too much stress is present, then a rational decision might be hard to come by. The more stress, the more likely the decision will be delayed or derailed altogether. In beginning to engineer commitment, it is helpful if you develop a decision-making profile of your client. This can help you anticipate selling strategies, your client's needs and any restrictions concerning the proposed purchase. The purpose of the profile is to help you to take preemptive action to control the buildup of undue stress surrounding the decision-making process. A decision-making profile includes the following elements:

- Authority to make decisions;
- Responsibility to carry through decision;
- Decision-making value (dollar amount and decision importance);
- Product or service familiarity levels (has he or she been here before?);
- Acceptance of your company and you personally;
- Budget capabilities (current, future, extraordinary, and importance of funds);
- Influencers required to support the final decision;
- Accountability for the decision (personal or purchasing process);
- Political atmospheres (entrepreneurial or institutional);
- Personality styles (Examiner, Impulsive, Relater or Victor);
- Personal stability (new to position, new to company or established and fixed in corporate process);
- Perceived risk of the purchase.

Authority

Authority is the most basic parameter with which you must deal. Is the person empowered to make an actual purchasing decision? Can he or she sign a requisition for a purchase order or sign the check? If not, that person doesn't have the authority to make the buying decision. You are probably dealing at the wrong level, and the time and effort you spend ultimately may be wasted. **Your first job is to determine if the person has the authority to purchase or cause the purchase to happen**; if not, then who does or how is the decision made? To find out, ask.

> *"Aside from yourself, Jayne, who else do you feel would be involved in the decision-making process?"*
>
> *"I wonder, Mel, if you could please show me how the purchasing process works here at Macdonald College?"*

Your responsibility on your first visit is to determine whether your contact is *in* the decision-making process or *outside* of it.

Responsibility

Does your prospect have the responsibility to carry the purchasing decision through to implementation? Will he or she be held accountable for the successful deployment of the product or service? If so, then you will want to assure your client throughout that you are there to assist on a personal level. Probe to determine the depth of the individual's involvement and to what degree he or she expects you to help.

> *"Mr. Lougheed, could you please tell me what the extent of your personal involvement with the implementation of the KT25 would be, and to what degree you would require personal assistance from our firm?"*

Let your client begin to set expectations concerning how you can help and assist. It's another area that can add height to your pyramid.

Decision-Making Values

Decision-making values relate not only to monetary amounts but also to the *impact* of the decision. What effect will the purchase have on your prospect's firm? A good example of impact occurred when I introduced the chemical security paint to one of Canada's leading petroleum companies. Although the dollar value was well within the prospect's authority limits, the impact of the product was company-wide, affecting every single employee, from the president to the mailroom sorter. The decision, therefore, had to go eventually to the presidential level for final approval before any purchase order could be issued.

Has your prospect made decisions of a similar value before? If so, how often? If you are dealing with a product or service that falls within the normal parameters of the prospect's purchasing habits, then expect no undue tension or stress. However, if your proposal approaches the upper levels of your prospects' authority (close to their signing limits), then expect some inner stress to build. If your proposal falls beyond the upper limits, then you will have to enact strategies to involve the process or the people who have the eventual signing authority.

> *"Mr. O'Reilly, every department has its purchasing limits. It is not uncommon to see our proposals to exceed departmental authorization limits. Could you show me some guidelines as to what our upper limits are in terms of your department making a purchasing commitment? If the accepted project happens to exceed these limits, then what escalation process can we look forward to?"*

Be careful to *de-personalize* the question: to use "departmental limits" or "regional restrictions" rather than refer to personal limitations. Be careful, however, to maintain the preferential communication system. Find out how far the prospect can take the decision and what lies beyond if it exceeds the prospect's personal or departmental limits. Find out who the *escalation* players are.

Product or Service Familiarity

Has your prospect purchased your type of product or service before and has it been a positive experience? When selling my security marking system to major industries, the product was perceived as untried, untested, and unfamiliar.

A whole process of education to make the customer familiar with the results of using the system had to be nurtured and expectations had to be built and monitored. The selling cycle was usually extended by a year or more while the educational process was being delivered. However, once several major industry players were using the system, the sales cycle was reduced dramatically.

If your product or service is unknown and untried, then you, too, must build familiarity as part of your selling cycle. You cannot expect a person who is charged with the responsibility of spending corporate funds (or personal funds) to make premature purchasing decisions just because you apply closing pressure. Decisions come more quickly in familiar situations.

Just think of how you react when faced with unfamiliar buying situations. Take, for instance, a restaurant: if it's your favorite and you've been there many times before, you know what you want to eat without a lot of stress or strain. However, if you are visiting a new restaurant with a different menu, or perhaps a type of food that is new to you, then you might struggle with your decisions. You feel higher stress and more anticipation or anxiety. The second time you go back, the choices are more familiar and the stress levels are much lower.

> *"Miss Winsor, what experiences have you had with this type of service in the past?"*

Acceptance

Many times, just the name of a well-known company can open doors and put the purchaser at ease. If you represent a brand name company with a well-established name, image and reputation, then it will be easier for you to establish a positive commitment profile. If, on the other hand, your firm is unknown or has a tarnished reputation, then you have some character building to do. Dealing with the unknown scares buyers. It creates personal stress that blocks buying decisions.

If either you or your company has sold to your client before and the relationship has been positive, then the commitment process has already begun. If the client has not dealt with you or your company, then the commitment process is missing the "who we are" cornerstone and you must ensure that you take the time and effort to construct it.

Budget Capabilities

If your prospect doesn't have the budget currently available for your purchase, there are always extraordinary funds available somewhere for exceptional needs. However, most of these situations will involve the next budget cycle. If the client is talking about purchasing far in the future and you feel that there is less than a 50% chance of it becoming a *real* budget item, then prioritize the sale accordingly. It is *critical* that you both you and your client identify the budget timing and parameters early. If you do, then this recognition becomes a foundation stone for purchasing commitment. Agree on the budget, and half your selling task is completed.

> *"Suzanne, what budget range do you see for this project and is it in the current budget cycle or can we look towards the next budget cycle?"*

Influencers

Often, there are people who act as influencers in the buying decision, advisors on everything from technical matters to finance. If the influencers are partial decision makers, then you must include them in the selling process from the beginning. Usually they require a different type of information or assurance than your key contact does. In order to engineer a complete commitment program, each influencer must be satisfied for the final, compound decision to be positive. Locate the influencers and their roles early by using an *"aside from yourself"* probe.

Personal or Process Decision

In most smaller firms, decisions are made on a personal level with personal accountability. However, in larger organizations, managers are assigned a process responsibility with no personal accountability for decisions other than for maintaining the integrity of the decision process itself. Is your contact responsible for making a personal buying decision or is the person responsible for assuring that a purchasing process is followed? Each position can represent a valid prospect. If you suspect that there is an institutional purchasing process to be met, then you must identify all the parameters of the process.

> *"Mr. Davidson, would you please outline the purchasing process involved for new products entering your system?"*

Political Atmosphere

New firms tend to be entrepreneurial; they are more risk-oriented and tend to make decisions on a personal basis rather than through a well-oiled and protected institutional process. If the firm is large, with more than four or five management levels, you can bet it has process oozing out of every department.

Anytime you find significant process, you'll find employees who do not take personal risks. You cannot expect them to take risks. Therefore, you must adjust your personal expectations to meet the actual operating environment and atmosphere of the client firm. You can get a square peg into a round hole, but it tends to wreck the peg and the hole, not to mention that it requires a lot of extra effort. Better to reshape the peg or find a square hole. Do not impress your corporate politics on your customers. They may do things in an awkward fashion, but you'll have to play along for the most part.

Personality Style
By now, the importance of personality style should be self-evident. If you are dealing with a Victor or Impulsive, then you can expect quicker decisions and a more personal interaction. If you are dealing with an Examiner or Relater, then expect a more process-oriented, structured sale that not will involve a personal decision: the process decides. Be careful when dealing with Relaters as you build your commitment strategies, for they tend to be more concerned with making friends than they are in purchasing the product or service and they are usually inconsistent decision makers.

Personal Stability
People who are new to positions might want to try to impress you and others with big talk, but they are usually pretty leery about taking too bold a step in terms of expenditures. If they are new to a company, the same thing applies. Sometimes, however, they are unaware of the political consequences and spend freely. Be sensitive to the person's position and where he or she has come from. Part of your commitment strategy may be to ally yourself personally with the newcomer.

Entrenched employees take few risks but hold many keys to your selling success. They tend to resist new associations and like to deal with well-known suppliers and products. Appeal to the stability and the non-risk (safe) areas of your product or service, and prepare documentation to support your claims. It is handy if you can have other recognized industry peers back your product.

Risk of Decision
The more risk that is involved in the purchase of your product, the harder it will be for process-oriented clients to purchase. Risk creates

negative stress for the process-oriented person. For the more spontaneous firm or buyer, however, risk-oriented decisions involve positive stress. Trying to sell a high-risk product to a low-risk firm is difficult. Analyze your product, your approach and your clients to see if the acceptable risk levels match.

Forestalling Objections and Concerns

One of the most important processes in engineering commitment is to eliminate as many concerns and negatives as possible before actually asking the client to purchase. The method for doing this involves drawing out expectations and setting new expectations. It also includes a process known as forestalling. Forestalling is the act of deliberately bringing up an area that may be traditionally voiced as an objection and resolving it before it becomes cancerous.

> *"Debbie, you know we've all heard the rumors that the silver market is too volatile to trust. Well, I'd like you to take just a few minutes to listen to the reports about the actual performance of the market and to hear about the investment results obtained by a number of our clients before we proceed any further."*

Every product, every situation has its share of negatives. Be they emotional, product-related, financial or hearsay, they all can influence the commitment process. Make a list of recurring objections and decide on ways to bring them up in a positive, constructive manner before the customer brings them up in a negative, defensive manner. If you are not afraid to show the customer that you are prepared to deal with both the negatives and the positives up front, then you will establish a more dialog-oriented consultative selling process.

Handling Unexpected Concerns

Many times clients will suddenly bring up unexpected objections or personal concerns. There are a number of areas from which these concerns come:

- Personal biases, opinions, style clashes, affiliations, loyalties and beliefs;
- Performance expectations or criteria that are not met, not filled, inappropriate or insufficient;
- Financial areas: price and value relationships, budget restrictions and expectations;
- Authority areas: not personally authorized to take action or make purchasing commitments;
- Insufficient time for analysis: information must be fully digested and claims corroborated before the decision can be approached or made;
- Overly severe decision intensity;
- Process not being followed correctly.

There are probably one or two other areas, but usually if an objection is encountered it will be coming from one of the above areas. The important part of your job is to determine which area it comes from. The prospect won't tell you when he or she first utters the objection or concern. The real reason is almost always concealed. Just think of yourself when you go shopping and you notice something you like. Then you notice the price and decide that there is not enough value for the money.

The salesperson catches you before you can move on and asks you if he or she can help. *"Nope, just looking, thank you,"* comes your reply. What you really meant was *"I like this but the price seems too high."*

We seldom tell the truth. We tell pseudo-truths, half lies, white lies and generally "excusify" our way past situations that we would rather not take the time to address. Your client or prospect does the same thing, but in a business context:

> *"Well, I like the look of your materials but I can't do anything right now. Thanks for stopping by."*

The client didn't tell you what was really on his mind. What he really meant was:

> *"I think your prices are too high and I don't understand how the new features will affect my operations."*

How do you get to the truth? First, assume that the objection you hear is not the objection that is really felt, heard or seen. Unless the client has been specific and given details as to exactly why and what is causing the concern, assume that the objection given is smoke. The real concern lies a probe or two deeper. To dig deeper, simply phrase bounce or use the *"Oh?"* query:

> *"Too high?"*
>
> *"Features?"*
>
> *"Oh?"*

Each time you reply with a puzzled probe, the prospect explores his or her position for a enhanced explanation. Eventually, the truth is revealed. Once you find out the real objection or concern, you can deal with it.

Key Objection Strategy: AGREE, RESOLVE, ASK

If you can first agree with the client or recognize why he or she has expressed a concern, then you will immediately begin to dissolve the inherent hostility found in almost any objection. Agreeing can be accomplished in many ways, but it is always done to put the client at ease and to diffuse a potential confrontation. My favorites have always been

> *"I'm glad you brought that up..."*
>
> *"That's good!"*
>
> *"You know, not many people question this point and I am really glad you brought it up..."*

Once you have agreed, then resolve the concern or objection by looking at the positive side rather than the negative. The key technique is using the word *however*, which bridges between the agreement stage and the resolve stage, turning the objection towards a solution.

> *"I'm glad you brought that up, Tom, because it is an area in which many people don't get a good feel for right away. However, it is the one area that contains an abundance of potential for the right person."*

The next key stage is to regain control by asking a question.

> *"Tom, how would you feel if I were to suggest that you could double your money in less than a year if you played your hand right?"*

These key objection techniques are the basic strategy for turning around most objections. The phrases may be substituted to reflect the type of objection received, but in a nutshell, *Agree-Resolve-Ask*. Let's examine in more depth the main areas from which objections arise.

Personal Reasons

For objections involving kinesthetic feelings, opinions, loyalties or beliefs, use the *Feel-Felt-Found* reply. I personally like this one because it allows someone to hold an opinion or belief without endangering the sale. It also gives assurance to those who feel that they might be entering new, uncharted waters by making a buying decision for a product or service about which they know very little.

> *"I know how you feel, Mrs. Bolton, and as a matter of fact, most of our satisfied customers felt exactly like you do right now when they made their decisions to buy a new Ham Hacker Deluxe. However, what they found was that after using it for just a couple of sandwiches, they wouldn't prepare their meats any other way. It's just that convenient! Now, how many sandwiches do you feel you currently prepare each week?"*

The visually-oriented prospect uses visual language and so you must convert the feel-felt-found strategy into something more understandable. Try *see-saw-discovered.*

> *"John, I can see how this affects you right now, and as a matter of record, most of our current clients saw this exactly like you do now before they made their decisions to buy a new Ham Hacker Deluxe. However, what they discovered was that after using it for just a few sandwiches, they couldn't see any other way of preparing their meats. It's just that convenient! Now, how many sandwiches do you see yourself preparing each week, John?"*

And then we have the audible prospect who likes to *hear* the demonstration and the future. Try *hear-heard-said.*

> *"Marthann, I hear what you are saying, and as a matter of record, most of our customers were heard saying the same thing before they made their decisions to purchase a Ham Hacker Deluxe. However, what they said was that after using it for just a couple of sandwiches, they wouldn't prepare their meats any other way. It's just that convenient! Now, how many sandwiches do you say that you currently prepare each week?"*

Finally, for the prospect using an intellectual preferential communications system, use intellectual terms. Try *understand, mentioned, concluded.*

> *"Skip, I understand your position. As a matter of fact, most of our satisfied customers mentioned the same concerns you have mentioned before they bought a new Ham Hacker Deluxe. However, what they finally concluded after using it for just a few sandwiches was that they wouldn't prepare their sandwiches any other way. Now, how many sandwiches do you think you might prepare each week?"*

Performance Criteria
For objections involving performance be sure to locate the exact concern before attempting to deal with it. If the performance concern is valid,

seek either a technical solution or a technical compromise. Obviously, if the customer requires a product that must peel 50 potatoes per second and you only can deliver one that peels five, then the performance problem is difficult to overcome. Try to seek or find a creative solution that can meet the client's needs. Also examine the expectational criteria for validity; it might be that it cannot be met by *any* product.

Financial Areas
Generally, price is an apparent problem when value has not been fully explained and interpreted. Relate price to function, advantages, benefits and added value. There is no such objection as the "price is too high." This is always a misunderstanding of relative value. When encountering a price objection, agree first with the customer and then move towards a value relationship:

> *"Yes, I hear what you're saying. The price is slightly higher than the average that you'd pay for a set of tires. But in this case, it's good value, and I'll tell you why....." (explain added value benefits, etc.)*

Other possible causes of financial objections include budgets not being set or approved, funds not being available (corporate or personal), new budget cycle not in effect yet, competitive prices are lower (or higher), etc. A financial objection is an opportunity to explore financial options. There are millions of us who have made purchases using finance plans or mortgages to make the financial burden lighter.

There are many ways to express price: easy payment plans, lease arrangements, residuals, interest rates, amortization schedules, non-taxable portions and many other financial terms that break "price" into less intimidating elements.

Authority Areas
When you continue to receive objections that seem to be unfounded, look for a lack of authority to make the purchase. This is an area where prospects can "lose face" if your detective work is not carried out with tact and understanding. Perhaps you forgot to ask, *"Aside from*

yourself, who else might be involved in the purchase?" Or, you could depersonalize the question by asking, *"What other processes must be completed before the final purchase decision can be confirmed?"*

In both cases, you must seek an alternative route to a decision if your prospect does not have the personal authority or ability to make the decision.

Insufficient Time
Allowing sufficient time for information to be examined and claims to be checked is particularly important for Examiners and for products or services that do not have track records or references.

Trying to rush your decision will only increase tension and trigger a closer examination of your materials. It could also result in a total sales failure, in that you alienate the prospect by applying closing pressure too early. Examiner individuals and industries like to take their time and make sure that they can spread the responsibility for the decision among as many players as possible.

This strategy protects the individuals in case there is a backlash from the product purchase. If it goes badly, no one person can be blamed; it was a group decision and every member shares just a bit of the responsibility, but not enough to incur serious personal retribution.

Understand the dynamics of Examiner types of organizations, such as banks, governments, large firms with more than five levels of management and institutions such as hospitals, universities and school boards. They work in a common fashion by spreading the liabilities through disseminating the decision. Thus, everybody gets to keep his or her job. This is one reason why decisions in institutional environments take so long to make. No one has clear-cut accountability so no one takes clear-cut responsibility. They play not to lose.

Your strategy should allow enough time to examine but not enough time to allow your proposal to find a comfortable resting place on the shelf. My favorite has always been to determine *who* is in the "group" and *when* do we meet and *what* will be accomplished.

> *"Mr. Wood, aside from yourself, who else do you see involved in evaluating the project as presented? How long do you see it taking you and your group to complete your studies? Exactly when can we meet again to look at the areas that need refinement and what would you foresee as our next agenda?"*

Just remember that all Examiners feel threatened when they are pressed for an actual decision. They believe that process makes the best decision.

Decision Intensity

If you make $1,000 decisions daily, then a $1,000 decision is easy for you. You know the situation, you've been there before. Faced with a $100,000 decision, you take additional appropriate steps to ensure that the decision is sound and proper and that your position is protected. Although the process of making a decision is not new, the amount involved in the decision is and, therefore, caution is exercised.

The type of objections that come from this area are "slow down," "spread the liability" and "insufficient time" objections. The decision level is too intense for the individual and so the burden is usually shared by others or by the process.

The other side is when you are dealing with a person who is not used to making decisions at all. This is common when dealing with the retail customer or with Relaters. If a person is not skilled at decision making and can't make a decision, then the objections again will seem inconsistent with the product's value or use. All things seem to point to a positive decision yet you keep getting nonsense objections.

Your strategy is to reduce the decision into something more appetizing, something more "bite size." Therefore, a $20,000 car becomes $400 per month, or it becomes the difference between the $18,000 and the $20,000 car: $30 per month. For some people, the decision has to be brought down to a level where their decision-making skills are active and refined.

This type of strategy, called "closing on a minor point," is used to replace large, unmanageable decisions with much smaller, digestible ones. This strategy can use money, features, functions, advantages or benefits as its structure; it generally uses a *"Which would you prefer?"* alternative choice probe architecture.

> *"Mr. Kolke, which would you prefer, the standard remote control unit or the one that also controls your DVD?"*
>
> *"Which would you prefer, the standard model as shown here, or do you like the look of the sports deluxe with all these added features at only $41 more per month?"*

It is not unusual, especially in some retail industries, even to vary the term of the financing package to dramatize the differences in benefits. For instance, a customer might be shown one product with a price tag of $4,000 and a 24-month finance program at 12%. The payments would be about $187 per month. Then he or she is shown a more deluxe version of the product at $6,000 and by using a 36-month amortization at 13.5% the payments come out to only $15 more per month! By manipulating the finance package, the value received for the increment charged is nothing short of "incredible."

Reduce the decision level and increase the value level until the decision is made. When selling aircraft, I sold more leisure aircraft by closing on a choice between colors than anything else. The important aspect to an alternative choice decision is that your client not be aware of the possible third choice: *none of the above.*

Process

If the sales process simply has not completed its procedural path, the objections will be fairly straightforward and will usually contain some form of request for additional detail. Generally in businesses where a definitive purchasing protocol is firmly in place, you can watch your efforts meander slowly through the process path until a decision is birthed in the form of a purchase order. To uncover problems within the process, simply ask.

"Julie, I have lost track of where my proposal now sits within your organization. Where are we in terms of seeing the proposal ratified and what steps still remain before we can expect to see a purchase order issued?"

QUICK CLOSING

Sometimes, a client will make a purchasing decision early and will not need to become involved in a drawn-out, expectational search. The danger in closing early is that a client may back off and be lost or may make the decision based solely on price rather than on explained and explored value. To test for early acceptance, cautiously probe.

"Jim, if I hear you correctly, it sounds as if you are familiar with this type of equipment. You seem to know exactly what you want and how much you want to pay. Why don't we get right down to the business of selecting the proper unit?"

Test your client by extracting opinions, feelings and thoughts.

"Sue, what's your opinion on having a matched pair rather than just a new washer?"

*"Barney, you seem to really like this model. How'd you feel about saving **$1,000** by considering a demonstrator?"*

"Sir, as you know, these compressors are in high demand by all industries and the wait for factory orders is now up to three months. If I could find a new unit at one of our out-of-town dealers, how would you feel about taking advantage of that by placing an immediate order?"

"Doctor, I appreciate that you have little time to spend on evaluating all the options and details of this unit. You can be assured just by its reputation that it does the job and does it well. How would you feel if we installed one next week, with the full understanding that if it is not what you expected or if does not do the job, then we will take it out, no questions asked?"

STYLE DIFFERENCES IN COMMITMENT

The Impulsive

Big dreams, big desires, big decisions: these are all a part of the Impulsive. They make irrational, emotional and flamboyant decisions that say, *"Look at me!"* In dealing with an Impulsive, throw out a challenge and build on a dream of what could be by painting vivid word pictures.

Be careful of the decisions made, however, because Impulsives tend to think decisions through only partially and to ignore many of the consequences, such as financing, implementation and impact upon others. They tend to make sudden and daring decisions and often exhibit a lack of maturity in the decision-making process. You might have to take on the role of devil's advocate to promote a rational and sound decision.

Because Impulsives tend to make hurried decisions, there are many cases of buyer's remorse and of sales unable to be completed due to missing detail or the company's purchasing procedures not being followed. (Impulsives cut red tape with swords, not scissors.)

Close early, be enthusiastic and get Impulsives physically involved with your product: they like to "experience" things. Personally pay attention to completing detail, because Impulsives will not.

The Victor

The results-oriented factual Victor looks for crisp, to-the-point presentations. They like to box and will dismiss an unworthy opponent with a quick verbal jab. Stand and deliver. You must show Victors that you can run with them, but don't take the lead away. Concentrate on impact and cost justification; present your product or service so that it makes or saves money in the final analysis.

Have references from associates and peers. Tighten the time frame. You do the leg work; let the Victor make the decisions. Be straightforward and bold. The decisions will be good and sturdy. Close early once your product's impact is understood and accepted. Don't bore Victors with detail and don't try to be friends. Just do your job professionally and with a sensitivity towards time and the Victor's ego.

The Examiner
Careful attention to detail; plenty of third-party, unbiased supporting documentation; and an appropriate portion of time are needed to satisfy the Examiner's need to be correct. Do your homework, prepare logically and carefully, and present in a methodical manner. Talk using process terminology. Explore the actual purchasing process with the Examiner and then follow it.

Do not expect personal help but do expect assistance to follow the purchasing process. Give Examiners time, but quantify it. Set a next appointment and discuss the agenda for the next meeting before you leave the present one. Get all the players involved, for it is rare to find an Examiner personally and solely risking a decision. Use the *"aside from yourself"* probes to locate the others involved. Follow the yellow brick road and you will eventually get to Oz.

The Relater
The weakest of the decision makers, the Relater tends to make emotional and pleasing decisions. Most Relaters are purposefully surrounded by process to protect them (and their companies) from themselves. Objections stem primarily from the inability to make personal decisions and from the lack of authority to make decisions in a corporate environment. To enhance the decision character of the Relater, gently suggest a decision for them and get them to adopt your suggestion.

Explore personal feelings and opinions that might lead them towards a decision. They require time but, more importantly, they require the support and understanding of others. Use word pictures that paint a safe, warm and harmonious product-use picture.

To help them make decisions, try increasing the conversational pace slightly and begin to change your vocabulary from personal, feeling-oriented expression to more factual expression. Try this only after you have achieved a solid rapport. If they follow your lead towards a more decision-prone style (Impulsive or Victor), making decisions will actually come easier and be less stressful for them.

Negotiating a Decision

Many customers enjoy negotiating a commitment – they seem to find it more businesslike. Instead of having to make a decision, they enter into a process of negotiation and discussion with the end result already concluded: a sale! It's not a complicated strategy nor is it a trick:

> *"Mr. Gilroy, I think we both agree that there will be a substantial positive effect once the training is completed and skills are effectively in use. But I personally feel that we need to negotiate some key items in several areas before the final course agenda can be set. The first area that we might discuss is ..."*

Negotiating assumes that a final result (a purchase) is already achieved; it just needs clarification.

The Non-Decision Decision

In institutions and institution-like businesses, most decisions are made by process and not by individuals. In these cases, do not set your personal expectations on getting a personal decision. Accept the process route to a sale and look for a sale occurring through the machinery of management. The decision evolves and a purchase order is the result.

Many times your contact will know that a decision has been made only after the purchase order has been issued and sent. This is a non-decision decision; it comes through meeting requirements, tender specifications or some other controlled means of purchasing. Play the game; don't play the person. Become a part of the process, but be sure you let the prospect know that you expect a *decision* to come from the process.

Commitment Action

It is extremely important for you to get your client to take personal action once a buying decision has been made. Signing an agreement, getting the next step defined, handing over the product, arranging for shipment or delivery, getting a deposit check, getting a purchase order number or whatever else the situation demands, get the client to take some form of commitment action. The only time when this is not important is when you are dealing with a process sale.

One important aspect of these final stages in the sale is to forestall *buyer's remorse.* If your customers make decisions that are unusually rushed, high-priced or difficult, then they will more than likely experience that *"Oh, no, what did I do???"* feeling.

> *"Jim and Wanda, you know this is a pretty important decision you've made and it's not unusual to feel a little uneasy about it when you get home. We don't usually make decisions of this magnitude every day and you're bound to feel some butterflies later on. But it's just natural to feel this way.*
>
> *ust remember that you have made a sound financial decision on a house with exceptional value and location. You'll be more than thankful that you've made this decision and if for any reason you want to see the property again before you take possession, you just feel free to call me and I'll make the arrangements."*

YOUR DOUBLING STRATEGY

Engineering a total commitment posture takes a lot of work and preparation, but the rewards are many. Most salespeople become superstars if they are just 10% better than the average. If you analyze what your actual closing average is currently (1 out of 10? 1 out of 5? 1 out of 3?) and determine where you want to be (doubling), then you know what kind of effort you must place into analyzing and preparing for incremental engineered commitment. If taken in small bites, a meal is delicious and appreciated; if taken in rushed gulps, it only leads to tummy aches. Don't depend on the skill of closing to make a good salesperson out of you. Depend on applying the strategies and preparation of an engineered commitment. *Bon appetit!*

DOUBLING

1. Look at your current style and selling approach to analyze where commitment building can begin in earnest. Are you applying pressure too soon? Do you force your clients into decisions before they are ready? Do you ask for a decision at all? Do you use closing as your primary selling skill and neglect most of the others? Rearrange your selling approach to reflect a more gradual, incremental commitment process by intentionally getting agreement as you discuss each expectation, feature, function, advantage or benefit. Each week, find a new way to get your clients involved in incremental agreement.

2. Analyze and arrange your sales and marketing materials to reflect an incremental approach. Each piece should logically lead to the next, and each piece should provide an opportunity for agreement. For each presentation, prepare your materials in advance for each client.

3. Examine how you build and maintain control of the commitment process within the context of the overall sale. Isolate the elements in your presentation or selling style that tend to abuse control or to lose control. Replace these elements with alternatives that seek to maintain control without appearing to take control forcefully.

4. For each of your clients and prospects, build a decision-making profile. Start developing strategies around each profile to engineer a commitment posture for the client. Review weekly how each profile is being met and adjust it accordingly.

5. List objections and concerns that seem to appear continually during your sales attempts. Structure a forestalling program for each major objection and begin introducing them one at a time into your selling strategies. Isolate one per week and master it.

6. Practice dealing with unexpected concerns or objections. If the concern is a recurring one, then develop a forestalling technique. Practice the Agree-Resolve-Ask formula for performance, price and timing concerns, and the Feel-Felt-Found/See-Saw-Discovered/Hear-Heard-Said methods for personal matters.

7. Practice turning price into value. Make a two-column list. On one side, put "price" and other adjectives relating directly to the price objection, such as "cost too much" or "can't afford it." On the other side, structure value resolutions explaining and offsetting the price concern. Each week, add a new resolution.

8. Build a battery of tactful questions that seek the decision making authority and process. Build one new personal probe and one impersonal probe each week that locates the real decision maker or the actual process route.

9. Construct some probes that attempt to locate the prospect's decision-making comfort zones in terms of dollars and function. Don't forget to include how often in your strategies. Then develop a program that converts major decisions into minor ones. Have several decision-making level options, such as $4,000 full price, $400 per month, $40 per month difference from basic model, etc.

10. Look at each style type and review all your commitment strategies to see what effect style has on commitment. Each week, review one style type and adjust all your strategies to fit the commitment expectations of that style.

CYCLE-SHORTENING STRATEGIES

THE SELLING SCHEMATIC

A sale tends to progress logically from the *initial contact*, through a qualification stage, to a needs analysis stage and then to an expectational analysis stage. After processing the information into a probable solution, the sale then proceeds to a presentation stage and then to the resolution or closing stage, which consummates the initial sale. The final stage is the follow-through, or linking stage, which bridges old or current sales to future sales with an existing client.

The selling process can be simplified into three primary functions: *input, process* and *output*. Although this progression seems logical, most sales involve repeating many steps, especially in a recall situation. However, from an overall perspective, the sales process will follow the above sequence. Let's have a brief look at the events in each section so that the schematic is more clear.

INPUT

Input is the initial contact, information-gathering, qualifying and expectation-setting phase of the sale, where customer objectives are explored, determined and set. During this stage, rapport is generally achieved or lost. Input involves some or all of the following elements. It may be achieved in just a few minutes or it may take several months and many visits.

Quick Qualify:

- Application scope
- Performance expectations

- Budget and financial expectations
- Decision-making process or path
- Timing
- Key features, functions, advantages and benefits sought
- Influencers involved
- Competition Involved

Analyze Needs:

- Application details
- Performance specifications, objectives and expectations
- Complete financial parameters and expectations
- Decision-making process, decision-making path and the person responsible for the purchasing decision
- Influencers and their expectations
- How often, when, and how soon the product is needed
- Required key features and functions
- Desired alternative features and functions
- Key competition
- Personal and political needs

Set Expectations:

- Set scope of purchase
- Set performance parameters
- Set budget range
- Set financial parameters
- Set decision-making process
- Set timing aspects
- Set key 20% performance expectations
- Set competition elimination parameters

- Set key spec areas
- Set influencers' involvement
- Set proposal scope expectations
- Set presentation expectations
- Set commitment and acquisition expectations
- Set next meeting expectations if necessary
- Reset or restate unrealistic expectations

Accept Expectations:

- Review each expectation
- Restate with benefit expectation
- Get client to agree with expectation
- Get client to accept expectation
- Summarize expectations and benefits

PROCESS

When you have fully explored and set expectations, you are then (and only then) positioned to process the information into a suitable presentation. The processing can be immediate or it may take days, weeks or months to conclude.

Construct Proposal:

- Personalized
- Background
- Summary of stated expectations and value
- Key expectations: met or exceeded and benefits
- Additional expectations met equals added value benefits
- Financial summary
- Implementation process, schedule, events
- Sample agreement and supporting documentation

Prepare Documentation:

- Style type orientation
- Overall scope of purchase
- Section details and specifications
- Costing analysis
- Return-on-investment analysis
- Warranty, guarantee and contract samples
- Testimonials, industry-related user list
- Technical liaison personnel

PRESENTATION, PREPARATION AND STRATEGY:

- Style type orientation
- Focus: improve, maintain, protect, save or gain
- Depth of information required
- Budget cycle or purchase cycle timing
- Which players are involved and when
- Where you will present (location)
- Timing for presentation
- Support personnel requirements
- Creating believability factors
- Printing materials, proposals and presentation graphics
- Equipment required to present (slides, overhead/video projector, laptop, etc.)
- Motivational factors
- Your personal enthusiasm and appearance
- Goodies (coffee, Danish, treats)
- Cycle-shortening tradeoffs
- Commitment program
- Added value/standard value relationships

OUTPUT

Once you understand your solution and have prepared to present it, then the output phase of the sales process begins. This is where you hopefully meet or exceed the client's expectations. If you have done a good job of exploring and setting expectations, then the presentation will flow smoothly and effortlessly. If you have short-circuited the input section and skipped the expectational development phase, then you can expect objection after objection. Garbage in = Garbage out.

Review Expectations:

- Summarize expectations and objectives
- Get client to agree and accept summary

Meet or Exceed Expectations:

- State expectation
- Link associated benefit, advantage, function
- Link feature
- Provide proof: demonstrate or document
- Repeat for each accepted expectation

Establish Value:

- Link price with performance
- Seek agreement and acceptance on value

Obtain Opinions:

- Use open opinion probes
- Use leading closed probes
- Obtain preliminary commitment on basic value

Add Value:

- Link subordinate expectations to increase value
- Add additional features, functions, benefits
- Link new performance with old price
- Prove using testimonials, documentation

Initiate Acquisition:

- Ask to initiate acquisition or purchasing process
- Ask detail implementation questions
- Assume purchase; seek purchase order
- Work both the process and the prospect

Get Commitment Action:

- Have "Accepted by..." area on proposal
- Have implementation date scheduled
- Get agreement on joint action

The sales process is simply the logical path to a selling conclusion. There are many areas in the selling process that tend to be repeated and can cause delay in the completion of the sale. Some areas can easily be missed or left incomplete, which also causes delays in the sale.

The focus of this chapter is how to shorten the selling cycle (the length of time it takes to sell a client), not shortening the selling process. If you shorten the process, you will generally lengthen the cycle. The question is: how can you do the required sales work in less time?

IDENTIFYING THE CYCLE

The sales cycle is the length of time between the initial sales contact and the eventual delivery of the product. The cycle is unique for each company, each product, each salesperson, each territory. The effect of decreasing the amount of time required to sell and deliver is dramatic: lower overall selling costs, lower inventory costs, more time to sell to others, better client response, larger client base and many other results that just improve everybody's position.

The starting point in any time study exercise involves identifying your personal sales cycle with each product and with each client.

TIGHTENING THE CYCLE

Use the schematic of the sales process and modify it for your particular selling situation. Identify the length of time it takes, on average, to complete each step. Then determine what you could do physically to consolidate or condense the time frame. If you are now making three calls to close a sale, could you do it in two? Are you constantly revisiting steps in the selling process, backtracking and wasting time on rebuilding to the point where you last left off? Are you leaving too early, before you have accomplished your call goals? Are the customers' meeting expectations similar to yours?

There are many questions you could ask yourself but, for the purpose of building a cycle-shortening strategy, let's categorize the critical areas.

- Schedule crystal-clear objectives to be met during each sales call.

- Decide how much time it will take to meet these objectives.

- Ask for this specific amount of time with the prospect. Ask if the meeting could stretch to ensure that all objectives are met by both parties if necessary.

- Prepare questions in advance and write them down in a logical sequence. Don't forget that you want to set expectation levels as well as to determine purchasing parameters.

- Prepare forestalling techniques to remove early objections.

- Get influencers and decision makers involved as early as possible; prepare materials for their specific roles.

- Do a group presentation rather than a series of one-on-one meetings. Bring in your experts to assist the influencers.

- Start setting the expected time frame for a purchasing decision by suggesting concrete dates and times.

- Provide an incentive for closing early and without having to make another visit. Alternatively, arrange to have agreements and documentation travel by fax, thereby avoiding additional personal visits and postal delays.

- Consider what other things you can do by phone, fax or courier rather than by a personal visit.

Most salespeople define the objectives of their sales calls poorly. Therefore, every call becomes a good call or a bad call, depending upon the observer. You goal is to create tangible call objectives for each and every call. It is more effective to plan carefully and then execute than it is to execute alone. Most Second and Third Dimension Sellers spend far more time planning than they do in actual execution.

Skills form a primary foundation upon which the cycle-shortening strategies can work. Without a solid base of probing and presentation skills, you will find it much more difficult to enact your strategies.

STANDARD TIME

One area that you can work upon immediately is erasing standard time from your thinking. Standard time in this context is not what you seasonally "fall back" to when resetting the clocks after summer; it is the time that is normally accepted by a prospect for evaluating and making a purchasing decision.

Time is always relative to a number of criteria: need, value, available resources, budgets, breakdowns, ego, competition, etc. For instance, if the fan belt broke on your car while driving to an important meeting, your need for a new belt would be immediate and critical, and whether the repair person charged you $5 or $50 wouldn't really matter. The important thing would be to get the repair done so that you could be on your way quickly. What would be important is time, not money (unless the repair price were ridiculous).

You always have an opportunity to create a new expected time frame. I say *new* because every buyer has an existing time expectation, whether it is conscious or not. Look at your currently acceptable time for the sales cycle, then determine just how you can "spring forward" into accelerated time.

ACCELERATED TIME

Simply put, accelerated time means *more done in less time.* Re-arrange the expectations of your client to focus on an accelerated time frame for acquisition. If the industry standard is a six-month evaluation, create a process in which the product can be evaluated within three months or less. If the prospect is working on next year's budget cycle, introduce extraordinary benefits provided that the product is purchased during the current budget cycle. Don't set your next meeting for next month; set it for next week. Don't make the meeting for a half an hour; make it for two hours and get the job done, if that is what's required to meet your call objectives. Accelerated time can be accomplished in many ways:

- Suggesting an accelerated meeting schedule;
- Suggesting longer, more productive meetings;
- Suggesting group meetings with influencers and decision makers present and participating;
- Suggesting an increased benefit for early decisions or added value areas that come from early commitment;
- Suggesting alternative financial arrangements that could give ownership now rather than later;
- Suggesting the emotional side of having "new" now rather than later;
- Suggesting the advantages of having a seasonal product for the beginning of the season rather than later on, or taking advantage of season-end bargains rather than waiting for next year's higher prices (a double savings);
- Outlining concrete meeting times and objectives and having all parties agree to an accelerated time frame;

- Preparing and providing documentation in advance of its being required;
- Forestalling objections that could delay the evaluation or commitment decision.

You choose the time and then make it appear that the customer is the one who benefits most from an early decision and implementation. It is entirely possible to double your sales just through initiating time acceleration techniques and expectations with only your major clients.

Standard Procedure

Every company has standard buying procedures that should be followed. If you can isolate these procedures and stay within their parameters, then your purchase will proceed along a normal and safe course. This is why it is important to identify the purchasing process within the company or institution. Play the game and you have a chance to win, but if you change the rules, you can easily become disqualified.

Most salespeople don't understand the purchasing process and try to circumvent the system by closing too early, applying undue pressure, or dangling incentive carrots when the system can't take advantage of them. This, in effect, is changing the rules for many purchasing agents and buyers. Change the rules and you lose, or the game is delayed because you've been handed a "roughing" penalty.

Most clients can be sold if you follow *their* rules of behavior. Most have standard buying procedures. Just by following the procedures, you can eliminate a lot of penalties. By eliminating the penalties, you can score more often.

Extraordinary Procedure

This statement may sound as if it contradicts the previous section, but all organizations (and individuals) have hidden procedures for handling exceptional situations.

Growing up in Montreal, I spent many hours watching hockey in my youth. During the last few minutes of most hockey games, extraordinary procedures became evident, as the team that was down by a goal or two attempted a final scoring blitz so as not to lose. Standard playing procedures were replaced by extraordinary procedures when the defensemen were pulled and replaced by additional offensive forwards. Then, as the final minute approached, the goalie skated furiously to the bench while another additional forward immediately leapt into action, thereby tipping the offensive manpower scales in favor of their team. The objective: score one goal before the clock runs out. It is an extraordinary procedure reserved only for do-or-die situations. Although extraordinary, it is valid and available for use when required.

Buyers have extraordinary procedures. They may not be as well defined as those in hockey, but they are there. Do not confuse them with breaking the rules: extraordinary procedures are defined by the buyer, not by the seller.

Extraordinary buying procedures are used when an extraordinary situation arises, such as an emergency, an unusual profit opportunity or a major change (management shift, corporate buy-out, death, etc.). If you have the capability of developing an unusual opportunity that can trigger the extraordinary buying procedure, then by all means demonstrate this to the buyer. You must first find out when and how the procedure is used, and then try to tap into it.

> *"Mr. Rausch, many of our clients have extraordinary purchasing procedures that address unbudgeted items such as major unscheduled repairs.*
>
> *Sometimes this procedure is also used to take advantage of unusual, time-sensitive opportunities that either increase the firm's profitability or reduce its risk.*
>
> *Could you please explain to me how your firm's non-budget policy works?"*

If you don't ask, you won't know. If you get an informative, cooperative result, then work upon it to see if your client would be interested in your extraordinary opportunity. Every purchasing situation could be made to exercise this option, but it would usually be at the expense of your product's profit margin, and this loss has to be weighed against the increased benefits of more rapid turnover and market penetration.

A warning accompanies this strategy: If the deal sounds too good to be true, it usually is. Suspicion is instantly aroused when the value seems to be worth considerably more than the asking price. What if a person approached you on the street and, after striking up a conversation, indicated that he had a new Mercedes-Benz that he just had to get rid of. He's so anxious that he'll let it go for one-tenth its normal price. Make up your mind: take it or leave it.

Well, if a Mercedes dealer were making the offer, I'd have few second thoughts. However, because it is a person you don't know and don't trust, it is obviously too good to be true. There has to be something wrong. Your suspicion is heightened. The car *must* be stolen.

Your customers can get the same feeling of apprehension and skepticism. Find a way to make it seem believable and safe, then maybe the extraordinary purchasing process could work for you.

PARALLEL OR SERIAL?

Parallel and serial are data-processing terms, but they mean more to a salesperson's strategy than just about anything else when it comes to shortening the selling cycle. If you've had any experience in the computer world, then the section title needs little explanation. However, for those not so experienced, a little review wouldn't hurt. It will help explain this valuable strategy.

When microcomputers were first introduced in the 1980's, there were two protocols for connecting a printer to the computer: *serial* or *parallel*. In the innards of a computer, information is stored as little electronic signals called *bits*. It takes a combination of eight bits to make up a logical piece of information, such as a letter, a period or a single digit (called a "byte").

The computer could send these bits one at a time in sequence down a single "serial" wire to the printer (picture a single-lane winding country road and eight cars following one another), or it could send them eight at a time down a special eight-wire "parallel" cable (picture eight cars abreast on an eight-lane expressway). The country road represents *serial* processing; the highway represents *parallel* processing. Basically, a parallel transmission is processed eight times faster than a serial transmission.

How does this relate to sales? Review the selling process to look for processes or actions that could be taking place simultaneously but that you now do serially. Your greatest immediate sales increase will come by accomplishing more in less time.

By arranging to do things in parallel as opposed to serial, you will speed up the selling process immensely. This is why you want to sell or influence a group rather than an individual. This is why you want to make one site call to visit all the players rather than separate site calls to each one.

This is why you want your proposals to address all the players rather than just the prime one. This is why you want to bring your support people to meet with your influencers in a group. It gets the job done faster. Scrutinize your selling process until you can streamline it to include as many parallel functions as you can.

I'S AND T'S - COMPLETENESS

Many sales are lengthened by salespeople or sales support staff who forget to include key elements in the preparation of proposals or responses to tenders. This includes simple things, such as forgetting to bring in product samples from the car while visiting a prospect on a call.

The dotting the i's and the crossing the t's are as important to the salesperson as making the initial contact or doing a super presentation in front of a board of directors. The more process-oriented your client, the more critical attention to detail becomes.

By making a checklist of all the physical and reporting things that must be done for each sale and by being sure that everything is followed up in its *expected* time, the little things that stretch a sale can be controlled. Review proposals and replies to tenders personally to ensure that everything is correct and complete before it is sent or delivered to the client.

INTRODUCING CYCLE-SHORTENING EXPECTATIONS

If you help set your clients' expectations concerning the time required to evaluate and decide upon your product, then generally that's what they'll use as their expectational boundaries. If you don't set the time expectations, then there may be a potential conflict of expectations: you expect to get the order in one month; the client expects to make a decision in six.

Ask your client what measures you could take to help shorten the evaluation and decision-making time frame. Give the client a good reason to use these strategies: saving time, money, manpower, lower price, saving interest or some other motivator.

> *"Mr. Karila, it's no industry secret that we tend to work closely with our clients to ensure that an appropriate amount of time is spent on the evaluation and decision making process. We understand that time equals productivity for most businesses, and because of the significant and immediate cost reductions associated with our product,"*
>
> *"I would like to work closely with you in finding methods by which we can tighten up the period normally associated with acquisition so that these benefits can start accumulating as soon as possible. What specific steps could we take to condense the evaluation process?"*

YOUR DOUBLING STRATEGY

It is totally up to you to control the tempo of the sales cycle. You must analyze, organize, prepare and control the selling process from marketing to after-sales service. Look at what you do and how you do it, not just today but for every sale.

There is always a shorter way but not always a safer way. You must balance the cycle-shortening techniques with the overall success probabilities of the sale. If you see an opportunity for shortening or condensing then explore it and, if possible, exploit it. Your task: *do more in less time and do it better!*

DOUBLING

1. Diagram your current selling process. Understand what you do, why you do it and when you do it. How does your selling schematic compare to the one presented in this chapter? What tends to make your process work and what keeps it from being more successful than it is now? Each week, take a portion of your personal sales process and refine it.

2. For each current client, chart the selling cycle in terms of how many calls have been made, what has been accomplished during each contact, who was present, etc. Take one new client each week and add this analysis to the growing client profile.

3. Assemble your client-call analyses into groupings to look for consistent areas of good performance and areas of poor or wasteful performance. It is hard to judge this area yourself, so you should use an objective outside opinion. Try to locate the things that you do (or don't do) that contribute to stalling, objections or anything else done by the prospect that lengthens the sale.

4. Set an objective to cut your call requirements by half. Start developing your strategies to put this goal into effect by the end of a specific period of time, perhaps three months. Build a whole set of strategies with one common objective: to reduce the number of physical calls on a potential client by half without reducing the effectiveness of your sales coverage or attention. Every week, review this goal and try to add one new strategy.

5. Each call, either by phone or in person, should have a specific set of objectives. Before making the call, determine exactly how you are going to achieve these objectives and what personal and corporate benefit it will have to your client if you can reach these objectives. Make sure your objectives include obtaining a referral name and number (or a direct introduction) from each of your customers and prospects on a regular basis.

6. What is the current standard time that your industry expects you to spend generating a sale? Make your personal goal to cut this time in half. Generate strategies that will set new expectations for your clients in getting the job done. One new strategy introduced each week will guarantee a cycle-cut of 50% within three months!

7. How can you introduce the strategy of accelerated time? Start looking at your industry, your products and your promotions to find the keys to unlocking the accelerated schedule. Which carrots can you dangle, which motivational materials will work, which promotional facets will make the client shift into high gear? Each week, develop one new strategy that will get your client to move at a faster and more beneficial pace.

8. Do your homework on your client's standard purchasing procedures. Add this to your client profile and fully explore the purchasing procedure for each current customer and each new prospect. Develop one new probe each week that helps to identify the process involved. Then make sure the purchasing process is followed. Analyze it to look for cycle-cutting opportunities.

9. Develop a probing sequence to introduce the area of extraordinary purchasing procedures. Find out if, when, why and how the procedure is used with each client.

10. Review all your selling actions and planning, as well as each client's profile to see if there are areas that could be linked or processed in a parallel fashion, as opposed to a one-at-a-time serial function. Each week, refine one area or one client profile into a faster paced, parallel sales process.

STANDING APART

SELF-IMAGE

There's a popular saying, *"What you see is what you get,"* meaning that your outside actions and appearances reflect your inside thoughts and beliefs. To a strong degree this is true, and we usually develop rapport based upon what we observe about a person.

However, there is one area that tends to control how and why we act the way we do. It is called self-image. Self-image is the heart's interpretation of who and why we are. It combines your attitudes, purposes, belief systems, the present, the past and the future into a complex picture of who you are.

The statement should probably be put, *"What you feel is really who you are."* It more accurately reflects the nature of your self-image as a deeply personal, powerful and controlling mechanism that leads you and directs you down a somewhat pre-determined path in life.

Your self-image constantly monitors your actions and the things that happen to you each day. It analyzes "input" against the complex image of who you feel you actually are in your heart of hearts. If the input matches the image, you feel comfortable. If the input falls outside the image then different feelings arise, either inferior to the image or superior to the image.

In either dimension, above or below the image, the "output" from your self-image mechanism makes you feel uncomfortable with yourself and issues self-correcting commands to your mind and body. This is one reason why it is so difficult to accomplish true and lasting change. Your self-image wants you to remain in a comfortable, known posture.

It's because of the ultimately controlling nature of your self-image that people seldom change permanently. This is why diets fail, New Year's resolutions are broken and addicts fall off the wagon. Your self-image wants to return to the comfort zone of life and makes you miserable until its demands to return to the "old" you are met or overcome. After all, which is stronger, old habits reinforced by 20 or 30 repeated actions each day for 20 years (like smoking) or a "new you" (smokeless) only one week old.

Old habits are like strong, thick steel cables pulling against a thin and delicate strand of silk. This is why change does not take place easily: it has a "foe" many times more mighty.

However, change *can* and *does* take place. It takes place when there is a conscious shift in self-image.

Change your self-image and you can change behavior.

Behavior comes about as a *result* of self-image. No change will be permanent unless the image held in your closest quarters is likewise changed and accepted. Change the image and the new behavior will begin to feel more comfortable.

The self-image is complete: it covers every area of your life. You feel comfortable when you are within its boundaries. You feel uncomfortable when you step beyond. Change the boundaries and you allow new behavior to become effective and comfortable.

It takes about three weeks, on average, of daily repetition to change a habit or develop a habit (or skill) so that it fits comfortably within the self-image framework. This is why three-day sales training programs don't work. They only poke at the self-image: they stand outside and say, "You can do this and you can be better and you can succeed." But they don't get inside the boundaries. They don't widen the horizons; they just make you realize you aren't yet equipped to be what you are expected to be by others. An assault on the self-image results in a retaliation by the self-image, commonly called de-motivation, despair and dejection.

For lasting change, for lasting skills, you must massage and reprogram your self-image to accept new skills, new attitudes, new actions and even new clothes, a new position or new responsibilities.

PROJECTED IMAGE

Projected image is the person you desire to be. It is the overhaul of the self-image in a conscious and positive manner with a goal to self-improvement. If you are a used car salesperson now and you desire to be a medical instruments sales professional, you must make the transition through a series of projected self-images, each representing a step towards the final self-image goal. You must construct the self-image for the next step and prepare the way before your current, comfortable self-image will allow you to change.

Who do you want to be? How do you want to feel? How will you act? These are just some of the questions that you must answer about yourself at each major plateau of personal accomplishment.

The important thing is to develop a projected self-image for each stage of transition. To become a professional in selling involves many intermediate steps, just as it does in any field. You don't inherit the position, you achieve the position. But you'll never achieve the position unless you master the intermediate steps. There is always a pattern to success and always a price to pay. Remember, the ladder that leads to the top floor is anchored in the basement. It may take years to climb to the top, but it only takes seconds to plummet to the bottom. Climb carefully.

If you asked Neil Armstrong how he got to be the first man to walk on the moon, it's unlikely that he would reply, *"Well I was just sitting down having a Big Mac when my good buddy Buzz said, `Come on, Neil, let's go to the moon tomorrow.'"* No, it was through many intermediate steps, many intricate skills, many failures, many successes, an incredible amount of practice and mostly plain hard work, all pulled by an ever-developing projected self-image of being the first man actually to walk on the moon.

Intermediate "plateau" goals (set for one or two years down the road) are the cornerstone to developing a valid projected image. Long-range goals (three years plus) are the keys to keeping your projected image in perspective and in line.

For instance, if your long-range goal is to become a general sales manager of a nationally recognized firm, then you have intermediate "plateaus" to achieve before you will be considered a candidate for the position. If you are a retail shoe clerk now, a wide gap probably exists between your current position (and self-image) and your eventual long-range goal.

Define the intermediate steps, positions, responsibilities, experiences, income, behavior and other factors of each major step along the way. Your long-range goals become the foundation for your long-range projected image.

Like the steps winding up a steep hillside to the mountain top, each step you take carries a new perspective, a different view and a fresh appreciation. As you climb higher, your vantage point allows you to see the lower steps and path in a more complete picture, in balance with the surrounding environment. Each step is an experience in its own right, and as you wind up the rustic staircase you notice paths that run off horizontally and small benches positioned for you to rest upon.

On your way up, you notice that some people have wandered off the main trail onto the horizontal trails towards other ventures, while some have elected to snooze on the benches meant for a brief stop only. As you ascend, it seems that each step requires more energy than the last. When you started out, there were many others who were eager to get to the top, many racing and running towards the staircase as if it were but a hundred-yard dash rather than a mile-high climb.

But now you notice that many have either quit and returned to the parking lot near the beginning of the trail, or they've left the main trail and staircase for other pursuits. Adjusting your pace for the long trek ahead, you put yourself into a position of organized achievement and press on, not resting too long, drinking cool water when appropriate and then resuming your climb. When you finally reach the top, there are only a few of the original group left, maybe only five of the original 100 who began. But the view is magnificent, the air is clear and the sense of accomplishment is overwhelming.

The climb reflects the aspects of projecting a modified self-image for yourself and taking the next step. You must feel comfortable as you climb higher. The next step is not the final step, but it is different than the previous one. Project, adjust, accept, react.

In developing a projected image to modify your current self-image, you should observe certain cautions.

1. Big Changes Evoke Strong Reactions

If you are anticipating a big change, a radically different approach to your life, then expect strong self-image reactions. You may feel great for a short period of time, but the steel cables of the self-image can spring back with devastating force. Oh, you can stretch and pull the self-image any way you want, but it always wants to return to its original shape.

The faster and harder you pull, the faster and harder it wants to put you back in your place. Do you remember Newton's Law? It states that for every action there is an equal and opposite reaction. Smaller changes tend to reshape the self-image gradually so that it respects its new form. They are not as hard for the self-image to deal with, and it can adjust without undue pain, stress or reaction.

2. Project a Complete Image

Many times when we seek change in our lives, we only look at one area, such as our business position or our marital status. Each change affects us in a much more total sense, with our emotions, our finances, our everyday activities, our personal habits, etc. In anticipation of the next step, develop a complete view of yourself, taking into account all those things that make up "you" from an inside and outside perspective.

3. Introduce the New Image Slowly, Gradually

When training salespeople, I know that it takes weeks of daily reinforcement to build new and permanent skills. I don't expect my students to be proficient in the first day or even the first week of trying a new skill. I wait for a full three weeks of daily, incrementally increasing practice before passing judgment. You, too, should not pass self-judgment on your new image before you have practiced daily on the changes involved. An incremental introduction of change accomplishes far more than a headlong rush into a new you.

4. Become Comfortable

Live in your new image for awhile before attempting to construct your next incremental projected image. Get used to what your new person can accomplish, what your new self feels like, how you react and relate to others. Make adjustments and improvements if necessary. Realize that you might have made a mistake in the projected image and that newer is not always better.

5. Keep the Standards Intact

It is fine to want to move ahead, but at what cost? I once experienced a corporate bulldozer who ran roughshod over anything and anyone who got in his way. The smile seemed sincere but there was a pinch of poison in his handshake. The position and the money were all-important to him: he used relationships only as stepping-stones to the top. When he finally reached the top, he had left a trail of broken and battered people, victims of a projected image that neglected the basic standards for decency and fair play.

Throw out your principles and you'll shoot yourself in your own foot. The basis for any self-image and projected image is solid principle, firmly understood and grasped with the fist of life-respecting determination.

You must respect the "unshakable unbreakables" of life: the axioms that you would not bend or break under any circumstances. Make your projected image work around your standards, not the other way around. Your foundation must be solid and reliable. It must be based on truth, God's principles and personal integrity.

STANDING APART

The emphasis in this chapter is on becoming different. To get to higher ground you must first reach for higher ground. Standing apart means becoming different. It might mean better, it might mean smarter, it might mean faster, it might mean finding a different way. It always means risk: personal, corporate, financial and emotional.

Without substantial risk, there are seldom substantial gains.

The key to standing apart successfully is to *manage* the risk and the responsibility of standing apart, for your actions not only affect you but they also affect all of those around you: family, business associates and friends.

To stand apart, you must know where you stand now. A self-assessment of the current you is hard to do and can easily be distorted by personal protective devices within your self-image mechanism. If you're a rotten salesperson but your parents have been stroking you with "how wonderful and marvelous their little son or daughter is," your self-image will reflect their influence and issue a personal assessment of "OK" for sales talent or skill.

Get an objective, third-party assessment of your abilities and talents, for it is what others see that is really true in terms of where you stand. You may see yourself as a giant, but the rest of your peers see you for who you really are. However, always consider the source: *you just might be a latent giant* and no one can see it but you!

To stand apart, you must know what it is you are standing apart from and what you might step into. Standing apart is not so much an action, but a way of thinking, a way of pursuing, a way of planning and a way of achieving. Look at how the majority act, and determine to act better. It might be that you refrain from the majority of time-wasting activities that 95% of your associates enjoy so that you can work on the future.

A good way to understand how to stand apart is to scrutinize and emulate those in your current or projected profession who stand apart. What do they do that is different than the crowd? If their actions fit within your standards, build a projected image and begin to integrate.

You won't be noticed unless you can be seen, and you won't be seen unless you make yourself visible. How can you be *different*?

YOU, NOT THE PRODUCT

Many salespeople get very attached to their products. Some get so attached that they rely totally on their products for personal success. That's fine, but products come and go and you could find many of your customers, so faithful over the years, rushing to dump your product in favor of a new, improved competitive model. You wouldn't be the first salesperson out of a job because your company failed to deliver the best product.

Rely on a safer foundation: your own skills, talents, integrity and determination. Build your personal resources, build your contact resources, build your experience, build your character.

Generally you know just about all that is important to know within one year concerning any product you represent. After that one year, it's just repetition and fine-tuning. If you've been selling the same product for ten years, you really only have one year of experience repeated ten times. Oh, sure, there are subtleties and relationships that build up over the course of hundreds of similar sales, but, all in all, you know most of it after year one.

I am not advocating that you quit your job tomorrow. I *am* arguing that you should have room to grow that is consistent with your goals and abilities. If you can't find it where you are after an honest search and evaluation, then consider moving on. The grass, however, isn't always greener, and to paraphrase Russell Conwell, there are acres of diamonds just waiting to be discovered in your present position if you will only take the time to look and to dig.

Changing products (or jobs) encourages growth in personal areas, expanding your experience and exposing you to varied and more challenging sales situations. If your company provides an upward career path, then lock on to it. If not, then you should renew the challenge involved in selling: reaching the next plateau.

To stand apart from the crowd means that *you* must be different. Your goals and your projected image must be the focus. Your integrity, accomplishments, skills, principles, talents, ideas, actions, honesty, and personal commitments make the difference. When you are building your projected image, it is the concept of how *you* fit in the picture that is important.

STOP, LOOK, LISTEN

It was the watchword when I was in kindergarten: stop, look both ways and listen carefully for cars before crossing the street. Most of my childhood was spent running from one place to another. My kids run from one place to another (except, of course, when you *want* them to). Just the other day my two kids ran smack into one another while they were rounding a hall corner from opposite directions. Sometimes we are so busy running that we forget the simple warning: *stop*, *look* and *listen*.

Stop

Stop because it breaks the routine rhythm of work. Practically, you can't observe, analyze and plan if you don't first stop what you are doing. Stop and then prepare yourself to look.

When taught in kindergarten how to cross the street, we were instructed to stop just short of the curb so that we could look without endangering ourselves. There were always a few cut-ups who had to poise on the edge of the curb or step boldly into the gutter, but a quick reprimand from the teacher brought them back into line because of the danger of being too close to the cars while attempting to observe.

Stand close enough, but not so close that you get hit. In this fashion, you can observe and decide on which action is appropriate and when to take it without fear of becoming a news item. Imagine yourself assessing the situation by standing in the middle of the road rather than from the safety of the curb: the scene becomes much more intense and it is critical to take correct and immediate action, for the wrong move or no move could lead to unpleasant, "page two" results.

Look

Looking from safe ground gives you time to plan and time to take constructive steps towards your future. It also gives you time to get a better perspective on the whole situation. Do you remember the illustration of a staircase winding up the mountain?

Imagine you are standing in the parking lot at the bottom of the trail and the winding staircase. You have a panoramic view of the path leading to the top. You can see it curl its way through the trees and rocks, disappearing for a moment only to reappear and continue upwards. You have a view of the whole.

However, as you climb, the view of the path is restricted to where you are. Having hiked many times in the Rockies, I know well how easy it is to lose sight of the path ahead and behind as you negotiate each local section of trail.

Once you are involved, you tend to lose perspective.

It is important to stop from time to time at a place where you can observe more of the scene than would be normally possible if had you kept yourself fully involved in the action of climbing. It's always handy and often wise to have a map and a compass on hand when you're in the bush.

Similarly, when you jump into a new, unfamiliar business or personal situation, it is hard to see past the present situation, hard to gain an overall perspective. The old saying, *"It's hard to remember that your mission was to drain the swamp when you're up to your butt in alligators,"* reflects this type of positioning and lack of overall perspective. Having a good overall plan and perspective helps immensely when you are in the thick of things. Think of your plan as a map to guide you through the "bush" of business. Look, observe, plan, make notes, select reference points, pick a path, act.

When I was 20, I was a bush pilot in northern Canada. The Cessna's compass and my trusty map were always important. But most of the time I navigated by using familiar landmarks. If flying low, I'd follow a river, logging road or train tracks that I knew would lead me to my next destination. If flying a little higher, perhaps it would be a distant lake or rock formation on the horizon that would act as the target. If flying in poor weather, an automatic direction finder's needle or the faint Morse sounds of an ever-beeping radio range leg kept me on course.

Without a path, every direction is *wrong*.

Without a map or overall perspective from which to select, each path could lead to disaster. If I lost direction, then I had to immediately take action to regain the right course or I would soon be an active contributor to the annual aviation statistics. The whole works for the parts and the parts work for the whole. Intermediate maneuvers work only if they fit within a master plan.

How does this relate to observation? You must look at the big picture to appreciate the immediate situation.

You must be able to give yourself reference points to mark your progress. You must take corrective action if you leave the path, and you must know *when* you have veered off course. Observing your career is as important as planning the next step or making the next move. You don't cross the street when the light is red or there's traffic approaching at an unsafe speed. The reason for looking is caution so that the action that follows can be constructive.

Listen

What does your heart say about your next move? What will other people say? What impact will it have on your life and the lives of your family and your friends? What about your finances? Listen while you're observing. What does it tell you about your next move? Will it be worthwhile to get to the other side of the street or should you stay where you are for now?

What risks are involved can you get back if it is not what you expected? Can you go only halfway and survive or do you need to get all the way before safety returns to you and yours? Who has to go with you: your family, your friends, your business associates? Are they willing to share the risk? Who gets left behind? What if someone you love gets run over when he or she hurriedly chases you across the street?

Your moves affect other people. Your moves affect *you*. How wide is the road that you are going to cross? When I was in kindergarten, the road was a country two-laner equipped with a traffic light. Little traffic, controlled intersection, crossing guard: little risk. No one ever was killed or injured crossing the street at that intersection as far as I can remember. Now, however, I often read of someone trying to cross the busy intercity expressway and not making it. Higher risk. I guess if there's one personal lesson from the many moves I've made, it is to assess the move more closely for its potential impact on others and yourself before making it.

If you don't like what you hear, ask yourself why. Is it because it is unfamiliar, or is it because it violates some of your principles or hurts others in the process? If you don't like the sound, will you accept the unpleasantness and expect that eventually you will grow to like it or will you take a different route altogether, one that is more likeable, more comfortable, more predictable?

The *intensity* of the next move is up to you. Take the time to ensure that it is made in the right direction, at the right time, and for the right motives.

COMMUNICATING

How do you look to your clients on paper? How do you sound to your clients on the phone? Are you an amateur or a professional when it comes to communicating with your clients? How do they perceive you from the direct communications they receive?

The small security paint company that sold its products only to the biggest firms in North America faced this problem. To get anywhere with the buyers, we had to make the correspondence and the communications appear as if they were dealing with a well-established organization. Dealing with established suppliers is just part of the "safety in buying" formula that large companies employ. They don't like dealing with mom-and-pop operations and little knick-knack enterprises. They like big, they like established, they like correct business etiquette. Part of the mix is the deliverables and part of the mix is the verbal communications.

We put a great deal of effort into making the deliverables appear businesslike and ensuring that all documentation, charts, graphs, specification sheets and articles were top notch. Nothing went to our clients that didn't appear first class.

When articles about our products didn't exist, I wrote some and had them published in trade magazines. I then used them for documentation. At one time, we even published our own industry newsletter that profiled our products from a third-party viewpoint, even though we wrote it totally in-house. This practice is now becoming commonplace – it's called an *advertorial.*

If you send a letter, proposal or documentation to your client, make sure that it meets the client's expectations for quality and content. Let the client's expectations determine the effort required for the communication piece. How often does the pinstriped, metro salesperson talk in vain to the farmer? If you don't have the materials necessary to influence your target market properly, then start making arrangements to get them.

Staying in contact is an important aspect of standing apart from the normal crowd. Each product and each client has its own time frame for the most effective communications. My suggestion is do *twice* as much contact as the average salesperson in your business. Have a purpose to each call; leave the client with the feeling that "I'm glad he or she called today." Work on it. Deliver benefits, advantages, and insights.

One of the worst things you can do to discourage and disgruntle clients is not to return their calls, emails or messages in a timely manner. Do not ignore or put off a tough call; it only gets tougher as the minutes tick by.

TECHNOLOGY AND COMMUNICATIONS

Technology continues to advance personal and corporate communications so fast that it is useless trying to identify or isolate specific technologies or products that help salespeople. The computer "revolution", which has brought immense technological power within the hands of the average salesperson, should be exploited for all it can deliver. If you are computer or social media illiterate, then eventually you will slip into the category of the business have-nots. People expect you to reply in kind, and if your clients use the latest technology, then you better get knowledgeable, and fast. Don't rely on your company to teach you. It *is* up to you.

THIRD WAVE

In the early 1970's, Alvin Toffler described a phenomenon that he entitled the "Third Wave." I used to teach from his book and have the extraordinary good luck to have been present to live out his predictions.

He saw the evolution in world business behavior and personal lifestyle changing in a dramatic fashion, a fashion so remarkable that it would affect literally every person in the civilized world within 30 years or so.

It involved a change from group dependency involving large manufacturing concerns to independent, individual and self-supporting "knowledge" workers using technology to bypass bureaucracy and change traditional employment relationships.

It meant people working, communicating and prospering through networked individual technological strength. The dependency on unions and traditional employer-employee relationships would diminish. Corporate and personal power would emerge and become established upon the technology that surrounds information interchange. A network of knowledge workers, using high-level technology to speed past conventional and traditional communication routes would replace traditional business formats.

The end result: the creation of a new class of enterprise, a global citizen without boundaries, and a culture linked by information technology. A new "have" class and a new "have-not" class would be created. In the early 1980's, I trained many salespeople in the technology of tomorrow, carrying myself into the depths of its course.

I remember making a prediction to my students, all of whom were new computer salespeople: *"The technology you see in this room will bring about a change in selling: one person being able to do the work of ten. One person replacing ten."*

It now is reality, as the technology-aided salesperson applies his or her trade. One replacing ten: it occurred by 1989. One replacing a hundred came six years later. One replacing a thousand: it's already happened - witness the power of the web! One replacing ten thousand – Amazon. What's next?

SWIM OR DROWN

Technological change leads you to a personal crossroads: surf the wave or be swept away and drown. Whether you recognize it or not, whether you accept it or not, the technological wave is upon you full force right now. You must make a decision: to become involved or to hope that someone will throw you a life preserver before you go under for the last time. This chapter is about standing apart: you can't stand while you're being tumbled and tossed by a tsunami. Swim or drown. Decide soon. Decide now.

SELLING TECHNOLOGIES

Selling technologies are those advances in communications that make your job "current" or "leading edge." Today's technology advances into tomorrow's with lightning-like quickness, and if you sell to leading-edge firms then you must be prepared to influence them using similar technologies.

One way of determining the technological advancement of a firm is to see or experience their sales presentation or materials. If your technology matches theirs, at least you're on common turf. If yours lags far behind, you and your company may be perceived as not being current, a negative impression.

Start advancing your presentation technologies and your communication technologies to match your client's technologies. If your firm isn't moving in that direction but you want to, then start prodding or start looking. Take an active lead in making new technological changes to the selling department and to your personal selling career.

KEEP UP WITH COMMUNICATION SYSTEMS

The post office dug its own grave, jumped in and pulled the coffin lid snugly in place, and nobody came to the funeral. First came the courier, then the fax and now e-mail and the web, but they all do something better than the post office once did: move hard-copy information quickly, reliably and much, much quicker. The post office thought that it was in the business of delivering mail. It was not. They were in the business of delivering information quickly; it just happened to be in the form of an envelope with a stamp. It lost sight of its purpose to the business public long ago and has been surpassed by technology and people willing to provide alternatives that can meet the needs of business.

Everything is subject to obsolescence – never forget that – and fight hard to stay on the leading edge.

E-mail, messaging, webinars, and web-hosted presentations are excellent candidates for "cycle-shortening award winners of the century." What once took weeks now takes seconds. And tomorrow? It's unimaginable.

The basic principle is to equip yourself *today* for the opportunities of *tomorrow*. The competitive edge means staying on top of everything.

MAKING IT STICK

Being unique offers an opportunity to step out and become unusual in many different ways. One way to be unique is through your personal correspondence. I used to hire a particularly astute public speaker named Don Hutson. Don was the past president of both Toastmasters International and the National Speakers Association. Every time I talked to Don on the phone, he would dash off a "thank-you" postcard to me highlighting the call information or some other useful ditty or action item.

The postcards were printed with his picture, phone number and return address and were made of high-quality glossy card stock, much like a long postcard. Don always carried a supply of these "ready-to-go-replies" in his briefcase, pre-stamped and just awaiting a quick two or three line note. It made him stand out! He was the only one who used "the card" and the only one who still stands out as a personal communications master.

I know it sounds "old school", however in today's world, a hand-written postcard is a novelty – it stands out as something thoughtful and personal.

Another way to get your name in front of your industry is to take out ads, with your photo, in trade magazines (on-line or in print), trade periodicals or on local social media platforms. Let people know who you are and why you're there. You must run the ads continuously, but not necessarily in every issue. There must always be something consistent about the ads you run, such as the photo, your name profiled, or your product. Something must be repeated in each successive issue. When you call on a new prospect, your name will sound familiar and your face will look familiar. Once the connection is made, you enjoy instant credibility.

Articles and Editorials

As I mentioned earlier, if there are no positive articles on your product (or you), write them or cause them to be written. I have done it many times and have had new products or services featured prominently within important industry trade journals. The publishers of trade magazines are always hungry for new information and, while they usually won't pay you for your efforts, it's a lot cheaper than advertising and a lot more powerful.

I've experienced a much higher response from a "free" two-column new product announcement than I've ever experienced with expensive, multi-column, multi-colored ads in the same publications. The best result is to have *both* published at the same time.

As long as your article is ready for the reader with little work or editing required to make it fit the periodical's format, then you can almost be assured of its being inserted. One caution: articles that sound like advertising will not be run. They must be of genuine interest to the reader.

I've had success with new product announcement notices and with feature articles published. The need is there, just fill it.

I wrote one of my most successful articles was when I was training computer salespeople using immersion training techniques at a remote conference center. A major sales management magazine contracted a writer to do an article on the program but they didn't like the way the article turned out. I offered to write the article and not only did it get published, but I was offered a columnist's position on sales training each month. For the next several years I wrote for a monthly publication and widened my personal reputation in the training industry. I did it because I saw an opportunity. You can do it because the same opportunity exists today for those who want to test the waters. To get known, step out.

TRAINERS

As a young salesperson, I was good, but not the top. Not great, not bad, just somewhere in the middle, struggling. I had attended one three-day course on sales training, like many have. I sold using just my personality. I knew that there were real skills that could be mastered, but I was lazy and didn't want to spend the time in solitude trying to learn anything new. I was solidly First Dimension, as most salespeople are.

Someone suggested to me that I should try to teach people to sell, then I would have to learn how to do it myself before I could pass the knowledge on. It sounded ridiculous enough to work. I contacted the local business college about offering a sales training program and they agreed. Within a month, I started teaching something I knew very little about. Talk about learning fast! I grew more in my sales career in those 12 weeks of trying to teach 35 other adults to sell than in any time before or since. It started a new career for me and it also showed me that a crazy idea, enacted with enthusiasm and a sense of adventure, *can* succeed. It can even change a life (and maybe 35 others as well).

The point to the story is that if you are looking for a way to increase your personal understanding of the sales process, teach someone else to sell. If you want material, see the appendix for information on obtaining workbook programs and a trainer's guide for Doubling, as well as other sales training materials you might like to use. You could repeat what I did many years ago. With every new evening class of adults, there's an opportunity for expanding your personal training business and expanding sales contacts as well.

As a salesperson, I made a comfortable living. As a high-profile sales trainer and speaker, I can make ten times as much, with half the work and twice the fun. Maybe it's your path. Call me; I'll talk.

YOU'VE GOT TO ACCENTUATE THE POSITIVE...

Accentuate the positive, *eliminate* the negative, *latch on* to the affirmative... This advice from an old time song seems self-explanatory, but it's amazing how much old, negative baggage we carry around with us when we attempt to move upwards and onwards. Look at the positive, constructive things you do. Realize that out of ten experiences, probably three are negative, six are average and one is really positive. Concentrate on the positives. Learn from the negatives but be careful not to dwell on them. Focus on the rewards of accomplishing your positive tasks and objectives and place the negative consequences of non-achievement out of sight.

Whatever you do, in whatever you say, build! Refrain from gossip, refrain from tearing down and finding fault. Always look for the good, the positive, and the pleasant. When you enter a conversation, smile and wait your turn. Leave something of value with everyone you meet; give freely of your experience and of your patience. What goes around, comes around. Remember, success and failure are not destinations; they are just perceptions.

YOUR DOUBLING STRATEGY

It is simple. Find ways that allow you to climb above the crowd. Be different, think strategically, stand apart. Anyone can run with the crowd, but people only cheer for those who pull away and race ahead. How are you going to do it? A personal decision, a personal effort, a personal triumph. It can be done, but you must take action.

DOUBLING

1. Make a list of those things you would like to change about your personal self-image. Realizing that it takes weeks of constant, gradual practice or reinforcement to create change in your self-image, design a daily program to enact the modification process.

2. Constantly plan and project a newer, more complete "you" to others and to yourself. Make your inside feelings and your outside image match by careful planning and paying attention to detail. Create a long-term plan for personal change, one year or longer, and then begin gradually to accommodate the new you inwardly and outwardly.

3. In planning for the future, it is important that you identify and solidify your personal standards. These are the principles of life and business upon which you stand and that you will not bend or break. Set them in areas of morals, ethics, business relationships, contracts (verbal and written), loyalties, philosophies, religion, marital commitments, faithfulness, finances and other areas that affect your life. The foundation you build will have to hold your future secure against hurricanes, tornados, floods and droughts, so build your base solidly.

4. Determine how and why you are going to stand apart from the crowd. What will make you different? What will make you unique? What will differentiate you from the next person? Make a list. Assign priorities to those areas that you can accomplish now or within the next three months and begin to implement your stand-apart strategy. Don't forget: when you stick your head out it might get noticed, negatively or positively.

5. Start to build a future apart from your product. Make a list of the things you could do to improve your future without linking it directly to your current product or service. Be a professional and learn your skills well enough that they could be used with any product or any service. Become transportable.

6. Stop and gather a panoramic view of where you're going and why you're going. Stop and look for the best path ahead. Most of us are so deep into the forest we can't see the beautiful fields and streams surrounding us. Stop. Take a break to survey your situation before making any decisions on the future.

7. Look for the logical, stand-apart way to get to your next objective. If you haven't defined your personal objectives yet, begin to isolate the things that are important to you and express them in concrete terms. Since the next chapter dwells in depth on personal achievement, just get a good "global" idea of where you are now and where you'd like to go. Select the mountain you'd most like to climb.

8. Discuss your future with those who can give you constructive feedback. Be aware that those who are mired in the mud along with you now might try to pull you back down to their own levels or comfort zones. Solicit opinions and suggestions but weigh them carefully for personal biases and hidden objectives.

9. Decide that you are going to be a top-notch communicator. List ten new ways in which you can improve your communications to your family, your friends, your business associates, your boss and your clients. Then enact each one on a scheduled implementation program, maybe one new method each month.

10. Ride the wave. Do not let another day go by without starting your personal program for understanding and using technology in your personal and business life. Draw up a long-range plan to involve yourself with telecommunications and information exchange technologies. Start tomorrow. Start today! The longer you put it off, the harder it will be to gain an understanding.

About the Author

A Five-Dollar Miracle

I was born in New Jersey in the waning days of 1945 – just a few weeks ahead of the baby boomers andgrew up in the wonderful town of Chatham, NJ. In 1959, my dad was transferred to Montreal and at age 13, I fund myself in the tiny hamlet of Baie d'Urfe, Quebec, Canada. I spent my formative teen years around Montreal and, after an unsuccessful stab at university, I found myself "on the street" at 19 years of age. I went to work in a low-paying factory job for $1.35 per hour and then as a construction laborer in a paper mill in Fort William, Ontario, living by myself in a dreadful cubby-hole apartment a thousand miles from "home".

I didn't know what I was good at and was depressed and unfocused. Laboring in a dirty paper mill was not glamorous or enjoyable – at all. I was lonely, disillusioned and mad at myself. Surprisingly, it only took a five-dollar bill to change it all.

While working high up in the paper mill's new addition, I watched student pilots practicing their landings at the airport that was about a mile away. So, on one clear, crisp Saturday morning, I drove over to the airport and took a "Discovery Flight" in a small four-seater airplane, a Cessna 172.

Thirty minutes was all it took to instantly rekindle my interests, ignite my passions, focus my attention and lift my battered self-confidence.

Within two months I had earned a private pilot's license. Several months later, I quit my paper mill job, returned to Montreal and completed my commercial license and instrument rating and went to work as a co-pilot for an executive charter firm, with an apartment in Montreal and corporate accommodations in New York City, right across from the Park Plaza Hotel.

It was less than two years from that initial five-dollar discovery flight and that hole-in-the-wall apartment in Fort William, Ontario. Instead of dirty overalls, I wore a crisp, tailored suit. Instead of steel-toe work boots, I could look down on a pair of fine leather shoes. Instead of beer with the boys at the tavern, it was dinner at the Park Plaza by Central Park. What a transformation. *Two years.*

I had proved to myself and to my doubting family that I could achieve. I could harness passion and learn new, complex skills quickly and competently. Most of all, I proved to myself that I was not a flunky, even though for a brief season, I wore the label of a dope, convinced that others thought that way about me too. But it was just for a season, as most things in life are.

Interestingly, I came to the conclusion several years later that I didn't enjoy flying at all, even though I was very skillful. But the experience taught me that tiny things sometimes have an incredible impact. In this case a single, blue Canadian $5 bill.

Life moved on, I returned to college and studied computer science. After graduating (magna cum laude, I might add: so much for the "flunky" label), I found myself leaning more and more towards being an entrepreneur. I learned to trust in my strengths as a visionary and over the years have been engaged in many new business start-ups and developments. I learned to write and have produced over fifty major sales and customer service-training programs and several books as a result. I became a pretty good motivational speaker and technical trainer. I never saw this in high school, not in college and not as a pilot.

As a professional workshop facilitator, I have had the incredible joy of training thousands of people how to sell and service clients in many different industries across North America. However, I have also visited the dark, lonely side of depression and self-doubt when ventures sputtered or finances vanished or investors turned on you. This too, is the life inherent of an entrepreneur and pulling oneself out of the abyss of deep depression is probably the hardest challenge of all.

I discovered over the years that I also had a significant technical side to me and this led me to work extensively in two areas that drew upon my training talent – the one talent that I am sure was God-given – to make the complex simple to understand – and to sell. As a result, I was fortunate to be profiled in Canadian Business magazine as one of Canada's "High Tech Entrepreneurs" for my unusually effective immersion sales training programs for the computer industry when it was exploding across the country in the mid 1980's.

Then, in a total departure from training and computers, I entered a new field and became known internationally for my work in creating forensic chemical marking technologies for use in major industrial loss prevention programs and in specific anti-counterfeiting and brand protection applications. The process saved corporations billions in losses over the years.

I co-founded a little start-up software publishing firm, Formgen Corporation, with friend Randy MacLean in 1987. Years later, Formgen grew to be the largest distributor of PC-based gaming software in North America.

Over the years, I have been a salesperson for everything from industrial soap to Boeing 747's and was the monthly columnist on sales training and feature article contributor for Sales and Marketing Management in Canada magazine.

My personal passion, however, is for training people. I have been described as an engaging workshop facilitator and an entertaining speaker, and have had the unbelievable good fortune to work alongside Earl Nightingale, Norman Vincent Peale, Art Linkletter, Don Hutson, Dottie Walters, Fred Herman and even baseball legend Mickey Mantle. I have been utterly humbled by the sincerity and deep conviction of wise preachers such as David Wilkerson and Billy Graham.

I am deeply grateful for the help of my close friend Cindy Anthony who helped me re-write the original manuscript for the Christian reader. She is a woman of deep spiritual depth and insight, and her task was to ensure that I stayed on the right side of the fence. My weekly breakfast buddy, Norm Sawyer – a devoted man of God – also helped me by reviewing the doctrinal areas in this book. And of course, I am thankful for my wife of 37 years, Suzanne, who stood by my crazy ventures, having to ride the wave along with me.

Selling is a tough job for most, rewarding for many but very difficult for others. My heart goes out to you, successful or not, for I know the highs and lows you experience, the times of frustration and the times of elation. I know the instability that can come from this work and I know the unbelievable rush that the big sale and the hard sale brings. It's one of the few professions that pays pennies and millions for the same effort.

I hope that something in this book makes a difference in your future. I pray that your family members gain understanding and insight into your private and unspoken world that's occupied by the obligation of having to constantly achieve.

Hypocrite? Unfortunately, Yes.

This book was shelved many times. Each time I began to explore ethics and personal behavior, I kept seeing myself in the reflection of my work. Not as a model of integrity, but as a person beset over his lifetime with moral failures, fleshly desires and ethical compromises. I kept feeling that I was just not worthy to write on this topic. It stalled the manuscript for years, multiple times. My heart kept saying, "hypocrite," yet for some reason, I was compelled to carry on, to add a paragraph at a time – to struggle over each phrase, over each critical word. My concerns finally were resolved when I realized that there is only one person who could write a manuscript based on a flawless life and that was Christ. *"No one is righteous, not even one"* declares the Bible in Romans 3:10. Pretty sobering. So even though I am flawed – and you are flawed – that does not excuse any of us from raising the bar concerning our own personal ethics and to strive for a cleaner life filled with good decisions and honorable behavior.

Personal Achievement Plans

Corporate training

The skill portion of this book is available as a companion workbook to help you achieve your doubling goals. *Doubling: Plan 30* contains a day-by-day plan for personal achievement in 30 days based upon the precepts in this book.

The purpose of Plan 30 is to get you immediately headed towards more and bigger sales. It starts the doubling process. The plan has a number of objectives to which you must commit if you wish to succeed:

> *1. To begin a process of change, to make change a matter of management and to master the effects of change;*
>
> *2. To begin to form the habit of extraordinary work, thought and action, and to realize and recognize that the true pinnacle of success is reached through a combination of extraordinary work, extraordinary thought and extraordinary action;*
>
> *3. To define and set tangible goals, to initiate the process of goal management and to begin to realize some goal rewards;*
>
> *4. To begin a skill- and strategy-building process that will eventually lead to the formation of a solid selling base.*

The Format

Plan 30 sets up a program that introduces and reinforces selling skills, positive and productive attitudes, selling strategies and personal goals. Each day's work, six days per week for 30 days, represents between a half an hour and an hour of solid, growth-oriented work. Every day you will be pressed a little harder than the day before. Every day you will be required to dig deeper, to draw from beyond the normal, to create and to confirm. It is a formula that I have used with hundreds of salespeople and there is no shortcut. It's hard, but it works.

Five Components
Any lasting change involves five primary elements: *actions, attitudes, goals, habits* and *skills.* Your actions are a direct result of your attitudes, goals, habits and skills. Your attitudes reflect the success of your actions and your grip on commitment. Your skills reflect the habitual repetition, practice and on-the-job experience that goes into their composition, as well as the strategic thought surrounding their development. The success of your actions is directly related to your skill and the direction of your actions towards your goals. The components are intricately linked together and together they must be developed if lasting change is to be achieved. Plan 30 involves these five elements linked together in an assault upon your future.

Each day in the workbook is divided into four portions: (1) attitudes, goals and objectives, (2) new skills and strategies, (3) reinforcement and (4) positive daily action.

Plan 30 is available as an excellent self-help program and as a powerful in-house training program. A corporate trainer's guide is also available (*Doubling: Plan 30/Corporate Trainer's Guide*).

CORPORATE TRAINING

Special "Doubling" programs are available from the author to suit every corporation's needs. Should you be interested in having the author as a guest speaker for your group meeting or as a special focus trainer, call the phone number below during regular business hours.

Doubling is available in several training formats.

1. Plan 30 Live

An instructor-based live presentation to your sales team Plan 30 Live lasts for one month. There is a full-day indoctrination briefing and then for every business day during the next 30 days the instructor will work with your sales team to build their skills and strategies. Each day features one hour of live instruction plus one-on-one consultation with one salesperson each day. The program ends with another full-day briefing that sets the pace for the rest of the year. The focus is to change the way your salespeople act and think. Anticipate a doubling in sales within 90 days for all salespeople.

2. Briefings, Workshops and Speeches

One-hour, half-day or full-day intense sales briefings, delivered personally by the author, will kick your training programs off with gusto!

3. Doubling Immersion

If you're really serious about overhauling your sales force, consider an immersion training program. We'd be pleased to sit down with you and organize an unforgettable experience.

4. Doubling for New Product Introductions

Have your new product introduction sales team drill to capture the excitement that surrounds a new product launch. Many times more powerful than conventional training!

5. Doubling Service Revenues

This program features an in-depth review of service offerings and focuses on building a new, expectation-oriented sales presence. Excellent, outstanding results reported from clients.

6. Selling at 60 DPPH (Doubling Points per hour)

A fast-paced presentation for sales groups large and small that feature the top 60 Doubling strategies in one hour!

If you are interested in any of the above programs or if you might have a similar training task in mind, send me an email at robertriker@sellegrity.com.

Many of the comments from participants in the Doubling seminars, workshops and courses reflect the timelessness of the program.

Doubling is not a light read; each page seems to have something of personal benefit. By the end of the six-week course, the DOUBLING paperback books have usually been re-bound with duct tape and most have multiple index tabs formed from Post-It notes marking the personal-impact areas. Some are restrained with a thick rubber band.

I hope that each reader could have the benefit of attending a Doubling six-week course. It helps so much. The most training I had as salesperson was a three-day Xerox PSS program in the early '70's: It wasn't enough. Doubling isn't enough, but it's a darn good start.

Here are some of the comments from salespeople who have attended the Doubling program.

DOUBLING as a Six Week Skill Development Program – Participant Comments

DOUBLING – The Course – had six, full-day workshops, spaced exactly one week apart, with a Daily Achievement Assignment required each day in between workshops (about an hour's work each day). Class size: 25 max; average class, 18. Some courses were industry-specific, some were product specific, some were open public programs, some were in-house corporate.

After six weeks of intense interaction and very demanding personal effort, these are the hand-written comments that participants provided. They are not as a result of an intense emotional process, such as found in a motivationally-charged seminar setting, but are more genuine, reflecting the effects of a sustained effort with lots of time for reflection.

These people grew. They worked hard and they achieved. Many changed their way of doing business and some had dramatic personal epiphanies. But the bottom line reflected the time-tested principle of spaced repetitious learning: there is no substitute or shortcut for old-fashioned hard work. Did they all double their sales? No. Did some? Yes. Did they all grow? Absolutely.

"If you want more than pep talks...I strongly suggest you invest in DOUBLING."

"I have already more than doubled my sales, but more importantly, I simply understand."

*"I was averaging **$1500** per month; I turned around, targeted customers, phoned, plotted and shortened a few selling cycles; I am expecting approximately **$13,000** for next month's pay check."*

"I'd say that DOUBLING was probably the only program from which I'd extracted anything positive. The length and content made it much more valuable than all the (other sales training) sessions put together."

"I'm much more motivated and confident. I'm also a lot more content within myself."

"November was my best month ever! December looks just as promising!"

"DOUBLING is a way to learn to sell with integrity, without compromising who I am or manipulating others."

"It's really helped me to add credibility to my profession. I believe that I can sell with integrity and be very successful."

"The program is quite intense."

"DOUBLING provided me with an insight into my personal life that I didn't expect and made me realize that life must be balanced."

"The Daily Achievement Assignments are very difficult but effective. It is something I will be able to refer back to many times."

"DOUBLING is an excellent program and I would recommend it to anyone considering a career in sales."

"My sales have increased because I waste less time and have better relationships with clients"

"Bob Riker is a captivating and entertaining speaker - obviously very experienced."

"I would say that DOUBLING is more than worthwhile..."

"DOUBLING is tough and it's hard work; you really have to want to improve, but it's worth the investment of time and money...and it's GOOD!"

"Can't call yourself a salesman until you know this stuff inside-out!"

"I have been inspired and motivated to undertake some important projects!"

"The Daily Achievement Assignments were very thorough. Doing them in repetition made me learn them."

"I expected to learn specific selling skills to apply to specific selling situations. My expectations were exceeded in this area. I did not expect to learn how to incorporate selling into my life...my hopes were turned into expectations...which were exceeded!"

"DOUBLING is excellent for the salesperson who needs a personal plan to survive. The ideas are so intense that you need to devote time to really thinking about them. It isn't a casual course. But once you grab even some of the concepts, your way of looking at sales will improve and your life will change for the better."

"Honestly, this is the toughest thing I have ever done..."

"After taking DOUBLING I know that I have the potential to be a great salesperson. There is a lot of hard work that goes along with it, but it is really worth the time and effort you put into it. Also, there is no other course that helps you gain inner peace without which you can't succeed."

"It will change your life and your way of thinking."

"This could be the one course that would make the largest impact on your business and personal life."

Doubling as a Four-Day Seminar – Participant Comments

The four-day workshop/seminar is not as developmental as the six-week program because all the spaced repetitious skill building process is left to the participants to accomplish after the instruction has concluded. Although it is a good seminar as reflected by the enthusiastic and supportive participant comments, the comments tend to express the emotional aspect of attending a motivationally-charged event for four days, rather than any actual personal achievement. It is an excellent program for strategy development, however. I personally am not a believer in using the seminar approach for developing skills – it doesn't work well. They're great for strategy and tactics discovery; excellent for recognizing strengths and weaknesses, but absolutely no good for long-term skill development or meaningful personal change.

"This is the best sales course I've ever been at. I know my capabilities will be increased..."

"Do it."

"Very worthwhile course. In speaking to other salespeople who have been with this company for several years they have also commented this is the best they have ever been through."

"Be prepared to really look at your life. The course goes very deep into what preconceptions you currently hold. It can also make you big dough!"

"If you're in sales and haven't take the DOUBLING program, prepare to eat our dust!"

"I expected more training in linear method selling. I am totally impressed with expectational selling!"

"I expected to be exposed to selling skills that would allow me to gain personally and financially. I also hoped to gain knowledge on how to become a better person. I wasn't disappointed!"

"I found (the seminar portions) very, very informative. Compared to some others I've been to, they were very satisfying! It also helps that they were a lot of fun!"

"Concepts are great..."

"We will be making and re-directing a lot of company objectives and goals (as a direct result of the DOUBLING program)."

"My sales group left with a better understanding of what is required to be a professional and we all left with a strong sense of purpose and a good foundation. Highly recommended." (From a regional manager)

"It showed me how to deal with different types of people and allowed me to see how I was both falling short in some areas and exceeding in others."

"I found the method very interesting after having been through the Xerox course - much more suited to my personality."

"I expected a typical sales course atmosphere, such as IBM, Xerox, etc. This was an excellent course and has helped me tremendously, and will have a significant effect with my customer relations. I would suggest that anyone who wants to really advance their sales career should attend this course."

www.ingramcontent.com/pod-product-compliance
Lightning Source LLC
Chambersburg PA
CBHW060318200326
41519CB00011BA/1764

* 9 7 8 0 9 9 5 8 4 8 0 0 9 *